Florida A&M University, Tallahassee
Florida Atlantic University, Boca Raton
Florida Gulf Coast University, Ft. Myers
Florida International University, Miami
Florida State University, Tallahassee
University of Central Florida, Orlando
University of Florida, Gainesville
University of North Florida, Jacksonville
University of South Florida, Tampa
University of West Florida, Pensacola

Music of El Dorado

The Ethnomusicology of Ancient South American Cultures

~

Dale A. Olsen

University Press of Florida

Gainesville · Tallahassee · Tampa · Boca Raton

Pensacola · Orlando · Miami · Jacksonville · Ft. Myers

First cloth printing, 2002
First paperback printing, 2005

Library of Congress Cataloging-in-Publication Data
Olsen, Dale A. (Dale Alan)
Music of El Dorado: the ethnomusicology of ancient
South American cultures / Dale A. Olsen.
p. cm.
Includes bibliographical references (p.) and index.
ISBN 0-8130-2440-4; ISBN 0-8130-2920-1 (pbk.)
1. Indians of South America—Music—History and criticism.
2. Musical instruments, Ancient—South America. 3. Ethno-
musicology—South America. I. Title.
ML3575.A2 O57   2001
780'.98—dc21   2001034780

The University Press of Florida is the scholarly publishing
agency for the State University System of Florida, comprising
Florida A&M University, Florida Atlantic University, Florida
Gulf Coast University, Florida International University, Florida State University, University of Central Florida, University
of Florida, University of North Florida, University of South
Florida, and University of West Florida.

University Press of Florida
15 Northwest 15th Street
Gainesville, FL 32611–2079
http://www.upf.com

Dedicated to the memory of

Eduardo Calderón and Guillermo Cano

Contents

Illustrations

Tables

Notated Musical Examples

All pitches produced and notated by Dale A. Olsen unless otherwise indicated.

Audio Examples

Each example is indicated as an audio track in the book. All examples were performed and recorded by Dale A. Olsen unless indicated otherwise. Examples may be heard on the Internet at http://otto.cmr.fsu.edu/~cma/Eldorado. Material may be downloaded without permission.

1. Demonstration of fingering methodology for tubular flutes, performed on three Tairona ceramic sausage-shaped tubular duct flutes with four fingerholes each (see fig. 10.9). Cano Collection.
2. Nasca human (?) bone tubular notch flute (see fig. 3.2 [top]). Olsen Collection.
3. First demonstration on Nasca human (?) bone tubular notch flute (pitches produced with a Western fingering method) (see fig. 3.1 [middle]). Private collection.
4. Second demonstration on same Nasca human (?) bone tubular notch flute (pitches produced with a Q'ero fingering method) (see fig. 3.1 [middle]). Private collection.
5. Nasca bird (?) bone tubular notch flute (see fig. 3.1 [top]). Private collection.
6. Nasca bird (?) bone tubular notch flute (see fig. 3.2 [middle]). Olsen Collection.
7. Nasca bird (pelican?) or camelid (llama?) bone tubular notch flute with internal diaphragm (see fig. 3.1 [bottom]). Private collection.
8. Chancay cane tubular notch flute (see fig. 3.2 [bottom]). Olsen Collection.
9. Early-period Nasca ceramic ten-tube panpipe (see fig. 4.1). Private collection.

10. Nasca ceramic fifteen-tube panpipe (see fig. 4.2). Delaney Collection.

11. Tairona ceramic globular-tubular duct flute in the shape of a two-headed snake, with two chambers (one fingerhole per chamber) and two mouthpieces (see fig. 5.1). Cano Collection.

12. Tairona ceramic three-duct, three-chamber globular duct flute in the shape of a jaguar god-man (see fig. 5.2). Museo del Oro, Banco de la República, Bogotá. Four musical demonstrations: (a) left and middle chambers; (b) right and middle chambers; (c) all three chambers with steady air pressure; (d) all three with varying air pressure.

13. Tairona small ceramic three-duct, three-chamber globular duct flute in the shape of a jaguar god-man. Museo del Oro, Banco de la República, Bogotá.

14. Nasca ceramic two-duct, one-chamber globular duct flute in the shape of a seated bird (see fig. 5.3). Private collection. Two musical demonstrations: (a) two pitches produced by closing each window; (b) improvisation of two pitches with difference tones.

15. Nasca ceramic two-duct, one-chamber globular duct flute in the shape of a human head (see fig. 5.4). Private collection.

16. Nasca ceramic two-duct, one-chamber globular duct flute in the shape of a human head. Private collection.

17. Moche ceramic two-duct/two-chamber globular duct flute in the shape of two owls. Calderón Collection. Four musical demonstrations: (a) both chambers together, (b) left chamber (with head), (c) right chamber, and (d) together.

18. Moche ceramic two-duct, one-chamber globular (nearly tubular) duct flute (see fig. 5.5). Calderón Collection. Four musical demonstrations: (a) both chambers together, (b) left chamber, (c) right chamber, and (d) together.

19. Chancay ceramic globular duct flute/container rattle in the shape of a dog, fox, or guinea pig. Private collection (see fig. 5.9).

20. Chancay ceramic globular duct flute in the shape of a small bird. Private collection.

21. Moche ceramic globular duct flute in the shape of a *pinto* bird (like a hummingbird). Calderón Collection (see fig. 5.10).

22. Moche ceramic globular duct flute in the shape of a sleeping pelican. Calderón Collection (see fig. 5.11).

23. Moche ceramic globular ductless flute in convex crescent shape (see fig. 5.12). Private collection.

24. Moche ceramic globular ductless flute in concave crescent shape (see fig. 5.13). Private collection..

25. Moche ceramic globular ductless flute in ovoid shape (see fig. 5.14). Olsen Collection; gift from Eduardo Calderón. Performed by Eduardo Calderón (see fig. 5.8).

26. Moche ceramic globular ductless flute in ovoid shape. Performed by Eduardo Calderón during 1974 interview (first short demonstration).

27. Moche ceramic globular ductless flute in ovoid shape. Performed by Eduardo Calderón during 1974 interview (second short demonstration).

28. Moche ceramic globular ductless flute in ovoid shape. Performed by Eduardo Calderón during 1974 interview (third short demonstration).

29. Moche ceramic globular ductless flute in ovoid shape. Performed by Eduardo Calderón during 1974 interview (fourth short demonstration).

30. Moche ceramic whistling bottle with head of large-beaked bird (see fig. 6.1). Private collection. Blown into.

31. Chimú ceramic whistling bottle with complete small bird (see fig. 6.2). Private collection. Blown into.

32. Moche ceramic whistling bottle with head of large-beaked bird (see fig. 6.1). Private collection. Water sloshed back and forth.

33. Chimú ceramic whistling bottle with complete small bird (see fig. 6.2). Private collection. Water sloshed back and forth.

34. Moche or Chimú ceramic tubular transverse ductless (cross-blown) flute (see fig. 7.1). Cassinelli Museum Collection, Trujillo, Peru.

35. Sinú ceramic tubular (double-cone) duct flute with cayman relief (see fig. 9.1). Cano Collection.

36. Sinú ceramic tubular (double-cone) duct flute with cayman relief (see fig. 9.1). Cano Collection.

37. Four Sinú ceramic tubular (double-cone) duct flutes in the shape of fish (see fig. 9.2). Cano Collection. Four musical demonstrations, one for each flute, from left to right.

38. Tairona ceramic globular duct flute in the shape of a frog or toad. Cano Collection.

39. Tairona ceramic globular duct flute in the shape of a turtle (see fig. 10.5). Cano Collection.
40. Tairona ceramic globular duct flute in the shape of a medium-sized flying bird. Cano Collection.
41. Tairona ceramic globular duct flute in the shape of a large flying bird. Cano Collection.
42. Three Tairona ceramic globular duct flutes in the shape of a standing bird (see fig. 10.6). Cano Collection.
43. Tairona ceramic globular duct flute in the shape of a flying bird-jaguar (see fig. 10.2). Cano Collection.
44. Tairona ceramic globular duct flute in the shape of a human with leaf-nosed bat face (see fig. 10.14). Cano Collection.
45. Tairona ceramic globular duct flute in the shape of a jaguar. Galería Alonso Collection.
46. Tairona ceramic globular duct flute in the shape of a mother opossum with a globular duct flute in the shape of a baby opossum on her back (see fig. 10.4). Cano Collection.
47. Tairona ceramic globular duct flute in the shape of a disfigured man (see fig. 10.15). Cano Collection.
48. Tairona ceramic tubular duct flute in the shape of a man (see fig. 10.7). Cano Collection.
49. Tairona ceramic globular duct flute in the shape of a priest/shaman (see fig. 10.16). Galería Alonso Collection.
50. Tairona ceramic globular duct flute in the shape of a man sitting on crescent-shaped throne (see fig. 10.10). Cano Collection.
51. Tairona ceramic globular duct flute in the shape of a man with a paddle who sits astride a crescent-shaped boat (see fig. 10.12). Banco Popular, Museo Arqueológico Collection.
52. Tairona ceramic crescent-shaped ductless tubular flute (see fig. 10.11). Cano Collection.

Acknowledgments

There are many people and institutions to thank for their generous support, advice, introductions, enthusiasm, and inspiration over the years that have led to the completion of this book. I sincerely thank my UCLA ethnomusicology professor Peter Crossley-Holland, for being one of the first to pique my interest in the systematic study of pre-Columbian musical instruments. Those many hours spent with him each week analyzing his collection will always be fondly remembered. I thank the granting agencies that supported my research: the National Endowment for the Humanities, the Fulbright-Hays International Exchange of Scholars, and the FSU Committee on Faculty Research. I am very grateful to the staff members of the Cassinelli Museum in Trujillo, Peru; the Field Museum of Natural History in Chicago; the Metropolitan Museum of Art in New York City; the Museum of the Banco de Oro in Bogotá; and the Moche Archive at the University of California, Los Angeles, for allowing me to personally study their collections. In particular I thank Peruvian scholars César Bolaños, the late Eduardo Calderón, Américo Valencia Chacón, and Enrique Vergara Montero for their inspiration, guidance, encouragement, and support of my investigations. I am forever grateful to the late Guillermo Cano, a well-known Colombian journalist, collector, and scholar whose death by an assassin's bullet ended a brilliant man's devotion to ancient Colombian cultures. His willingness to allow me to study his vast private collection will always be remembered. I am extremely thankful to Christopher Donnan, Ellen Hickmann, Kenneth Moore, Michael Moseley, and Douglas Sharon, for their assistance, moral support, sharing of ideas and materials, and permission to study the collections that they have cared for or worked with. To Alicia and Ernesto Maúrtua, and their son José, I am grateful for kind hospitality in Peru. To my students and colleagues at the Florida State University, especially Jennifer Ladkani, Laurie Semmes, José Maúrtua, Dr. Mary Pohl, and Dr. Mary Glowacki, I give thanks for comments on various drafts of the book; and to Karyn Hahn for her tonometric analyses I am appreciative. Finally, I thank my wife, Diane—anthropologist, archaeologist, instructional designer, Latin Americanist, musician, and best friend—for reading and critiquing the final draft of this book, for offering ideas and strategies, and for always being there with her support and love.

Finally, I acknowledge the following for permission to reprint portions of my publications:

Smithsonian Institution Press for "Implications of Music Technologies in the Pre-Columbian Andes," in *Musical Repercussions of 1492*, edited by Carol Robertson (1992), pp. 65–88.

Libreria Musicale Italiana for "The Flutes of El Dorado: Musical Guardian Spirit Effigies of the Tairona," in *Imago Musicae: The International Yearbook of Musical Iconography* 3 (1986), pp. 79–102, published by Barenreiter Verlag and Duke University Press (1987).

The American Musical Instrument Society, Inc., for "The Flutes of El Dorado: An Archaeomusicological Investigation of the Tairona Civilization of Colombia," *Journal of the American Musical Instrument Society* 12 (1986): 107–36. Copyright 1986 by the American Musical Instrument Society, Inc.

Verlag für Systematische Musikwissenschaft GmbH., Bonn, for "The Magic Flutes of El Dorado: A Model for Research in Music Archaeology as Applied to the Sinú of Ancient Colombia," in *The Archaeology of Early Music Cultures*, edited by Ellen Hickmann and David W. Hughes (1988), pp. 305–28.

Part I

≈

Prelude

1

≈·≈·≈·

Background

Gold is the most exquisite of all things. . . . Whoever possesses
gold can acquire all that he desires in this world. Truly, for gold
he can gain entrance for his soul into paradise.

CHRISTOPHER COLUMBUS

These words characterize the attitude of many Spanish conquistadores.
When these fearless and often ruthless men began exploring the regions
of the Americas that they had claimed for the king of Spain beginning in
1492, they had but one real purpose—to find gold. While they found a
vast wealth of precious metals and stones, they also discovered that the
Indians (as the native people were to be erroneously called) did not place
the same value on it as did they, the Spanish. The native people, for example, did not kill for gold, except when they were attacked by the foreign intruders.

Probably more important to the native Americans at the time of their
encounter with the Spanish was their music. It provided them with supernatural power because it was a vehicle for transcending their mortal
world, curing their sick, and creating stability in their universe. Music
accompanied them in war, into the afterlife, during their dances of death.
Music offered protection, guaranteed fertility, provided pleasure. These
things we learn not through the pen of a conquering ethnomusicologist
aboard a Spanish galleon but from the hundreds of ancient native American musical instruments and music-related icons left in ancient tombs,
temples, and terraces. If the indigenous people from the ancient realm of
the fabled El Dorado could have edited Columbus's words, perhaps they

would have said the following: "Music is the most exquisite of all things. ... Whoever possesses music can acquire all that he desires in this world. Truly, for music he can gain entrance for his soul into paradise." Indeed, native Americans before Columbus placed great value upon music, musical instruments, and music making. Music (or what we would call music) after 1492 and into the present continues to have value for all native Americans. It is, for them, a ritual commodity, not to be sold, traded, or exchanged.

For most of the Spanish conquerors, however, native American music was meaningless sound used to conjure up devils and assist in "pagan" rituals. Even into the colonial period, Catholic clergy considered indigenous musical instruments to be such a detriment to conversion that in the early 1600s Catholic missionaries destroyed thousands, as explained by Nicolas Slonimsky: "During the early centuries after the conquest of South America, the ecclesiastical authorities tried in vain to suppress the native drums and flutes, which were regarded as accouterments of pagan ritual. A seventeenth-century Jesuit missionary in Peru proudly reported to his superiors that he had personally destroyed 605 large and 3418 small drums and flutes in the Peruvian villages. In 1614, the Archbishop of Lima ordered the confiscation and destruction of all Indian musical instruments in his bishopric. Those found in possession of the forbidden objects were punished by receiving three hundred lashes in the public square, and then led through the streets on the back of a llama" (1946, 47).

One of the driving forces of the Spanish conquerors was to find the fabled El Dorado, the Golden One, and his city of gold. Encouraged by stories they had heard from the native people about such a person and his realm, the Spanish invaders constantly pressed forward throughout the coastal and highland regions of present-day Venezuela, Colombia, Ecuador, Peru, and elsewhere, in their search for the land of El Dorado. I have chosen this term, El Dorado, to represent the ancient native American cultures from those lands. Other designations I use for these regions of South America are the northern and central Andes, although I use those terms very loosely because many of the archaeological cultures thrived in coastal regions.

Geographic and Historical Background

For the purposes of this book, I define South American archaeological cultures as those polities prior to the Spanish conquest that existed primarily in the greater Andes and their watersheds to the Pacific Ocean and the Caribbean Sea, stretching from northwestern Venezuela and northeastern Colombia to the tip of Tierra del Fuego (fig. 1.1). Considering the total length and breadth of the Andes enables us to view not only the vast areas of the central Andes that came under the domination of the Incas (from southern Colombia to the Maule River in central Chile) but to also include such northern cultures as the Colombian Sinú and Tairona that, in many ways, shared music technologies with other pre-Columbian Andean peoples.

Within this vast area, the central Andes have been the most studied, and its music today reaches far beyond its borders. The central Andes include much of Ecuador and Peru, northwestern Argentina, western Bolivia, and northern Chile, a region that rises from the Pacific coast to heights exceeding 20,000 feet. It is an area rich with music, and even in ancient times music was important in the mortal and immortal worlds of native people. The Spanish conquerors, accompanied by Catholic missionaries and African slaves, introduced additional musical elements into the region, beginning in the early 1500s.

Although the cultural geography of the central Andes reveals considerable diversity, the area is today somewhat united by several factors: the Quechua language in the north and south and the Aymara language in the south; religious festivals that reveal a fusion of Roman Catholicism and indigenous beliefs; *huayno* (*wayno*) dance music and its variants; the guitar and other stringed instruments introduced by the Spanish; and, since the 1970s, a pan-Andean musical style that originated in southern Peru and Bolivia and spread into many of the cities and towns in the central Andes. While this book concentrates on music before the "discovery" of the Spanish by the native Americans, the music of today often continues as a legacy of the past.

I use the term *El Dorado* metaphorically to emphasize several characteristics about the South American cultures studied in this book. First, all the cultures existed in northern and western South America, in the areas that were originally included under the Viceroyalty of Peru until the early 1700s (including the *audencias* of Santa Fé, Quito, and Lima) and

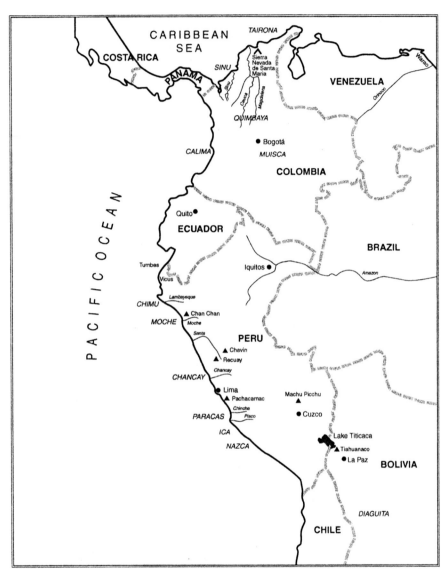

1.1. Map of western South America from northern Colombia to northern Chile, showing some of the main archaeological cultures. Cartography by Robert Burke.

later under the Viceroyalty of Nueva Granada (New Granada, consisting of present Colombia and Ecuador) and the Viceroyalty of Peru (consisting of present Peru) by the colonial administrators (Lombardi and Lombardi 1983, 29, 32).

Second, the myth of El Dorado conjures up great wealth, and it is used here as an icon for the highly developed cultures in the regions of northern Colombia and the central Andes. For example, the civilizations of the Sinú (ca. A.D. 1000–1550) and Tairona (ca. A.D. 500–1550) in northern Colombia, two cultures that fed the myth, were elaborate city-states or complex chiefdoms (see chapters 9 and 10). Likewise, the Chibcha or Muísca (ca. A.D. 650–1550) near present Bogotá were highly developed (all Colombian archaeology dates are from Dickey, Man, and Wiencek 1982). Continuing southward into present Peru, there were many great ancient cultures (or styles), such as the Chimú (ca. A.D. 900–1430), Lambayeque or Sicán (ca. A.D. 900–1370), Moche (ca. 100 B.C.–A.D. 700), Recuay (ca. 200 B.C.–A.D. 550), and Vicus (ca. 300–100 B.C.) from the Peruvian north coast; the Chancay (ca. A.D. 900–1430) and others from the central coast; the Ica (ca. A.D. 900–1550), Nasca (ca. 200 B.C.–A.D. 600), and Paracas (ca. 800–100 B.C.) from the south-central coast; and the Inca, lasting into the early 1500s (all Peruvian archaeology dates are from Donnan 1992, except Nasca, which is from Silverman 1993, 30).

Third, the native peoples of South America included in this book, like the Spanish, placed great value on gold (also silver and precious stones, such as jade and turquoise). For ancient Americans, however, the value was religious rather than monetary.

The Musical Background

The main title of this book, *Music of El Dorado*, refers to my explorations of the South American past by seeking answers to the questions who made music, where was it made, how was it made, and why was it made. The book's particular focus is on several archaeological cultures in the northern and central Andes (and adjacent areas) of Colombia and Peru, respectively. Archaeological studies have revealed that edge-blown aerophones, what we would call flutes in the broadest sense,[1] were the predominant melodic musical instruments of the ancient people from the realm of El Dorado. My musical explorations are informed by studies (my own and those of others) of (1) ancient native South American flutes (and to a lesser degree drums, rattles, conch shell trumpets, whistling, and singing, because they were often used in conjunction with flutes) of the greater Andean region; (2) iconography depicting flutes, other instruments, and their performers; (3) what archaeologists, art historians, historians, and other scholars have said about flutes and related instruments; and (4) current native South Americans from the greater Andean region who play and have ideas about similar instruments.

The book's subtitle, *The Ethnomusicology of Ancient South American Cultures,* refers to the musical-cultural study of numerous pre-Columbian (also called pre-Conquest, pre-Encounter, and pre-Spanish) peoples from northern Chile and Bolivia to the Caribbean coast, including certain regions of the Pacific coast and highlands of South America (loosely called the Andes for the purposes of this study). For this type of investigation I have coined the term *ethnoarchaeomusicology* (a combination of ethnomusicology, ethnoarchaeology, and archaeomusicology), by which I mean the scientific, cultural, and interpretative study of music from archaeological sources. This term could also be defined as the ethnomusicology of archaeological cultures, meaning more specifically the study of people making music for themselves, for other people, or for their gods, as determined from the investigation of archaeological artifacts.

Ethnohistorian and anthropologist Arjun Appadurai, in *The Social Life of Things: Commodities in Cultural Perspective,* presents the following paradox that is relative to this study:

> Even if our own approach to things is conditioned necessarily by the view that things have no meanings apart from those that human transactions, attributions, and motivations endow them with, the anthropological problem is that this formal truth does not illuminate the concrete, historical circulation of things. For that we have to follow the things themselves, for their meanings are inscribed in their forms, their uses, their trajectories. It is only through the analysis of these trajectories that we can interpret the human transactions and calculations that enliven things. Thus, even though from a *theoretical* point of view human actors encode things with significance, from a *methodological* point of view it is the things-in-motion that illuminate their human and social context. (1986, 5; emphases Appadurai's)

Archaeological artifacts, however, are not "things-in-motion"; moreover, they were probably not commodities, and we do not know their trajectories beyond what is depicted in iconography or where they are found in archaeological sites. Therefore, ethnoarchaeomusicology is challenged by two questions: What is culturally significant about musically related artifacts lost in time, and how can we obtain ethnomusicological information from them? The primary purposes of this book are to provide a methodology for such a study and to present data and conclusions derived from the applications of my research, which is based in musicology (by which I mean the study of any music from all conceivable approaches) rather than archaeology. This book, as a musicological investigation of archaeological cultures, also suggests ideas about interpretation of pre-Columbian musical instruments to students of archaeology who lack the musical training to (1) produce sounds on the musical artifacts they discover, (2) understand how sounds are produced on musical instruments, (3) classify musical instruments according to the tenets of organology, (4) analyze pitches, intervals, and tone systems, and (5) be sensitive to the importance of music as sound within indigenous cultures. Each researcher approaches his or her study with a particular expertise or set of intellectual tools. Interpretation, especially, "is open to individual manipulation to some degree" (Appadurai 1986, 17), and many of my interpretations (my manipulations) in this book are derived from ethnomusicology and flute performance, two areas that require and are based on sensitivity for music as culture, sound, and performance. My approach is intended to breathe life into ancient musical artifacts, many of which were most certainly constructed for the purpose of making sounds.

Why is sound important? "Sound identifies and gives shape to societal values and structures" (Sullivan 1986, 15). Because pre-Columbian musical instruments were intended to be heard, I have recorded a compact disc to complement this book, whose contents are available on the Internet through a link at the website of the University Press of Florida <http://www.upf.com>. The recorded examples (called audio tracks in this book) include performances by Eduardo Calderón and myself on many of the ancient musical instruments I studied. It is my conviction that many wind instruments of pre-Columbian native Americans were used for or represented supernatural power derived from theurgical communication. The best way to appreciate them, and perhaps grasp their musical beauty and power, is to hear them.

This book, therefore, is flute oriented because those breath-sounding musical instruments were the most common melody producers of ancient South Americans and are, I believe, holders of significant information for understanding some of the human and spiritual behavior of ancient South Americans who lived in the realms of the mythical El Dorado.

The Roots and Routes of My Research

The inspirations, research, and collecting of data for this book have occurred over the past thirty years or more, and because I consider many of these roots and routes relevant to this study, they are presented here as a short autobiography. My background interests and experiences with the musical instruments of ancient South America began when my wife, Diane, and I were Peace Corps volunteers in Santiago, Chile, from June 1966 until December 1968. As a volunteer I performed for two seasons as principal flutist with the Philharmonic Orchestra of Chile. As a sideline I developed a fascination with the traditional flutes of the Andes, largely because of music I heard at various patronal festivals I attended in northern Chile (La Tirana, Aiquina, Andacollo, and others), and the pan-Andean music we heard at La Peña de los Parra in Santiago (a folkloric nightclub-coffeehouse, begun by Violeta Parra and continued by her children, Angel and Isabel). Also in Santiago, *quena* flutes and *siku* panpipes played by members of Inti-Illimani, Quillapayún, and many other young musicians who performed with Angel and Isabel Parra intrigued me. Vacations from the Philharmonic Orchestra in the summer (December and January) and winter (July) gave us time to travel within the country, and the northern Chilean Andes (the home of several ancient cultures) were accessible by bus or train. I first encountered South American pre-Columbian flutes and pottery in the small but wonderfully cluttered museum in San Pedro de Atacama, in the province of Antofagasta.

On our way home from the Peace Corps we traveled to several archaeological centers in the altiplano between La Paz (Bolivia) and Puno (Peru), such as Tiahuanaco and Siscuani, and in the Cuzco department of Peru, such as Machu Picchu, Pisac, Ollantaytambo, and other sites in the

Sacred Valley of the Inca. These places fascinated me and added historical, environmental, and contextual aspects to my interests. But it was the collection in the National Museum of Anthropology and Archaeology in Lima that introduced me to the possibility for scholarly study of pre-Columbian musical instruments and musicians through their depictions (the ancient iconography) that were etched into, painted upon, or modeled as pottery vessels.

Upon returning to the United States in the spring of 1969, I secured a summer position as second flutist in the Chicago Grant Park Symphony. The Field Museum of Natural History is just a short distance from the Grant Park band shell where I rehearsed and performed nearly every day. When I discovered the large displays of pre-Columbian ceramics from Peru in the Field Museum, I was also introduced to other cultures, such as the Sinú and Tairona of northern Colombia. John Alden Mason had worked with the Field Museum, and the collections from his archaeological investigations in northern Colombia are there, with many of the most important pieces (including ceramic musical instruments) on display. These collections, and others at the Art Institute of Chicago, further inspired and intrigued me.

Diane and I spent the summer of 1970 in Mexico, before moving to Los Angeles to attend the University of California, Los Angeles (UCLA), where Diane would pursue a master's degree (1972) in Latin American Studies and I, a doctorate (1973) in ethnomusicology. Our goal in Mexico was to visit every archaeological site in that country, a goal we soon realized could never be attained during one summer. Nevertheless, the many days spent in the National Museum of Anthropology in Mexico City introduced us to the rich music archaeological collections from Middle America (Mexico and Central America) and South America. Additionally, the many trips to Michohuacán, Yucatán, Oaxaca, the Gulf coast, and elsewhere in Mexico provided additional historical, environmental, comparative, and contextual fuel to my interests in archaeomusicology.

At UCLA one of Diane's teachers was Professor Christopher Donnan and one of her classmates was Douglas Sharon, two scholars of Peruvian archaeology and cultural anthropology who have been extremely influential in my own work. Another of Diane's professors, for whom she worked as a research assistant, was Johannes Wilbert, then head of the Latin American Center. Dr. Wilbert became one of my major professors as I conducted research and wrote my dissertation on the music of the

Warao of Venezuela. It was through him and his writings that I was introduced to South American shamanism and the works of Reichel-Dolmatoff (known for his archaeological studies of the Sinú and Tairona of Colombia).

Christopher Donnan and I assembled a slide-audiotape documentary of a Los Angeles private collection of pre-Columbian musical instruments from Peru. I recorded myself playing, among others, several bone and cane tubular notch flutes from the Chancay and Nasca (also spelled Nazca) cultures, ceramic globular duct and ductless flutes from the Moche (also called Mochica), Nasca, and Chancay, panpipes from the Nasca culture, and whistling bottles from various ancient Peruvian cultures, while Professor Donnan and I photographed the artifacts in an artistic yet scholarly fashion. This was my first introduction into the realm of archaeological archiving and documentation. It was also during my tenure at UCLA that I first worked with the Moche Archive established by Donnan. In addition, I often traveled to the University of California, Berkeley, to work in the R. H. Lowie Museum of Anthropology, where I met John Rowe, Dorothy Menzel, Laurence Dawsen, and others whose publications were informative. Moreover, these scholars were enthusiastic about my ability to play the museum's ancient Peruvian flutes. For two years I worked with ethnomusicology professor Peter Crossley-Holland, measuring, performing and recording, and helping him classify the many pre-Columbian musical instruments in his private collection. This work was continued by Linda O'Brien and ultimately published by UCLA (Crossley-Holland 1980).

After graduation in 1973, Diane, our son, Darin, and I moved to the Florida State University (FSU) in Tallahassee, where I was hired as assistant professor of ethnomusicology. I went to Bogotá in 1974 on a summer stipend grant from the National Endowment for the Humanities (NEH). There I began my first systematic study of over 400 ceramic globular and tubular flutes from the Sinú, Tairona, and other ancient Colombian cultures. Dozens of antiquities store owners, private collectors such as Guillermo Cano, museum curators, and others were extremely helpful in allowing me to photograph, measure, document, and record myself playing musical artifacts from their collections.

I was also able to travel to Lima on the NEH grant, where I photographed more ancient musical instruments and related artifacts, working primarily with César Bolaños in the National Museum of Anthropology and Archaeology but also studying artifacts in other museums. I also traveled to Trujillo, on the north coast, where I spent several weeks working with Eduardo Calderón (a shaman or *curandero* [curer] living in the village of Las Delicias near Moche) and Dr. Michael Moseley and his Harvard crew, who were excavating Chan Chan. It was in Trujillo that I also conducted research in the Cassinelli Museum and other repositories of pre-Columbian musical artifacts.

At FSU, Diane received a contract to document and write an exhibition catalogue (Diane Olsen 1978) of the university's John and Mary Carter Collection of pre-Columbian artifacts. While helping her organize that collection, I studied numerous musically related ceramic vessels from ancient Peru, including many whistling bottles.

In 1979, I received a Fulbright-Hays International Exchange of Scholars Fellowship to teach and conduct research in Peru. While in Lima I continued my study of ancient musical instruments and also traveled extensively throughout the Peruvian highlands from Cajamarca to Puno, always seeking out more musical artifacts to photograph and study, and absorbing more of the geographical, historical, and contextual data of ancient Peruvian cultures. I also spent more time with Eduardo Calderón.

I received a Committee on Faculty Research Award (COFRS) from the Florida State University in 1982 to conduct research at the Field Museum of Natural History in Chicago. There I worked exclusively with John Alden Mason's original field notes, documentations, and Tairona musical instruments that he had collected decades before in northern Colombia. I was privileged to work again with Michael Moseley, who was the curator. During the summer of 1983, I studied the pre-Columbian musical instrument collection in the Metropolitan Museum of Art in New York, Kenneth Moore, assistant curator of musical instruments. I also spent several weeks studying pottery making in Tallahassee, primarily attempting to make ceramic globular flutes with duct mouthpieces and four fingerholes. Since then I have had opportunities to photograph pre-Columbian musical instruments and artifacts in museums in Amsterdam, Berlin, Chicago, Gainesville (Florida), Hamburg, La Plata (Argentina), London, Los Angeles, Minneapolis, New York, Paris, Venice (Italy), and other cities in the Americas and Europe.

In 1991, out of a collection of more than 125,000 photographs of Moche art pieces in the UCLA Moche Archive, collected and organized by Dr. Christopher Donnan, then director of the Fowler Museum (Donnan 1990, 23), I studied all that pertained to music and dance. In 1996, I returned to Trujillo, Peru, where I again spent several days with Eduardo Calderón at his home in Las Delicias, reading to him several chapters of my manuscript that pertain to the Moche culture. His corrections and additional explanations and interpretations were extremely important to the completion of this book. It was just several months after that visit that he died.

Archaeological field investigation (that is, excavation) has not been a part of my research, and I do not consider myself to be an archaeologist in any sense of the word. I am an ethnomusicologist and a flutist interested in exploring the ethnoarchaeomusicology of the great musical cultures of ancient South America. It is my belief that an ethnomusicological approach to the archaeological past is valid and potentially productive. In an earlier publication I wrote, "Ethnomusicology is the study of a culture's music undertaken to learn something about how that culture thinks about itself and the world it lives in. . . . An important question the ethnomusicologist must ask is, what can music tell us about a civilization, a nation, a tribe, a village, a person, that nothing else can tell us?" (Olsen 1996, xxv). While the first part of this quotation relies on folk evaluation, something that is impossible to achieve with cultures lost in the past, the second part, as a broad question, can be answered by analytical evaluation (Merriam 1964, 31–32). What can we learn about South American archaeological cultures through music? That is the question I propose to answer in this work.

As my summary reveals, fieldwork has been a part of my research, as it is of any ethnomusicological research. Because there are no consultants from the past, however, conclusions in this book have been informed by outsiders such as Calderón and other shamans, archaeologists, anthropologists, ethnographers, ethnomusicologists, historical musicologists, art historians, art collectors, and curators, and by my own critical analyses. In many cases, and not surprisingly, my conclusions are personal because "ethnomusicological fieldwork is personal—it must be, or it would be pointless" (Bohlman 1997, 147). Moreover, the conclusions made by Calderón and other shamans are personal because the archaeological musical instruments they use are power objects that assist them in their curing rituals. My conclusions are personal because they are often based on my understanding of the archaeological musical instruments through my performances on them. While some may interpret my performance of the musical instruments of El Dorado as exoticizing the past, I feel it is breathing some life into the past after millennia of silence; such musical life can be very rewarding and revealing, both personally and scientifically.

Formal Structure

Chapter 1 explains the various backgrounds that form the foundation of this book (geographic, historical, musical, and research), and chapter 2, "The Theory and Methodology of Ethnoarchaeomusicology," establishes the frameworks for the approach of the study. The five chapters that follow (3–7) are musical topical studies of five pre-Columbian types of edge-sounding aerophones found in many South American archaeological cultures: tubular notch flutes, panpipes, ocarinas or globular flutes, whistling bottles, and transverse flutes. The last three chapters are musical case studies of three archaeological cultures in South America: the Moche (including Vicus, which was related to early Moche) of northwestern Peru, the Sinú of northwestern Colombia, and the Tairona of northeastern Colombia. In these musical case studies I present particular ideas and develop specific hypotheses that pertain to the significance of musical artifacts in those great archaeological cultures. The Moche (chapter 8) native Americans were among the greatest artisans in all of ancient South America, and their pottery is like a ceramic ethnographic textbook. The Sinú (chapter 9) were probably the greatest duct tubular flute manufacturers in all of ancient South America, and the Tairona (chapter 10) manufactured tubular and globular duct flutes of all types and in incredible numbers.

All the musical topic and case study chapters either systematically or loosely follow a methodological model for ethnoarchaeomusicological inquiry, which I explain in detail in chapter 2. I have purposely chosen to apply the methodological model in a mechanical and systematic way throughout this book, except in chapter 8, where I blend the investigative process into a more fluid discourse based largely on interviews and discussions with Eduardo Calderón.

Throughout the book I present many original photographs of archaeological artifacts. While other photographs of some of these artifacts appear in archaeological publications, many have not been published be-

fore. In addition, fifty-two audio examples accompany this book (indicated as audio tracks in the text), available on the Internet at <http://
www.upf.com> (these audio examples are also on a compact disc available from the author for a nominal fee <dolsen@mailer.fsu.edu>). My
main desire with the audio examples is to demonstrate the musical beauty
and technological complexities of the ancient musical instruments that
form the basis for this book.

2

_~·~·~_

The Theory and Methodology
of Ethnoarchaeomusicology

Archaeomusicology, or music archaeology as some would call it, is concerned with the ancient material objects themselves. Appadurai refers to a concern about material objects as a "methodological fetishism," explaining that "things in general [including musical instruments] . . . are the stuff of 'material culture,' which unites archaeologists with several kinds of cultural anthropologists [including ethnomusicologists]" (1986, 5). For the archaeomusicologist, the primary sources of material culture are ancient musical instruments and the ancient iconography that depict their use.

Musical Instruments of Ancient South American Cultures

Ancient South American musical instruments are aerophones (air sounders, or wind instruments), membranophones (membrane sounders, or skin instruments), and idiophones (self-sounders, or hard instruments). Prehistorically, as today, the greater Andes were primarily flute and drum oriented, with trumpets, bells, and rattles also used secondarily as sound makers. This book principally pertains to the first category: edge-blown (flute-type) aerophones, the most prominent and melodic of instruments. Flute-type aerophones were not usually played in isolation, however. Many membranophones or drums accompanied them, such as a small-frame drum with two skin heads known as _tinya_ in Quechua; a deep-frame drum with two skin heads called *huancar* (*wancar*) in Quechua and *bombo* in Spanish (an onomatopoeic name for a similar deep-frame drum, also with two heads); a ceramic kettle or vase drum with a single skin head; and a ceramic hourglass drum with two skin heads. Moreover, they were perhaps also occasionally accompanied by or complemented with a number of idiophonic sound makers such as container rattles made from ceramic, metal, gourd, calabash, or rafted cane tubes filled with seeds or small stones.

Many excellent studies of musical instruments from the ancient cultures of the central Andes have been done, beginning with Charles Mead's (1903) seminal descriptions at the turn of the century, Raoúl and Marguerite d'Harcourt's monumental study (published in French in 1925 and reprinted in Spanish in 1990), and Robert M. Stevenson's thorough musical analysis (1968). Shorter and more specific studies of ancient Peruvian music have been done by Arturo Jiménez Borja (1951), Jorge Silva Sifuentes (1978), and César Bolaños (1981, 1988a, 1988b). Other noteworthy studies of pre-Columbian Andean musical areas include María Ester Grebe's (1974) survey of Chile, Segundo Luis Moreno Andrade's (1949) study of Ecuadorian music and dance, and the more recent and ongoing work of Ellen Hickmann (1986, 1987, 1988, 1990), whose book *Musik aus dem Altertum der Neuen Welt* (Music from the antiquity of the New World) is the most thorough catalogue of musical instruments from ancient Colombia, Ecuador, and Peru. Useful surveys of pre-Columbian musical instruments in South America are included in volume 2 of *The Garland Encyclopedia of World Music*, entitled *South America, Mexico, Central America, and the Caribbean* (Olsen and Sheehy 1998). In particular, portions of entries by Olsen (in "Approaches to Musical Scholarship," 6–12), Henry Stobart ("Bolivia," 282), John Schechter ("Ecuador," 413–14), and Raúl Romero ("Peru," 467) provide recent summaries from certain areas. The volume also contains entries pertaining to Mexico, Central America, and the Caribbean that provide useful comparative materials. The archaeological portions are by Arturo Chamorro ("Mexica [Aztec or Nahua People]," 555–57), E. Fernando Nava L. ("Mixtec," 563–64), Daniel E. Sheehy ("Mexico," 601–3), Linda O'Brien-Rothe ("Maya," 650–51), Oliver Greene ("Belize," 667), Carlos Fernández ("Costa Rica," 680–81), Salvador Marroquín ("El Salvador," 706–7), T. M. Scruggs ("Nicaragua," 747–48), and Martha Ellen Davis ("Dominican Republic," 846–47).

The most useful application of the comparative method in South American archaeomusicological research, as in any scientific study, is to compare sets of information that have common points of origin, both in space and time. This is not always possible, however, because the lack of documentation of many pre-Columbian artifacts has made exact provenience difficult to determine. Due in part to grave robbers and others who are unskilled or uninterested in scientific documentation, to a lack of funds of many museums for proper classification of artifacts, and to falsifications in pre-Columbian art, such lacunae of information about provenience makes scientific studies difficult if not impossible. In addition, the quests of some scholars for pan-Peruvian, pan-Andean, or other types of universals, have led to incorrect generalizations. The pentatonic myth of the Andes that abounds in much early literature (Castro 1938; Harcourt and Harcourt 1925; Giacobbe 1936, 230; Lacroix 1843, cited in Stevenson 1968, 246; Sas 1935) and which was finally laid to rest by Stevenson (1968, 246–52) and Joerg Haeberli (1979), is a good example of such an incorrect generalization. My model for a musical atlas of Peru (Olsen 1986b) provides a paradigm for the classification of music information, based on a schema for determining the proper information to be compared.

Wendell C. Bennett and Junius B. Bird's early study *Andean Culture History* (1964) is based on a common attitude that regards the technical accomplishments of the ancient peoples of the central Andes as superior to those of other ancient Andean peoples. For example, after a few pages about the northern Andes where they write, "The Chibcha and Tairona cultures present some evidence of complexity" (1964, 50), and even fewer pages about the southern Andes, they devote most of the remainder of their book to the central Andes (for them Peru and Bolivia). It is perhaps true that up to 1949 the central Andes had been studied in much more depth than the other areas; in addition, Bennett and other scholars at that time were interested in cultural diffusion and the idea of information disseminating from major centers to outlying ones (Mary Glowacki, pers. comm., 1999). Nevertheless, their criteria for conclusions about technical development and complexity of cultures are often based on either size of cities, number and size of monuments, variety in ceramics and metallurgy, or color and texture of textiles. Because little was known about arts and crafts at the time of Bennett and Bird's seminal study, I propose that another subject be considered: musical instruments. Musical instrument classification, or organology, is a useful criterion for attempting to understand more about ancient Andean cultures, one that can be used in addition to the usual criteria listed above. Ethnomusicologist Judith Becker describes the importance of musical instruments in the human symbolic system: "Musical instruments, throughout the world, come to have meanings associated with them that far surpass their pure physicality as sound producing objects made of wood, metal, or clay. . . . As zoomorphic representations of deities, or as metaphors of sexuality (flutes or drums), their physical shape may make them suitable objects through which or by which to worship spiritual forces. Outside of ritual, instruments nearly always have associations of class, or hierarchy, thus reinforcing the rankings of men and women within a society. Everywhere, musical instruments are embedded within the systems of thought that organize and give coherence to a particular worldview" (1988, 385). Although Becker is referring specifically to the musical instruments of Java, her profound ideas pertain to many other regions of the world, and particularly to South American archaeological cultures. To clarify how musical instruments in South American archaeological cultures can be classified, I delineate the following organological categories (throughout this book, the first term in each category may be used interchangeably with the term following it in parentheses):

(1) *ductless tubular flute (notch flute)*—a single-tube (open distal end), ductless (with a notch for a mouthpiece), vertical or end-blown, edge-sounding instrument with fingerholes, similar to the present Andean *quena (kena)* and its variants;

(2) *duct tubular flute (duct flute or recorder flute)*—a single-tube (open distal end), duct (with a fipple mouthpiece, like an American recorder or Irish pennywhistle), vertical or end-blown, edge-sounding instrument with fingerholes, similar to the present Andean *pinkullo* and its variants;

(3) *ductless transverse tubular flute (transverse flute)*—a single-tube (open distal end, although some variants are closed), ductless, horizontal or cross-blown (with a mouthpiece like an English fife or European orchestral flute), edge-sounding instrument with fingerholes, similar to the present Andean cross-blown *flauta* or *pífano* and their variants;

(4) *panpipe*—a multiple-tube (closed distal ends, joined together in a raft shape), ductless (open proximal ends only, no notches), edge-

sounding instrument without fingerholes, similar to the present Andean *antara, rondador,* or *siku* (consisting of two halves) and their variants;

(5) *ductless globular flute (ocarina-type flute)*—a single-chamber globular, ductless (with a cross-blown mouthpiece or embouchure hole), edge-sounding instrument without or with fingerholes, similar to the present ductless ocarina made in northern Chile;

(6) *duct globular flute (ocarina-type flute)*—a single-chamber globular, duct (with a fipple mouthpiece), edge-sounding instrument without or with fingerholes (the former instrument is often called a whistle in the literature), similar to the present duct ocarina made in northern Colombia;

(7) *multiple-duct globular flute (double or triple ocarina)*—a multiple-chamber globular, duct (with a fipple mouthpiece), edge-sounding instrument without or with one fingerhole (one chamber may have a single fingerhole), similar to the present multiphonic ocarinas made in Peru;

(8) *whistling bottle (whistling pot, whistling vessel)*—a globular aerophone without fingerholes, consisting of one or two chambers with a single internal duct sounding device (the bottle is the duct, and the player's mouth never touches the sounding apparatus).

There are perhaps several reasons why Andean archaeological musical instruments have not previously been considered in archaeological theory for studies relating to dating, diffusion, and cultural development: (1) most pre-Columbian musical instruments lack accurate provenience, which makes dating problematic; (2) the cultural contexts of many ancient musical instruments are difficult, if not impossible, to determine; (3) many archaeologists do not possess sufficient musical skills to study ancient musical instruments; (4) Andeanists have had more fundamental issues to address than ancient musical instruments; and (5) a nearly universal attitude exists among industrial nations that music making is diversion and not worthy of serious study. Relevant to this last point, until musical instruments and music making in ancient native America (and even present native America) are considered integral and significant aspects of South American society, ritual, and politics, on par with other human products such as textiles and metal objects, the musical artifacts will remain obscured as mere whistles of the past. The following words of Karl

Marx, although written about contemporary material culture or commodities, are pertinent to an understanding of ancient musical artifacts: "A commodity appears at first sight, a very trivial thing, and easily understood. Its analysis shows that it is, in reality, a very queer thing, abounding in metaphysical subtleties and theological niceties" (1970, 76). In early 1998, Dumbarton Oaks, in Washington, D.C., made a serious effort to elevate the study of pre-Columbian musical instruments by conducting a conference titled "New Research in Pre-Columbian Music." In attendance were North American and Latin American scholars, collectors, and musicians who presented papers on their most recent research.[1] Thus, interest in the archaeomusicology of Middle and South America is growing. By writing this book I hope to add to the serious study of the music from the realm of El Dorado.

The Theory and Methodology of Ethnoarchaeomusicology

Ethnoarchaeomusicology, the cultural and interpretative study of music from archaeological sources, could also be called the ethnomusicology of archaeology, meaning the study of people making music for themselves, for other people, or for their gods, as determined from the investigation of archaeological artifacts. My ethnoarchaeomusicological investigative approach employed in this book has been loosely inspired by ethnoarchaeology and experimental archaeology. Ian Hodder defines ethnoarchaeology as "the collection of original ethnographic data in order to aid archaeological interpretation" (1982, 28). It is also explained by Carol Kramer: "As a research strategy, ethnoarchaeology . . . [is] designed with a view to aiding in the collection and analysis, as well as in the interpretation, of archaeological remains" (1979, 7). Ethnographic analogy, however, is the only aspect of ethnoarchaeology that I employ in this book, and it is mostly for the purpose of interpretation.

Experimental archaeology is defined by Sara Champion as "A term used to describe attempts at the reconstruction of past processes" (1980, 45). I include my performance on ancient musical instruments within this definition because I believe that the musical instruments were made to be played and that their sounds can possibly tell us something about the cultures that manufactured them. Both of these subdisciplines of archaeology are aspects of the so-called New Archaeology, which is based on the premise that through archaeology it is possible to learn about the social organization and religious beliefs of ancient people (Renfrew 1987, 80).

A Methodological Model

To find answers to questions about the music cultures of ancient cultures requires an interdisciplinary approach that goes beyond the description and analysis of the artifacts themselves. It requires the thorough exploration of all facets of knowledge that pertain to the object or subject of study. For the purpose of making ethnoarchaeomusicology a systematic study, I have organized a schema based on four modes of inquiry that feed into and interact with the ultimate goal, musical knowledge. I call my approach a methodological model, rather than simply a model, because it refers to an approach or sets of approaches, rather than a theory. My methodological model, which is based on common practices in New Archaeology, is best viewed in the cruciform diagram in figure 2.1. The four extremities of the cross pertain to four steps that lead toward the accumulation of information relating to the center, musical knowledge. The center of the cross could also be labeled to reflect a specific objective—knowledge of a culture, musical instrument, tone system (scale), and so on.

In some instances my specific objective will be knowledge of musical

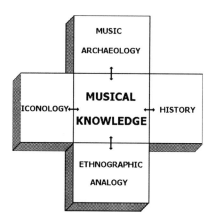

2.1. Olsen Methodological Model for Ethnoarchaeomusicological Inquiry

instruments while in others it will be musical-cultural knowledge. In my quest for knowledge about ancient musical material culture, for example, I am inspired by the words of Judith Becker quoted above, and by the following passage written by Alan Merriam, in which he advocates a holistic approach to the study of musical instruments, one which far surpasses normal organological approaches:

> In addition to . . . primarily descriptive facts about music instruments, . . . there is a further range of more analytic questions of concern. . . . Is there present in the society a concept of special treatment of musical instruments? Are some revered? Do some symbolize other kinds of cultural or social activity? Are particular instruments the harbingers of certain kinds of messages of general import to the society at large? Are the sounds or shapes of particular instruments associated with specific emotions, states of being, ceremonials, or calls to action? The economic role of instruments is also of importance. . . . Instruments may be considered as items of wealth; they may be owned by individuals; their ownership may be individually acknowledged but for practical purposes ignored; or they may constitute an item of village or tribal wealth. The distribution of instruments has considerable importance in diffusion studies and in the reconstruction of culture history, and it is sometimes possible to suggest or to confirm population movements through the study of instruments. (1964, 45)

While many of Merriam's questions cannot be answered for archaeological musical instruments, it is the purpose of my methodological model to provide a basis for such a study.

My methodological model comprises four steps.

1. *Music Archaeology.* I define this step as the descriptive study of the musical-cultural remains of a people. As a mode of ethnomusicological inquiry, it includes a complete description of the musical or musically related artifact in question, ideally based on scientific dating techniques, physical measurements, photographs from all angles, x-rays, audio recording of pitches, and measurement of pitches (if it is a musical instrument) in a scientific manner. This step can also be called archaeomusicology, which is more specifically music centered.

In any archaeomusicological study there are numerous variables that must be given careful attention. Most important are the authenticity and provenience of the archaeological sources themselves, because a certain number of the ancient artifacts available for study may be fakes. This is especially true for archaeological remains from Colombia, where grave robbing is rampant and copies of ancient artifacts are constantly being manufactured for the tourist market. Not only are fakes often cleverly made to look old by being buried and dug up after weathering has taken place, but some reproductions are actually inventions of their modern creators (some contemporary Colombian blackware artifacts, for example, even resemble Godzilla). Furthermore, many archaeological specimens found in commercial stores, private collections, and museums are poorly documented because they were purchased from grave robbers uninterested in documentation. Even some of the ceramic objects carried from northern Colombia to the Chicago Field Museum by John Alden Mason in the 1920s were purchased from grave robbers (according to his field notes, now in the Chicago Field Museum archive), making their authenticity and provenience unknown. Gerardo Reichel-Dolmatoff, in a private conversation with me in 1984, pointed out the problems of authenticity and provenience in Colombian archaeology. Colombian grave robbers are well organized into their own unions, and although many claim to employ archaeological field methods (according to Guillermo Cano, private conversation, 1974), this claim is highly questionable.

Other variables involve laboratory analysis of the objects. While it is true that laboratory analysis can support scientific statements about certain musical characteristics (such as the pitch possibilities) of ancient flutes, the obvious question is: Who produces the sounds? One approach is to use a mechanical device. Garrett and Stat (1977), for example, in a study of pre-Columbian whistling bottles, employed a scientific blowing apparatus that was able to provide consistent air pressure. While their machine was useful for their study of whistling bottles, because each artifact has a duct whistle in its spout and no fingerholes, the same apparatus would not work for notch flutes with fingerholes or for panpipes.

A more practical approach is to use human air pressure. I argue that the most logical person for studying pre-Columbian musical instruments of the flute type is a flutist trained in ethnomusicology, because a flutist-ethnomusicologist has a stable embouchure (pitch and breath control) and is familiar with flutes from different cultures and understands their fingerings, embouchures required to play them, and blowing techniques. Likewise, a flutist has finger coordination for playing flutes with fingerholes, although any fingering skills other than coordination are of no use to a scientific study of pre-Columbian flutes: the fast-fingering technique of the Western flutist, for example, serves no analytical purpose. Furthermore, it is ethnocentric to consider only the standard Western fingering pattern of lifting one finger off after the other, from the distal to the proximal end of the instrument. For example, I have found that a careful study of the flute fingering techniques of several present native South American cultures is useful for determining alternative fingering methods. The Warao of the Orinoco delta region (Delta Amacuro) of Venezuela, for example, finger their three-holed deer-bone flute one (and only one) finger off at a time (Olsen 1978–79, 588–94; 1996, 72). Thus, their sequence would be typically all fingers on, bottom off, all on, middle off, all on, top off, and so forth. Another fingering method is found among the Q'ero of southern Peru, high in the Andes, who play their four-holed flutes by removing two fingers (never one) at a time (Cohen 1966, 7).[2] Another fingering method is used by pinkullo players in Conima, Peru, on the northern shore of Lake Titicaca, whereby the upper fingerhole is always closed and the lower one always left open (Turino 1993, 49). Thus, to employ a Western flute-fingering technique on the Warao and Q'ero flutes, and by extension, pre-Columbian flutes, would be ethnocentric and of questionable value.

Therefore, my field method includes my "objective" recorded performances on hundreds of pre-Columbian musical instruments from museums and private collections in Colombia, Peru, and the United States. This objective performance approach can be partially heard in audio track 1, which demonstrates my fingering method as applied to three ancient tubular flutes from the Tairona culture (see fig. 10.9).

I have carefully measured my recorded pitches with tonometric devices (e.g., Stroboconn and Korg tuner) and frequency counters. The systematic measuring of pitches, when combined with the other three modes of inquiry, enables us to distinguish certain correlations or relationships within the sampling.

2. *Iconology.* I define iconology as the scientific study of representation in the plastic arts. Another term, *iconography,* refers to the material objects (artifacts or representation of artifacts, such as painting, etching, relief, and so forth) themselves that are the objects of study; it "concerns the nature of the objects *per se,* their formal characters, the technique of production, their distribution in space and time, and their stylistic affini-

ties to similar productions elsewhere" (Grottanelli 1961, 46, cited in Merriam 1964, 34). Iconology, as a broader and more holistic study, includes the above definition of iconography, but goes beyond it to include a description and analysis of artifacts as depicted in painting, sculpture, or other iconographic sources. It also includes a study of the exterior and interior designs of the artifact, following Erwin Panofsky's three steps: "the description of the design motif thoroughly in *objective* terms, . . . the complete analysis of the motif just described, . . . [and] the interpretation" (1962, 3–17, cited in Cordy-Collins 1977b, 421; emphasis Cordy-Collins). Most important, iconology "has to do with the meaning of the representation, the nature of the beings it purports to portray, and the underlying system of conceptions and beliefs in which it is integrated—the world of ideas and symbols in a given culture" (Grottanelli 1961, 46, cited in Merriam 1964, 34). Iconography and iconology are vital to this study of the interpretation of ancient music cultures from archaeological sources. An attempt to understand the significance of ancient musical artifacts through their representation, however, must also rely on history and the use of ethnographic and ethnohistoric analogies for interpretations.

3. *History.* I define history as the descriptions of musical artifacts or musical occasions written by chroniclers. Such historical writings (sometimes called ethnohistory) can be emic (insider, or folk, evaluations) or nearly so, such as those by El Inca Garcilaso de la Vega (1966) writing about the Inca culture in the sixteenth century; more often, however, they are etic (outsider, or analytical, evaluations), such as those by Felipe Huamán Poma de Ayala ([1615] 1978) writing about ancient American civilizations, in which case the information may be highly biased.[3]

The historical record for archaeological interpretation must be carefully analyzed, because written information often varies: some will be objective and others subjective. Cordy-Collins, for example, warns of the dangers of ethnohistorical bases for interpretation of ancient artifacts: "The Spanish chronicles or ethnohistories of the Colonial Period are far from complete. If we rely on these ethnohistories . . . to interpret Andean iconographic motifs, we run the risk of disjunction (cultural disjunction occurs when a new people move into an area, adopt a motif developed in that area, but fail to adopt the meaning and, instead, substitute their own) or of descendants having forgotten what a motif originally represented" (1977b, 421). Likewise, Patricia Netherly warns us: "It is . . . necessary to know something of the culture of these who write down the original observations about a given society. As readers of such written records, we can observe the object of our study only indirectly through the eyes of another individual, frequently from a culture and time quite different from our own" (1988, 260). In spite of these admonitions, history can perhaps tell us something, as we endeavor to attain musical knowledge about ancient cultures.

4. *Ethnographic Analogy.* I define ethnographic analogy as the study of possible parallels between an ancient culture and a living culture or cultures, while an ethnographic analog is the thing, part, or culture that is analogous. Ethnographic analogy is a common interpretative technique in archaeology and provides the basis for the field of ethnoarchaeology. Hodder (1982), for example, has presented several ways in which ethnographic analogy can be applied with success in archaeology. These include the methods known as *formal analogy* and *relational analogy.* He defines formal analogy as the "direct comparison . . . of the forms of archaeological and ethnographic artifacts," such as "in the interpretation of tools" (1982, 68). Many of the comparisons using the method of formal analogy, however, are often made between cultures geographically very distant, such as Iron Age England with modern Kenya. A relational analogy is defined by Hodder as a comparison of "parallels of past and present technical processes," providing means thereby to understand "why a particular procedure should lead to a particular end result" (1982, 72). Such comparisons are also often made between cultures geographically distant, thereby weakening the analogy.

If the analogy is made between an ancient and a modern culture where the latter either geographically parallels the former, or when the inhabitants of a modern culture are thought to be descendants of the ancient culture, the approach is called a *direct historical approach.* The opposite of this is termed a *general comparative approach* (Chang 1967), "which involves selecting analogs not necessarily restricted to the same geographic area as the archaeological data with which they are compared" (Kramer 1979, 2). Although both of these approaches to ethnographic analogy can be applied, careful consideration should be given to the following two variables that function as constraints: *spatial proximity* and *temporal proximity.* The first refers to the distance (space) between the primary culture and the secondary culture that functions as an analogy, and the second refers to the time between them.

These variables are important because of the problems of cultural disjunction (Cordy-Collins 1977b, 421) and probable lack of continuity when comparing ancient cultures with those in the twentieth century. Often, colonial and postcolonial events and developments have had tremendous effects on the people who are most often approached as ethnographic analogies or links to the past. Nevertheless, as Kramer writes, "Observations of contemporary behavior can facilitate the development and refinement of insights into past behaviors, particularly when strong similarities can be shown to exist between the environments and technologies of the past and contemporary sociocultural systems being compared" (1979, 1). This view is supported by Frank Hole: "Now archaeologists realize that the study of human culture history requires more than just arranging artifacts in chronological sequences, and that there are circumstances when it is most efficient to study living people if we wish to rediscover the past" (1979, 193). Likewise, Patty Watson explains, "the use of analogies derived from present observations . . . [aids] interpretations of past events and processes. The reason we archaeologists do this . . . is to provide ourselves with as many and as varied interpretive hypotheses as possible to help us understand (explain and predict) archaeological remains" (1979, 277). In a type of reversal of the concept Peter Roe argues that "archaeological evidence, however tentative, seems to indicate a world not unlike that seen from the ethnographic evidence of the same and neighboring areas and gives a very respectable antiquity of some 3,000 years for the growth and development of the cosmic zygote" (1982, 305). Thus one epoch can inform the other, whether from antiquity to modern times or vice versa.

Researchers in ethnoarchaeology are not alone in studying the present to learn about the past. Ethnomusicologists also use the approach occasionally, as Philip Bohlman explains: "Through the experience of oral tradition in the field, the ethnographer tries to create a text for reading culture by moving backward through time. By interpreting the music of the present as linked to something previous through processes of either stability or change, it becomes possible to read backward through the past to a moment, perhaps, when only oral tradition existed. In this way, oral tradition may even render the past timeless. . . . Frequently, in the popular imagination, it is oral tradition that allows a community or culture to believe that some core of musical practices from the past—some essence of the past—remains intact in the present" (1997, 151). I hope to demonstrate in this book that oral traditions, interpretations, and other types of knowledge derived from present comparative ethnographic and ethnomusicological research are of value for the study of pre-Columbian musical contexts, behaviors, and significance.

The four modes of inquiry chosen for my ethnoarchaeomusicological research and delineated in this book represent the ideal, and the complete methodology is not always possible to apply. Because data are usually incomplete, for example, certain modes of inquiry may have to be omitted. In some situations music archaeology and iconology may not yield much information because incomplete field research has not produced many artifacts or because relevant exemplars do not exist. In other situations history or ethnographic analogy may not be possible because of a lack of information. Each mode of inquiry, however, must be thoroughly explored because each is seen as a step toward focusing on the ultimate musicological goal; until all four are explored thoroughly, in-depth knowledge and understanding will not be possible.

My research aim in the thorough exploration of all four modes of inquiry is related to the concept of complementarity, which refers to "the multiple parallel interactions and engagements of concepts, metaphors, or frameworks" (Plotnitsky 1993, xiv). It is further ethnomusicologically inspired by Izaly Zemtsovsky's concept of the "synthetic paradigm," whose "aim is to see the subject in its fullness, to enjoy the abundance of qualities" (1997, 189). These concepts of completeness are similar to the approach I took in my study of the Warao of Venezuela: "the ethnomusicologist must think of the subject of study as akin to the hub of a bicycle wheel, with the many spokes of information and knowledge leading to and supporting that hub. Several of these spokes can include music as sound, music as communication, musical instruments as material culture, musical instruments as symbol, dance as music, religious expression as music, music and myth, a specific music within the world of music, and so forth" (1996, xxv–xxvi). In other words, an ethnoarchaeomusicological study must be interdisciplinary and holistic, with music as the focus and point of departure. Furthermore, the approach must be systematic, following the modes of inquiry of the ethnoarchaeomusicological methodological model in the order suggested. Netherly explains a similar approach with regard to ethnohistorical investigation: "The point to remember is that the primary and secondary modes of analysis must occur before proceeding to a processual analysis, or instead of science we will find ourselves in the realm of fantasy" (1988, 260). Likewise, Richard Burger argues, "Ethnographic analogy—extrapolating from contemporary data what may have existed in the past—is a difficult and even dangerous approach, but it can be an effective tool for penetrating the alien and often mysterious world of the ancient Andes, when linked with critical archaeological and historic evidence" (1997, 21).

It is my desire to carry the study of ancient South American music beyond the purely descriptive stage (this is music archaeology) into analytical and hermeneutic levels (this is ethnoarchaeomusicology) whereby interpretation can suggest something about ancient music cultures in South America.

Part II

≈

Musical Topical Studies

3

Notch Flutes of Life and Transcendence

Within the worldview of traditional native South America, the concepts of life and transcendence are often of great importance. Transcendence has two realms: during life and after life. Transcendence during life is associated with shamanism and other theurgy (communication between mortal and immortal), while transcendence after life is associated with eschatology (the soul's ultimate destiny). This is corroborated by Peter Roe (1982, 303), who is in turn inspired by Elizabeth Benson: "The image of decay in life and vitalism in death from lowland cosmology is nowhere better stated visually than in Mochica art (Benson 1972:154, 1975:140)." While Benson is referring directly to Moche art, the idea of decay in life can generally be applied to South American shamanism, because symbolic death or near-death is often a part of a shaman's initiation in many cultures and is generally a slow process that takes place during the initiate's drug- or tobacco-induced trance state (Sullivan 1988, 398, 639, 648, 652).

Two types of vertical flutes seem to be closely linked to concerns with transcendence among ancient South Americans. These are the notch flute and the duct flute, which perhaps can be loosely called *quena* and *pinkullo*, respectively, after the terms employed in the central Andes of southern Peru at the time of the Encounter, as explained by colonial Spanish chroniclers. While I prefer not to use these terms for pre-Incan flutes, most archaeologists refer to the common archaeological variety with a notched mouthpiece (i.e., a cut in the proximal or mouthpiece end of the tube where the air is directed) as a quena (or kena). Since we do not know what the ancient, pre-Incan people called their flutes, I will, therefore, refer to them as notch flutes because of the highly visible notch-shaped cut used as a mouthpiece. Most pre-Columbian vertical tubular flutes in the central Andes were constructed with notched mouthpieces, although Hickmann (1990, 262) provides evidence for a bone duct flute with four fingerholes from the Chancay culture. Duct mouthpieces were commonly used on ancient coastal Peruvian globular flutes, proving that the principle was also known among the Moche and Nasca as well (but not for their tubular flutes). The Sinú and Tairona of northern Colombia, on the other hand, used the vertical duct flute concept almost exclusively (see chapters 9 and 10).

According to early colonial Quechua and Aymara dictionaries, the word *kena* or *quena* simply meant flute, and not specifically the type with a notched mouthpiece commonly known as quena today. Stevenson (1968, 258–61) has studied several colonial Quechua and Aymara dictionaries in great detail, and has discovered the following about vertical tubular flutes: "The best dictionaries of these two tongues were published in 1608 at Lima for Quechua (Diego González Holguín) and in 1612 at Juli on the shores of Lake Titicaca for Aymara (Ludovico Bertonio). In both tongues . . . *pincullu* = *pincollo* meant flute. . . . The Aymara also distinguished between bone flute (*cchaca pincollo*) and cane. The cane variety they called *quenaquena* or *quinaquina*, meaning 'full of holes.' They also knew it as *tupa pincollo*. Bertonio . . . repeats *Flauta de caña: Quenaquena; Qenaquena* (!) [sic] *pincollo: Flauta de caña*" (1968, 259). Therefore, the terms *kena-kena* (or *kina-kina*) and *pinkullo* (or *pincollo, pinkollo, pinkuyllo, pincullo, pingullo, pingollo, pinquillo, pinkillo,* and others) were used interchangeably in ancient times in the central Andean highlands during the colonial period (and probably before among Aymara and Quechua speakers) to indicate the notch flute.

Music Archaeology

Notch flutes (which always have fingerholes) existed from pre-Columbian times in ancient Peru, Bolivia, Chile, Ecuador, Venezuela,[1] and probably elsewhere. In coastal Peru, ancient tombs and ceremonial sites (Quechua: *huacas,* "sacred places or things") of the Chancay, Chimú, Ica, Moche, Nasca, Paracas, and other cultures have yielded notch flutes made from numerous tubes, including vegetable (e.g., various types of cane), animal (e.g., human, deer, llama, and pelican bones), and geological (e.g., clay, silver, and gold) materials. Izumi Shimada (1994, 213, fig. 9.30) excavated llama bone flutes from Moche V (late period) ceremonial centers near Chiclayo (Huaca del Pueblo Batán Grande in La Leche Valley, and Pampa Grande near the Chancay River) in northern Peru. Some were found complete, while others had been broken; all were on the floors of the sites, indicating possible ceremonial use. Most archaeological notch flutes are currently housed in museums, where outsiders are not usually permitted to play them.

In ancient times the notch on tubular flutes from the central Andes were most often carved or modeled from the inside of the tubes (similar to the Chinese *hsiao*), either in the shape of a V or a U, or any gradation in between. The notches were constructed as if they were filed inside the tube (undercut), rather than outside, like today's quena flutes. Most of the undercut notches are found on ancient cane instruments.

Generally, the early pre-Columbian flutes from the central Andes have two, three, or four fingerholes (such as those from Moche and Nasca, respectively), while those from later periods have more. Bird bone notch flutes from the coastal Ecuadorian Valdivia culture, for example, have two, three, or four fingerholes; Nasca instruments have three or four; some Ica flutes have five fingerholes; and Chancay flutes may have as many as seven. The fingerholes are arranged rather evenly throughout the front (i.e., facing away from the player) of the flutes, rather than in the lower half of the tube as are European, Asian, Middle Eastern, and most other mouth-blown flutes that require the fingers of both hands to cover the fingerholes. This unique characteristic allows the flutes to produce nearly two octaves without overblowing (many other world flutes produce an octave by overblowing each fingerhole). Additionally, the tone systems (scales) produced on these ancient flutes are only rarely similar to those used in Western (or Eastern) cultures.

The Pentatonic Myth

One of the oldest and most prevalent stereotypes about ancient Andean music is that it was pentatonic (Mead 1903; Harcourt and Harcourt 1925) (i.e., that pre-Columbian music and musical instruments were based on five tones that were arranged within an octave, like the black keys of a piano). Although the pentatonic scale can be produced on some ancient

Andean flutes, Stevenson (1968) and others have shown that pentatonicism did not reign supreme in the ancient Andes. I will also demonstrate that its existence as the musical foundation of ancient times is not based on empirical evidence, although much of today's music in the central Andes is pentatonic. The idea that pentatonicism was the norm in the ancient Andes, however, has been somehow perpetuated by a romantic impression of the Inca, according to John Cohen in his film *Mountain Music of Peru* (1966).

Evidence reveals that most of the scales of ancient Andean flutes were constructed to emit pitches not found in Western pentatonicism. Mead (1903), for example, published scales (and photographs) of twenty-five pre-Columbian Peruvian bone and cane tubular flutes from the collection at the American Museum of Natural History, and his notations indicate that only two of the flutes produce Western pentatonic scales. The remaining twenty-three flute scales he notated are far from being pentatonic, yet so strong was the pentatonicism in his hearing and thinking that he wrote, "It has been believed commonly that they employed the five-toned or pentatonic scale, so widely used in the primitive music of various peoples. . . . Many of the scales given in this paper seem to indicate the use of this five-toned scale" (1903, 31). Mead must have overlooked the evidence in his own notations, although he added, "there are some puzzling exceptions."

Even if pentatonic scales could be produced on these ancient flutes by using a Western fingering system, other fingering possibilities result in other scales. Several ancient tubular Peruvian flutes (figs. 3.1, 3.2) that I played and whose pitches I measured with a Stroboconn tuner, for example, yielded some intervals that are similar to several intervals of a European pentatonic scale when I played them with Western fingering. When fingered with the one-finger Warao method or the two-finger Q'ero method, however, the results are not pentatonic (audio tracks 2–6 and musical examples 3.1a–c). In addition, in audio track 8 you can hear an improvisation played on the Chancay cane flute pictured in figure 3.2 (bottom), in which the bottom fingerholes approximate a pentatonic scale while the upper fingerholes produce microtones and other pitches (musical example 3.2b).

An additional characteristic existed in south-coastal Peru that also questions the use of pentatonicism: the insertion of an internal diaphragm within the flute tube that alters the scale, providing a completely different

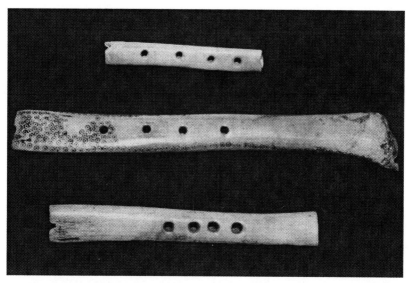

3.1. Three tubular notch flutes from Peru: *top,* bird (?) bone, Nasca (listen to audio track 5); *middle,* human (?) bone, Nasca (listen to audio tracks 3 and 4); *bottom,* bird (pelican?) or camelid (llama?) bone, with internal diaphragm, Nasca (listen to audio track 7). Private collection. Photograph by Christopher B. Donnan.

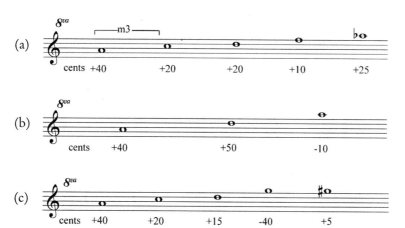

3.1. **(a)** Five pitches produced on a Nasca human (?) bone tubular notch flute with a Western fingering method (see fig. 3.1 [middle] and listen to audio track 3); **(b)** three pitches produced on a Nasca human (?) bone tubular notch flute with a Q'ero fingering method (see fig. 3.1 [middle] and listen to audio track 4); **(c)** five pitches produced on a Nasca human (?) bone tubular notch flute with a Warao fingering method (see fig. 3.1 [middle]).

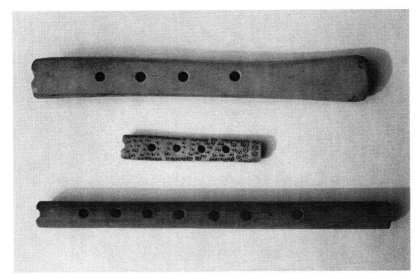

3.2. Three tubular notch flutes from Peru: *top,* human (?) bone, Nasca (listen to audio track 2); *middle,* bird (?) bone, Nasca (listen to audio track 6); *bottom,* cane, Chancay (listen to audio track 8). Dale A. Olsen Collection.

view on melodic complexity in ancient Peru. For example, the Nasca bone flute in figure 3.1 (bottom) has four equally spaced fingerholes that are clustered very closely together near the center of the tube, and between the second and third fingerholes is an internal wax diaphragm that is pierced with three small holes. When I play this flute in a Western manner, the diaphragm acoustically alters the instrument's tone system. For example, when I open the third fingerhole in succession after opening the first and second fingerholes, the pitch descends rather than ascends. The resulting sounds are very disjunctive, like the twittering of a bird (audio track 7 and musical example 3.2a).

Pre-Columbian Peruvian musicians appear to have prominently employed microtones rather than pentatonic scales, as suggested by my tonometric measurements of several ancient Peruvian flutes (musical examples 3.2b–d and audio tracks 8, 5, and 6). Furthermore, my analysis of Mead's notations (1903) also indicates an ancient use of microtones. At a certain level Mead seems to have shared my interpretations when he wrote the following about the microtonal characteristics of the flutes he studied: "Many of the tones produced from these instruments only approximate, in pitch, to some one [*sic*] of the notes of our familiar twelve-tone piano scale. In many instances the variation amounts to nearly a quarter of a tone" (1903, 20). His conclusions, however, reveal an ethnocentric reasoning: "We are led to the conclusion that these ancient flutemakers were not governed by set laws, but that each made his instrument according to his own idea. That the tones produced are in false key-relationship is not to be wondered at when we consider the imperfections in their construction; in fact, the flutes are sadly out of tune" (1903, 18–19). On the contrary, the pre-Columbian flutes are happily in tune when their tone systems are considered within the contexts of the cultures that produced them. Unfortunately, we may never know exactly what those contexts were, and we will never know what the musical meaning was behind the intervals produced by the ancient musicians. Writing in 1609, Garcilaso de la Vega explains that the Colla native Americans "had flutes with four or five holes, like those played by shepherds. But since these were never played on in concerts, each player carved his own in his own manner, according to what suited him best. With this flute he accompanied his

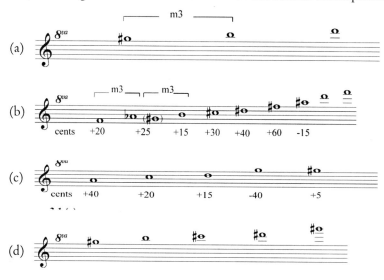

3.2. (a) Three pitches produced on Nasca bird (pelican?) or camelid (llama?) bone tubular notch flute with internal diaphragm (see fig. 3.1 [bottom] and listen to audio track 7); (b) nine pitches produced on Chancay cane tubular notch flute (see fig. 3.2 [bottom] and listen to audio track 8); (c) five pitches produced on Nasca bird (?) bone flute (see fig. 3.1 [top] and listen to audio track 5); (d) five pitches produced on Nasca bird (?) bone flute (see fig. 3.2 [middle] and listen to audio track 6).

love songs, which recounted, in even meters, the favors or disfavors of his ladylove" (1966, 78). This clearly suggests that each flute was in tune with itself, and that flute melodies were recognized as having the ability to communicate specific ideas, such as love. Historical accounts such as that of Garcilaso, combined with iconography, suggest various cultural contexts of ancient musical instruments.

Iconology and History

Certain types of cultural information can be learned from the iconography of pre-Columbian pottery, and when combined with writings from early chroniclers, it is possible to make interpretive suggestions about the use and significance of musical instruments and musical contexts. From Moche pots and figurines, for example, it is possible to interpret a variety of religious contexts for music making on vertical notch flutes. Inspired by Donnan, who wrote, "I now realize that art expresses the religious and supernatural aspects of Moche culture and that virtually nothing of everyday life is illustrated for its own sake" (1990, 23), in the following pages I present two broad interpretations of the significance of notch flutes among the Moche. The first has to do with music and male symbols, which I believe contribute to life-giving power; the second involves the shaman's trance state as a musical flight of ecstasy, which I see as a form of shamanic transcendence.

Music and Male Symbols: Life-Giving Power

Pictures, reliefs, and modeled figures on pre-Columbian pottery from the central Andes, especially among the Moche and neighboring cultures, portray notch flutes with three or four (and even five or more) fingerholes played by males who may be either priests, shamans, prisoners, ill, or dead. Women are never depicted playing flutes, although Felipe Huamán (Guamán) Poma de Ayala writes that virgin girls "who had musical talent were selected to sing or play the flute and drum at Court, weddings and other ceremonies and all the innumerable festivals of the Inca year" ([1615] 1978, 85). Huamán Poma, writing about the Inca in southern highland Peru, a much later culture than the Moche, presents a puzzling anomaly for early Peru, because there is no iconographic evidence of female flute players among the Moche or any other pre-Columbian culture in the Andes.

Much of the Moche iconography that depicts notch flutes seems to pertain to some aspect of supernatural communication involving fertility, as Benson suggests: "Two quena players have a design of beans on their headdresses. . . . Quenas . . . are sometimes played by anthropomorphic vegetables . . . , and one potato figure with a diseased face and a headdress tied under the chin holds what may be a quena. . . . Music . . . ties in with fertility. . . . all of these things are part of a closely woven system of beliefs" (1975, 120–21).

The notch flute–playing iconography of the Moche, however, also shows warrior or warrior-priest flutists with elaborate headdresses, earlobe plugs (also called ear spools), weapons, and fierce expressions (fig. 3.3). Some of the flute-playing priests appear as wrinkled elders with ear-

3.3. Moche ceramic vessel depicting a warrior-priest playing a tubular notch flute. National Museum of Anthropology and Archaeology Collection, Lima.

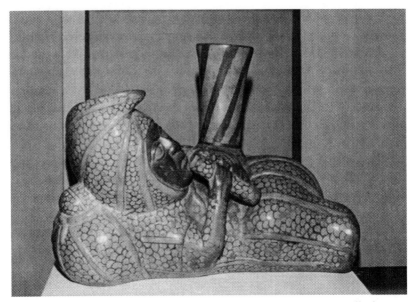

3.4. Moche ceramic vessel depicting a reclining priest or prisoner in *ulluchu* costume playing a tubular notch flute. National Museum of Anthropology and Archaeology Collection, Lima.

lobe plugs, and others have lima bean designs on their headdresses. Some flutists appear as *ulluchu,* or peanut men, who are wearing capes and pointed hoods, which seen together resemble the hanging *ulluchu* fruit (a member of the papaya family) or a peanut. The ulluchu, or peanut flutist, seen in figure 3.4 is completely covered with scales or scabs; even his flute is covered. Yet others depict mutilated or diseased flutists without eyes or lips, dressed in capes and hoods without pointed tops. What does this diversity of flute-playing individuals mean? Donna McClelland explains that the iconographic attempt to relate a multiplicity of activities that something is associated with, "will not necessarily provide a definition of its meaning" (1977, 449). Therefore, I will only generally suggest that the vertical notch flute, perhaps as a phallic icon, is a symbol of fertility or exclusive male power such as military aggression, warriors going into battle, the priesthood, or some other male role. This symbolism appears very commonly in the native Americas and, indeed, throughout the non-Western world.

From the iconography of the Moche, however, there is little evidence that proves a direct reference to fertility and only indirectly can it be suggested. It is perhaps better to use the term *life-giving power* with reference to the use of the vertical notch flute in Moche art, and in so doing, an argument can be made for transcendence—that is, moving from one level to the next. Relating this hypothesis to the above Moche figurines, we can speculate that the warrior-priests (fig. 3.3), who are in combat with or rely on the powers of the mountains (perhaps a male symbol, where the sun rises) or the sea (perhaps a female symbol, where the sun sets), or both, use their flutes as power implements to sustain or restore life; this could be a similar role for the flute-playing, wrinkled, elder priests. Perhaps the lima bean designs on the headdresses of some flute-playing priests are symbolic of germination (as seeds), a life-giving process. The reclining flute-playing man (fig. 3.4) who is dressed in a cape and top-knotted hood and seems to resemble an anthropomorphized ulluchu fruit or peanut (Berrin 1997, 125), could be a symbol of transcendence because the ulluchu fruit is thought to have been associated with the ritual drinking of a prisoner's blood, as Sidney Kirkpatrick writes: "A prominent theory held by [Walter] Alva and other Andean scholars suggested that the *ulluchu* had anticoagulant properties that were useful in preventing clotting before a human or animal's blood was consumed" (1992, 206; see also Alva 1990). McClelland (1977, 449) suggests that the ulluchu had an ancient role for curing illnesses (life giving), and it could have been a narcotic (an outside inducer of transcendence). The scale-covered flute players wearing ulluchu, or peanut, suits who appear as prisoners with deformities may symbolize transcendence into the afterlife as they prepare to be sacrificed, die, and have their blood drunk.

Jiménez Borja (1951, 35) has speculated that the notch flute in ancient times was a symbol of fertility, often by virtue of the number of flutes found in ancient graves. His inference (inspired by Curt Sachs) is that the tubular flute (male symbol), when buried in a tomb within Mother Earth (female symbol), insures procreation, meaning eternity. He elaborates on the phallus metaphor when he writes the following about the use of flutes during funeral celebrations: "the quenas that resounded around the dead during indigenous celebrations did not probably have a mournful intent but were, instead, enchantments of life and resurrection."[2]

An important but unprovenienced rustic piece of sculpture from Peru's south coast, featuring a human face with an actual cane notch flute hanging from the mouth, has been interpreted by Helaine Silverman (1993, 192, fig. 13.44) as an ancestor post. She relates this figure conceptually to the *mallki,* or cultivated tree, which is an ancestor symbol in the Andes. Quoting Sherbondy (1986), she writes, "the cultivated tree . . . lends itself for symbolism of ancestors, women, and men of a family, and above all the fruit tree as a symbol of the family which produced its fruit: children" (Silverman 1993, 192). The notch flute attached to the ancestor icon's mouth perhaps further symbolized fertility or transcendence.

Magical fertility-power aspects of the vertical tubular flute persisted into the historical period in certain areas of the Andes, as reported by Spanish and mestizo chroniclers. Especially prevalent is the role of the vertical flute as a love charm, as Garcilaso de la Vega wrote: "With this flute [the Indian] accompanied his love songs. . . . The story is told of a Spaniard who, one evening, upon meeting an Indian girl of his acquaintance on a Cuzco street, urged her to come home with him. 'Señor,' she replied, 'kindly let me go my way. The flute you hear is calling me with such tenderness and passion that I can't resist it. Leave me, for your own life's sake; my love is calling me and I must answer him, that he may be my husband and I his wife'" (1966, 79).

More recent is an account described by Jiménez Borja, who writes about the "phallic connotation of the instrument, whose magic voice defeats death and promotes life"[3] (1951, 36), as exemplified in a folktale well known in the southern region of Peru. The story involves several personages who probably lived over a century ago in the town of Yanaquihura, department of Arequipa. A certain Don Gaspar, in love with a woman named Ana, traveled some distance to visit her. When he arrived, however, she had died and been buried in the church. That evening he disinterred her and dressed her in the fineries he had brought for her. Suddenly he, and the rest of the village, heard the passionate sound of a flute. Tracing the music to the priest's house in Yanaquihura, the people forced open the door and found the priest playing a quena into a clay pot, a "strange conversation between Life and Death" (Jiménez Borja 1951, 36). In another version of the tale Don Gaspar arrived many months after the death of his beloved. Thereupon he disinterred her bones, fabricated a quena from her tibia, and played it into a clay pot.

Whether these narratives represented true events or not, they convey the ritual significance and transcendental quality attributed to flutes in the Andean worldview. Jiménez Borja (1951) published a photograph and gave a detailed description of such a vessel found in Huamanga, department of Ayacucho. According to him, the large pot has a small opening at the top for inserting a flute, two larger openings in the sides for the player's hands, and two eyelets on the sides so the vessel can be suspended around the quena player's neck. He further explains that the vessel should have a certain amount of water in its bottom, but not enough to touch the flute (Jiménez Borja 1951, 37 and unnumbered photo). Paredes (1936, 80), writing about Aymara (Colla) musical instruments, briefly mentions a similar tale about a small animal bone flute called *manchaipuito* that is played into a clay pot. The Catholic Church considered this apparently ancient technique of playing a quena within a clay pot sinful, because it was a clear symbol of the sexual act and the power of procreation.

These narratives, while removed in time and space from the Moche and other pre-Incan cultures, nevertheless represent a certain continuity of thought regarding the fertility or life-giving essence of vertical tubular flutes in Peru. I have argued that fertility symbols imply transcendence, or the movement from one level of existence to another. Certainly the creation of life, the growing of crops, and the symbol of germination are actions of transcendence or moving beyond oneself. The realm of the shaman is another type of transcendence for which flutes or flute sounds (such as whistling, as discussed in chapter 8) are important.

There is yet another context for notch flute performance with the Moche: dance. Numerous scenes occurring as fineline drawings on Moche ceramic pots depict notch flute players providing accompaniment for Moche men who are interpreted as dancers (Donnan 1982a). In addition to the flutists, who are usually in groups of two or three, several drummers often provide accompaniment. Because of their importance in my analysis of cultural context and human transcendence, those fineline drawings (in Donnan 1982a, figs. 1, 6, 7a, 7b, 11, 12) that depict notch flute players are included here. I have arranged them into three groups based on my names for the participants (Donnan's "dancers"), whom I shall call climbing dancers (fig. 3.5), temple dancers (fig. 3.6), and cloth dancers (fig. 3.7).

The climbing dancers (fig. 3.5), all male, appear to be climbing, or "spiraling upward," as Donnan writes (1982a, 106), guided by the musicians who are shown facing them. It is not known what the actors are climbing, if they are indeed climbing. Perhaps the spiral technique is simply the artist's convention for depicting a lengthy horizontal procession that happens to be going around a circular pot. Nevertheless, the spiral aspect that makes it ongoing gives it the appearance of climbing. Not only do

3.5. Fineline roll-out drawings from two Moche ceramic vessels depicting (*top*) climbing warriors led by a drummer and a notch flute player (drawing by Donna McClelland) and (*bottom*) climbing, processing, or dancing warriors, accompanied by drummers and notch flute players (drawing by Donna McClelland).

3.6. Fineline roll-out drawing from a Moche ceramic vessel depicting warriors (on the middle platform) approaching a chief accompanied by a drummer; two notch flute players are above them, and another drummer leads the procession in the lower tier (drawing by Donna McClelland).

the musicians face the dancers and musically lead them on, but a lead climber (dance leader?) faces the others as if he is pulling them. All the male dancers are attired in battle dress and are holding hands. It should also be noted that all the personages in these scenes are depicted as alive (to be contrasted to the "death" actors in the next chapter), and their seemingly upward progression could be related to the climbing of a sacred Moche mountain for the purpose of gaining life-sustaining power.

The temple dancers (fig. 3.6) and musicians (two vertical-flute players and two drummers) perform on three level planes. This scene takes place within a templelike structure, suggested by the platform and the steep sloping ramp leading up to the second level. The lower level shows dancers accompanied by a single drummer (second from right); the middle level includes a minor figure in front of a drummer presenting something in a bowl to a major figure with a huge headdress; and the upper level depicts flutists. The middle level may be an example of what Donnan (1975) calls the Presentation Theme, or Sacrifice Theme, especially because the major figure holds a rope around a prisoner's neck (Donnan 1982, 99).

The cloth dancers (fig. 3.7), which Donnan calls ribbon dancers, proceed in a line like the climbers; however, they are on a more level plane

3.7. Fineline roll-out drawings from two Moche ceramic vessels depicting (*top*) four warriors carrying a long banner or piece of cloth, accompanied by two notch flute players who face them (drawing by Donna McClelland), and (*middle and bottom*) a line of eight warriors carrying a long piece of cloth, accompanied by notch flute players and a trumpeter in the background (drawing by Donna Mc-Clelland).

and connect themselves by holding a long piece of cloth. Judging from their feet positions, the dancers appear to be progressing forward, sometimes led by flute players who face them (fig. 3.7 top); other times they are by themselves, with musicians in the background (fig. 3.7 middle and bottom). In the second of these two fineline drawings the musicians appear to be in the background by virtue of the artist's use of perspective (the musicians appear slightly above the dancers, and are about one-half to one-third of the dancers' sizes; I believe this is indicative of their distance away from the dancers rather than their lesser status). The cloth dancers may also be cloth presenters, whose presentation may be a form of gift giving, a common act of celebrating life.

In many of these small fineline drawings of vertical-flute players it is not possible to distinguish the mouthpiece type of the instruments, as can be done in the sculptured artifacts of flute players already seen and others soon to be discussed. In many instances, in fact, the mouthpieces seem to be detached from the musicians' mouths as if the flutist is caught in the process of taking a big breath. In other instances a musician's mouth is open so wide that he appears to be singing. While these anomalies can be explained as examples of artistic license, the art tells us little about the actual instruments other than that they are vertical flutes, also suggested by numerous dots that probably represent fingerholes. Because one of the instruments seen in figure 3.7 bottom (lower left) is conical rather than cylindrical, however, and is held by one hand while the other hand holds a rattle of some type, it is perhaps a trumpet rather than a vertical flute. To summarize, the musicians appear to be accompanying the dancers rather than participating directly as members of the dancing groups. The contexts themselves are interpreted as scenes of life-giving activities because the actors and musicians are drawn as being alive.

Musical Flights of Ecstasy: Shamanic Transcendence

A unique recurring theme found in the iconography of certain ancient Peruvian ceramic vessels and figurines is the three-dimensional representation of a man lying on his belly, knees bent with feet up, and neck bent with head up. He is usually playing a notch flute, a unique musical motif that appears only in Peru, but with several variations (figs. 3.8, 3.9). I associate this motif with shamanic flights of ecstasy and transcendence from one level to another (i.e., from earth to cosmos) because of the body position of the flutist and his occasional assistance by helpers, who either accompany him in flight or aid him with offerings of what is perhaps a hallucinogenic brew. Figure 3.8 is a Recuay pot that depicts a flying flutist accompanied or assisted by six individuals (one is broken) holding containers. Figure 3.9 is a figurine from Chincha that is completely molded into a representation of a flying flutist.

That these flute-playing individuals are simulating a position representing ecstatic flight is based on conjecture; nevertheless, a horizontal

3.8. Recuay ceramic vessel depicting a notch flutist in flying position, flanked by five men (one broken) holding flasks. John and Mary Carter Collection, Florida State University, Tallahassee.

3.9. Chincha ceramic figurine in the shape of a notch flutist in flying position. National Museum of Anthropology and Archaeology Collection, Lima.

body position with belly down, legs up, and head and shoulders raised is an abnormal pose in everyday human life. It is a body position that seems impossible except for someone adept at yoga. By eliminating other obvious human activity, this position suggests either flying or swimming. However, because no water is evident, and since the figures' posture suggests elevation because their bodies are often set upon tiny pedestals, ecstatic flight seems to be the most plausible explanation.

Ethnographic analogy with close geographic proximity (direct historical approach) to these areas offers detailed information about ecstatic flight, but nothing about the flute's role in such journeys of the soul. Although today's descendants of the ancient flying flutists are acculturated mestizos (people of mixed race and culture), several published ethnographies that discuss shamanistic magical flight might offer important comparisons. Douglas Sharon (1978, 113), for example, describes the shamanic flight of Eduardo Calderón (see also chapter 8), who is from a region not very far from where several of the ceramic vessels depicting magical flight have been excavated. Calderón's magical shamanic flights are aided by the ingestion of a hallucinogenic brew made from San Pedro cactus, as Sharon writes: "San Pedro is a cactus that contains an ingredient that, upon ingestion, produces the opening of the subconscious and . . . the telepathic sixth sense of the individual [which allows him] to transport himself, to sublimate himself across matter, time, and distance" (1978, 113). This explanation, in particular, describes a situation that is perhaps ethnographically analogous to the scene depicted on the Recuay vessel in figure 3.8. The five individuals who are flanking the flying flute player and holding containers are perhaps representative of the ancient shaman's helpers; they are perhaps holding vessels containing the hallucinogenic drink of the San Pedro cactus.

Ethnographic analogies can be made between the Wari, Recuay, and Chincha cultures and several cultures that are not very geographically distant from them. For example, shamans from several Peruvian *montaña* (eastern slopes of the Andes) and Amazonian cultures employ music with their magical flights. Specifically, shamans of the Campa, who live almost directly east of the Recuay area, have described their shamanic flights of ecstasy to Gerald Weiss, who writes, "Even while the shaman is singing, his soul may go on a flight to some distant place, returning later" (1973, 44). Additionally, Fred Katz and Marlene Dobkin de Rios describe the shamanistic use of high-pitched flute sounds, which in one ethnographic analog actually includes human whistles. Some of the native Americans and mestizos in the vicinity of Iquitos, Peru (also east of the Recuay region), ingest *ayahuasca,* a hallucinogenic drink made from a vine (*ayahuasca* means "vine of the dead" in Quechua), as they continue to explain: "Since much of the music found in ayahuasca sessions consists of whistling incantations, it is important to mention the widespread belief in the area that whistling is the way in which the spiritual forces of nature and the guardian spirit of the vine, itself, can be evoked by the healer" (1971, 324). These ethnographic analogies may aid in the interpretation of the Peruvian iconographic theme of musical magical flight because of seemingly similar circumstances. The Recuay vessel in figure 3.8, especially, seems to relate to the ritualistic use of the ayahuasca brew and high-pitched whistle sounds described above. Indeed, the flute that the central ceramic figure is playing and the whistling incantations of the current native Americans and mestizos of Iquitos can perhaps be understood symbolically as the same. That the brew suggested by the small containers depicted in the Recuay vessel could be ayahuasca is supported by that hallucinogen's common occurrence in the Andes, which includes a large region from northwestern Colombia to the lowlands of Bolivia, both east and west of the Andes (Harner 1973, 1).

The ethnographic analogies discussed in the present chapter seem to support my interpretation that these Peruvian artifacts represent shamanistic musical flights of ecstasy, often accompanied by hallucinogens and whistle sounds, the latter represented in ancient Peruvian iconography by a tubular notch flute. Calderón, however, disagreed with me when I read him this chapter and showed him my photographs in 1996:

Figure 3.8. "He is not flying. This flying stuff is very Spanish. It is not a trance state. This is a reunion, with the chief in the middle. He is not lying on the sand, just on a flat surface."

Figure 3.9. "He is lying on his belly. He is not flying, but lying on the sand, calling the animals and the birds. This is a very special custom."

Nevertheless, and in spite of Calderón's analyses, I still believe these figures *are* indicative of ecstatic flight rather than some type of normal human activity for the following reasons: (1) lying on the ground on one's belly with elbows, shoulders, knees, and feet in the air is not conducive to playing the notch flute, or any other type of vertical flute; (2) a flute cannot be played while swimming and will not sound under water; and (3) while a human cannot physically fly, even if he (i.e., the male flutist depicted in these artifacts) is calling birds with his flute, he may still be representing magical flight. Calderón went on to explain: "In the pictorial shamanic representations of the Nasca and Paracas cultures, yes, they are representing fliers. They show the cosmic effect of the drink made from the *chalaco* fish. This is a hallucinogenic fish, very strong, like eating mushrooms." Certainly intertribal contact and exchange existed during pre-Columbian times in Peru, making Calderón's analogy with the Nasca and Paracas cultures relevant.

Additionally, a comparison of the Peruvian ecstatic flying flutists with certain archaeological artifacts in Mesoamerica shows the existence of a similar bodily formation. In Guatemala and southern Mexico, for example, such contorted musicians are referred to in English as acrobats (Mary Pohl, pers. comm., 1999). While it is possible that there was intertribal contact between ancient Peruvian and Mesoamerican cultures, scholars have not explored such diffusion. Moreover, the substantial distance between Peru and central Mexico weakens the possibility of such an analogy.

Identification of a Musical Forgery

Inspired by the proceedings of a conference at Dumbarton Oaks entitled "Falsifications and Misreconstructions of Pre-Columbian Art" (Boone 1982), and especially by Donnan's paper "The Identification of a Moche Fake through Iconographic Analysis," I realized that iconology can also be used to determine the authenticity of certain ancient artifacts that portray musical themes.[4] In the preface to the above proceedings Elizabeth Boone writes, "A surprising number of falsified . . . objects do exist in public and private collections, [and] . . . many have been published in the literature as representative of Pre-Columbian artistic forms. The danger is that these recreations, unless identified as such, can distort our understanding of Pre-Columbian art and can lead to erroneous stylistic and iconographic interpretations" (1982, v). Indeed, as Appadurai explains, "copies, forgeries, and fakes, which have a long history, do not threaten the aura of the original but seek to partake of it" (1986, 44); in other words, the copying or faking potters take advantage of the originals, usually for economic reasons, making interpretative archaeological conclu-

sions difficult. Boone continues, "forgeries can most efficiently be de-
tected, not through scientific testing, which is often financially unfea-
sible, but through an experienced comparison with objects known to be
authentic. And here the stylistic and iconographic integrity of an object
in question is crucial [because] . . . the irregularities of the objects are
subtle and are identifiable only because [of certain individuals who are] .
. . well versed in the rules governing that particular form of visual presentation" (1982, vi). Indeed, knowledge of musical rules by scholars of pre-
Columbian art is rare, and archaeologists, art historians, antiquities collectors, and others untrained in the current or historical music of related
or proximate cultures often misinterpret musical instruments and musical events depicted on authentic pre-Columbian pottery.[5]

This topical study is based on a double-chamber blackware vessel
from the John and Mary Carter Collection, currently the property of
Florida State University. This artifact, cataloged as Lambayeque with a
question mark (fig. 3.10), is termed "unusual because [the] strap handle is
turned sideways, [and it depicts a] musician playing drum and quena,
standing on one of two clam-shaped objects" (Diane Olsen 1978, 104). In
addition to the perhaps uncommon construction of the vessel's handle,
the musical situation molded into clay is indeed unusual, suggesting one
of at least three possibilities: the artifact is an example of artistic license
(the artist was perhaps not a musician); the musician depicted on the artifact is symbolically performing an impossible musical act; or the artifact
is a fake and is not pre-Columbian.

There are two reasons why I believe this artifact to be a fake: notch
flutes are never played in a pipe-and-tabor fashion, and the upper fingerhole of the instrument in the artifact is represented as open (a tubular
flute played in that manner would not produce any pitches beyond its
highest pitch).

Iconology reveals that numerous artifacts found today in Peruvian
museums contain representations of musicians that are similar to the subject matter depicted in the ceramic vessel at the Florida State University.
These could have provided a modern forger with authentic sources from
which to make his careless copy. The similar vessel is from Chimú, which
depicts a player of a tubular notch flute with a small membranophone
attached to his waist. While this is related subject matter, the musician is
not playing both instruments at the same time. Another similar artifact
(fig. 3.11), from Chincha (Peru) shows a panpipe player playing a drum at

3.10. Lambayeque (possibly fake) ceramic double-chamber vessel showing notch flute and drum player. John and Mary Carter Collection, Florida State University, Tallahassee.

the same time, a very common occurrence that is substantiated by ethnographic analogy with the Aymara in southern Peru and northern and central Bolivia. The common practice of simultaneous panpipe and drum playing by the same musician may have inspired a nonmusician potter to depict someone playing a notch flute and drum at the same time. The post-Columbian or modern potter could have been further confused by the common pipe-and-tabor practice in southern Ecuador and northern Peru, whereby one musician plays a duct flute and drum at the same time.

Indeed, the particular organological anomalies of the Lambayeque vessel seen in figure 3.10 are subtle, and only someone who is very familiar with the present Andean notch flute and pipe-and-tabor traditions (such as the *pingullo* and drum in southern Ecuador, the *roncador* and drum in northern Peru, and others) would be able to detect them. Iconology, verified by ethnographic analogy, reveals this particular potter's

3.11. Chimú-Inca ceramic double-chamber vessel showing panpipe and drum played simultaneously by one individual. National Museum of Anthropology and Archaeology Collection, Lima.

creation to be wrong, strongly suggesting that the artifact itself is a post-Columbian reproduction.

The preceding topics, studied through the iconology and history modes of inquiry, can perhaps be further explored by ethnographic analogy. Let us now look at the ethnographic data about quena and pinkullo flutes in the central Andes.

Ethnographic Analogy

Today, the Aymara word *kena* (*quena* in Spanish orthography) is used by Aymara, Quechua, and mestizo people for the notch flute, while the Quechua term *pinkullo* and its many variants are used for the duct flute.

Also today, notch flutes have a variety of names. Paredes (1936, 80), for example, describes four notch flutes in Bolivia during the first half of the twentieth century whose names reflect their differing sizes and number of fingerholes: kena (50 cm in length, six fingerholes and a thumb hole), *kenacho* (44 cm long, four fingerholes and a thumb hole), *kenali* (thinner than the rest, with six fingerholes and one thumb hole), and *pusi-p'iya* (meaning four holes, i.e., three fingerholes and one thumb hole), the largest of the Aymara quena types, measuring up to nearly 70 cm long (pictured in Buchner 1972, fig. 117). The Bolivian Chipaya also have a very large notch flute, *lichiwayu*, which they use mostly from May through July (Baumann 1981, 182). Additionally, quena flutes come in three sizes within many of the groups (González 1937, 27): *taica* or *jajcha* (mother), *mala* or *malta* (middle, two-thirds the size of the mother, a fifth higher in pitch), and *kallu* or *chchiti* ("son"; small, half the size of the mother and an octave higher in pitch).

Because the duct flute was perhaps contextually interchangeable with the notch flute during the colonial period in the Andes, one can surmise that its significance today is probably similar to the quena's significance in ancient times (again, since the former probably did not exist). In many regions of the Peruvian Andes the pinkullo is seasonal, meaning it is played only during particular calendric periods, such as the rainy season from October through March. Jiménez Borja, for example, writes,[6] "This flute is played during the season when the great rains begin. . . . Before playing the instrument it is moistened in chicha, alcohol, or water. The coincidence of . . . festivals with the arrival of the rains, the moistening of the wood before making the flutes, and the moistening of the instruments before playing them, is very significant" (1951, 45). The pinkullo and its music are believed to cause rain in the central Andes. Because the rains are necessary for agriculture, the pinkullo and its music are indirectly associated with the fertility of crops and, by extension, of animals and humans, as the symbolism suggested above would indicate. The wet season is the season of life throughout the Andes.

More overtly, the pinkillo flute in highland Bolivia is used in the *k'illpa* animal fertility ritual. Its sound is believed to make the animals fertile (Stobart 1998, 289). Notch flutes are also played during the llama fertility festivals of the Q'ero of highland southern Peru. To further support the fertility metaphor of the Andean tubular flute, especially as an instrument used during planting and animal fertility festivals, both *pinga* and *ullu,* the Quechua words from which *pingullo* is derived, mean "penis" (Carvalho-Neto 1964, 342).

These ethnographic analogies from the highland central Andes (southern Peru and northern and central Bolivia) offer some evidence to support my argument that native vertical tubular flutes are givers of life; they are flutes of transcendence and life. While it would be desirable to have concrete ethnographic analogical evidence that is closer in time and space with the Moche and other ancient cultures of Peru's northern coast, where the bulk of the iconographic data are found, it is my belief that the northern pre-Incan cultures, by being conquered by the Inca or before them the Wari (Huari), provided the inhabitants of southern highland Peru with outside musical knowledge. The first school of music in the Americas is believed to have been in Cuzco, established by the Inca Roca around 1350 (Garcilaso de la Vega, cited in Stevenson 1968, 274–75). With the assistance of musicians from cultures assimilated by the Inca, such as those from Peru's northern coast (Moche, Chimú, and others), it is possible that notch flute technology and beliefs were either introduced into the southern Peruvian highlands or, if they already existed, were reinforced, allowing them to survive in the central Andes today, where they are continued by the descendants of the Inca and those whom they conquered.

In spite of the apparent frequent use of the notch flute among the Moche, Chimú, and other ancient cultures from northern Peru, it is particularly noteworthy that the notch flute is not common in northern Peru today. When it is used, it is by young people who perform the music of southern Peru in ensembles consisting of quenas and *charangos* (armadillo carapace guitars). In addition, some elementary schools in Ancash today (I observed this in 1979) are teaching music by using plastic quena flutes (rather than Western recorders or traditional roncador flutes). It seems that the notch flute may be making a complete circle by returning to its ancient place of greatest dispersion: northern coastal Peru.

The next chapter explores another important pre-Columbian melodic instrument type from the central Andes: multitube flutes known in English as panpipes. While their frequency of use makes them analogous to notch flutes, I will argue that their significance is transfiguration and death rather than transcendence and life.

~·~·~

Panpipes of Transfiguration and Death

As important as life and its transcendence are in the worldview of traditional native South Americans, transfiguration and death are equally important because life and death must be held in balance. Between life and
death is often a state that I refer to as transfiguration, which in its simplest
definition is "a change in form or appearance" (Merriam-Webster 1994,
1253). While in Christianity transfiguration refers to Christ's physical-
spiritual change, and therefore is usually glossed as a change for the better, Moche transfiguration, as we learn from their pottery, can be seen as a
change for the worse (at least from the Western perspective). The changes
occur in degrees, from seemingly diseased facial parts to bodily skeletonization, and such Moche human figurines are almost always playing panpipes.

A panpipe is a multitube flute that consists of a series of vertical, tubular, ductless, and closed pipes without fingerholes. Its sound is produced
by blowing air across one of the open ends of the tube (or sometimes two
tubes simultaneously, as with the present rondador of Ecuador), which
functions as the embouchure hole or mouthpiece. Like the notch flute,
panpipes are known from pre-Columbian times in ancient Peru, Bolivia,
Chile, Ecuador, Colombia, and elsewhere. Also in coastal Peru, ancient
tombs of the Paracas (ca. 800–100 B.C.), Nasca (ca. 200 B.C.–A.D. 600), and
Moche (ca. A.D. 400–1000), in particular, have yielded panpipes made
mostly from ceramic, but also of cane and silver.

Music Archaeology

In the central Andes today, panpipes can be classified into two groups: single unit and double unit. The former instruments are usually called *antara* in Quechua, while the latter are called *siku* in Aymara. Because pre-Columbian terms are not known (except for the Quechua and Aymara terms provided by chroniclers; see Stevenson 1968), the terms *single-unit panpipe* and *double-unit panpipe* will be employed for ancient exemplars.

Ancient Single-Unit Panpipes: Tiwanaku (Tiahuanaco), Paracas, and Nasca

Single-unit panpipes (i.e., its single part is capable of producing a complete melody), which are constructed mostly from ceramic ductless closed tubes joined together as a raft, have been found archaeologically in a number of places, including the following: (1) Tiwanaku (A.D. 500–1150) in the southern basin of Lake Titicaca in northern Bolivia; (2) Paracas and Nasca in the south coastal Peru department of Ica;[1] (3) coastal Ecuador, where two varieties of pre-Columbian ceramic panpipes and one type of stone panpipe are mentioned by Carlos Coba Andrade (1981, 1:99); (4) Atacameño and Diaguita in Argentina and Chile; and (5) Inca, possibly the Cuzco region of Peru. The last two regions have produced panpipes made from stone, and the best-known example of a stone panpipe, the so-called Rawdon Syrinx, has been studied in depth by Francis Huxley (1955) and Ellen Hickmann (1990, 278–81). So unique is this instrument and the story behind its discovery, disappearance, and rediscovery, that I quote Huxley's commentary:

> The Rawdon Syrinx is a fine instrument of eight pipes, carved out of blue-veined steatite and covered with a dark brown patina. It was discovered in a Peruvian huaca ore grave mound, lying on the body of a mummy, and obtained by General Paroissien "as an article of value and great rarity." In 1820 Paroissien gave it to Joshua Rawdon; at some date plaster casts were made from it and were put on show in several Museums, while the original was lost sight of by archaeologists. The original, however, was being safely kept by the Rawdon family until this year [1955], when Major Rawdon sold it to Liverpool Museum. Paroissien unfortunately did not record the

place where the syrinx was found, though it is usually thought to be in Highland Peru—Cuzco, perhaps. The syrinx is certainly of Inca style, dating some time between A.D. 1300 and 1600, but it may owe a lot to the contemporary cultures in Chile and Argentine [sic], for it is there, among the Atacameno [sic] and Diaguita, that stone Panpipes . . . are most common. (Huxley 1955: 17–18, cited in Hickmann 1990, 281)

Stone panpipes, however, are rare, certainly owing to the difficulty of their manufacture. More common, perhaps, but rarely found archaeologically, were panpipes made from bones.

A late-twentieth-century discovery of cut and polished camelid bone tubes in Misiton, a household site in Lukurmata within the greater Tiwanaku archaeological region, have been interpreted as tubes for panpipes, according to Janusek: "Each group of tubes was characterized by a graded variation in length that corresponded to tone variation; tone variation emphasized the notes E, A, B, and C-sharp. . . . Further, the tubes were all within the size range of known contemporary and prehispanic panpipes, and all that were intact produced a clear musical tone" (1999, 119). While tone production by itself is not a basis for tubes being musical instruments, Janusek argues that their "tuning lengths" suggests their use as flute tubes rather than snuff tubes, containers, or handles (1999, 120). Assuming they were panpipes, their discovery in a household site has inspired him (1999, 119) to argue that the venue itself was a craft production center specializing in the manufacture of panpipes.

Throughout various regions of Tiwanaku, evidence of craft production appears to have existed for the purpose of providing goods for ruling elites, rather than for individual household use (Janusek 1999, 109). He further argues that such craft production may have had festival use: "In Tiwanaku, we can hypothesize, feasts would have been times when style actively helped group members mark their identities or promote their prestige relative to others" (1999, 111). While such contextualization is conjectural, the importance of this discovery is the possibility that the location was a panpipe factory that supplied such instruments to musicians in the vicinity.

There is one admonition and perhaps even a flaw to Janusek's argument, however. A careful examination of his drawings reveals that the tubes are all open-ended rather than closed, unlike today's panpipes, and open-ended tubes do not produce sounds when blown in a rafted-panpipe fashion. Individually, an open-ended tube will produce a pitch, but the musician's embouchure must be similar to the embouchure required to play a Middle Eastern *nay* or Yugoslavian *kaval*. In other words, an open-ended tube requires the musician to pucker the mouth and bring it into contact with the open (playing) end of the tube at an angle. Not only is this impractical, it is impossible when a series of pipes are rafted together to form a panpipe. As the section on ethnographic analogy will show, open pipes are sometimes attached as a second row behind closed pipes in some current panpipe traditions; however, their function is simply to add resonance to the full sounds of the closed pipes. It is difficult for me to believe that all the intact tubes in Janusek's sample produced a clear musical tone if they were played in a typical panpipe fashion. This is an instance where an audio example and further explanation are of vital importance.

Other recent and earlier findings in coastal Peru are more convincingly of panpipes because of their similarity with current panpipe models (i.e., they consist of closed-end tubes that are rafted together). Scholars (Bolaños 1988a, 33–44; 1988b, 29; and Haeberli 1979, 58) have determined that (at least) two types of ancient panpipes existed in the region of southern coastal Peru, categorized by their tube shapes: (1) Paracas, the older, slightly conical (almost bulbous) near the proximal end, becoming narrower and cylindrical at the distal end, and also tapering slightly at the embouchure hole; and (2) Nasca, the newer, cylindrical with a slight taper at the embouchure hole. Within these periods, however, are numerous phases, making cultural identification difficult without adequate documentation; Nasca pottery, for example, has been classified into nine phases (Silverman 1993).

Archaeologist Jorge Muelle (in Stevenson 1968, 246) suggested in 1939 that the ancient Peruvian panpipes (especially the Nasca instruments) were made from molds, assuring precise and predetermined tuning. Dawson, however, claimed in 1964 that slip casting was the method used. Haeberli (1979, 61) agreed, and further surmised that mouth-end tapering was a way of tuning the instruments during their construction. Peter Kvietok (cited in Silverman 1993, 241) refuted those construction theories, however, claiming the panpipes were hand modeled over a template. His reasoning is based on the fact that Nasca panpipes were apparently made with precise tuning in mind, an idea supported by Stevenson, who wrote the following about Nasca panpipes that were duplicated precisely at the octave: "No two instruments sounding the same series of ten letter-name pitches, but at an octave's distance, can have been fashioned haphazardly" (1968, 246).

While many panpipes have been tonometrically measured (Bolaños 1988a; Haeberli 1979), most of them are characterized by various tubes that are not playable, resulting in the measurement of incomplete scales. While it has not been my purpose to study a representative sampling of panpipes, the two I have been able to play and measure are in perfect condition (figs. 4.1, 4.2), offering additional pitch relationships to analyze with those in other studies.

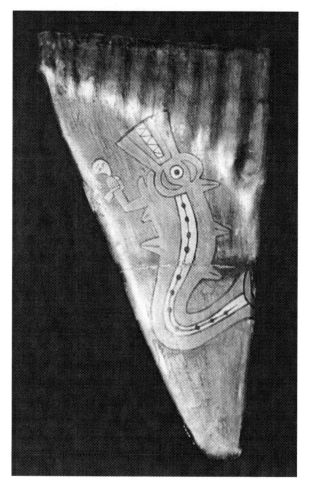

4.1. Early-period Nasca ceramic panpipe (listen to audio track 9). Private collection. Photograph by Christopher B. Donnan.

4.2. Nasca ceramic panpipe (listen to audio track 10). Charles Delaney Collection, Tallahassee, Florida.

In 1972, I recorded and measured the pitches of an early Nasca (perhaps phase 3) panpipe with ten tubes (fig. 4.1) from a private collection in Los Angeles. The pitches I produced on this instrument can be heard in audio track 9 and seen in notation as musical example 4.1. My transcription reveals several characteristics that I consider highly significant with regard to tuning possibilities. First, tonal measurements, made with a Korg tuner set at –50 cents flat (–50 was set as the standard, in order to give 0 cents deviation from the lowest tube), reveal that the lowest (and longest) tube (tube 1; A = 0 cents deviation) and its octave at tube 7 (a = 0 cents deviation) are perfectly matched (using a Western equal-tempered standard, one would say precisely in tune). Second, tonal measurements reveal that tube 3 (D♯ = +50 cents deviation) and tube 10 (d♯ = +50 cents deviation) are also perfectly matched. Third, tubes 2 (C = +15 cents deviation), 4 (E = +20 cents deviation), 5 (F♯ = +10 cents deviation), and 6 (G♯ = +20 cents deviation) are similarly tuned because they are only between +10 and +20 cents from the standard, a difference that is minimal and

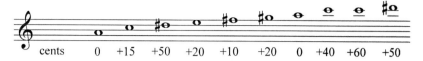

cents	0	+15	+50	+20	+10	+20	0	+40	+60	+50

4.1. Ten pitches produced on a ten-tube Nasca panpipe (see fig. 4.1 and listen to audio track 9).

hardly noticeable by the lay person's ear when the pitches are played in sequence. These characteristics lead me to conclude that tuning was indeed a concern with the panpipe makers, as suggested by Bolaños, Haeberli, and Stevenson.

Another conclusion I make from this panpipe, contrary to what Haeberli (1979, 71) concludes, is the apparent importance given to the interval of a fifth. For example, the interval between tubes 1 and 4 is only 20 cents larger than a perfect fifth, and the interval between tubes 7 and 10 is only 50 cents smaller than a perfect fifth. This panpipe, in fact, seems to emphasize the intervals of the octave and the fifth. The other relationship I consider noteworthy is that of the foundation interval (between tubes 1 and 2), which is a minor third (see Olsen 1996).

Microtones occur between individual tubes of this panpipe, with its higher-pitched tubes. Tubes 8 (C = +40 cents deviation) and 9 (C = +60 cents deviation, which can also be interpreted as C♯ = –40 cents deviation) are essentially the same note tuned 20 cents apart. Because their tuning difference is so minimal, it is noticeable only when the two notes are played in sequence. Stevenson noticed the same characteristic among the panpipes he studied, and explained: "Where such microtones do insinuate themselves, they always come in the upper half. These fine pitch distinctions near the top of a series must obviously have cost the maker some pains. Just as it is easier to fret microtones near the pegbox than near the bridge [referring to a violin], so such fine distinctions would have taxed the antara maker less at the bottom of his series than at the top" (1968, 252).

cents	0	+18	-35	+45	-45	-33	-18	+20	+20	-20	+20	+40	+25	0	+30

4.2. Fifteen pitches produced on a fifteen-tube Nasca panpipe (see fig. 4.2 and listen to audio track 10).

In 1999, I recorded and measured the pitches of a fifteen-tube Nasca panpipe (perhaps phase 5 or 6) belonging to Charles Delaney, professor of flute (retired, 1999) at the Florida State University (fig. 4.2). The pitches I produced on this instrument can be heard in audio track 10, and are included in notation as musical example 4.2. My analysis of this panpipe reveals several characteristics that I believe are also highly significant. Tonal measurements made with a Korg tuner set at 0 cents deviation (A = 440 Hz) show that the first and lowest tube (F♯ = 0 cents deviation) and its octave at tube four (f♯ = 45 cents deviation) are nearly a quarter tone apart. By Western equal-tempered standards this octave would be out of tune, but by other standards (systems), it is possibly acceptable. In addition, tonal measurements reveal that tube 2 (A♯ = +18 cents deviation) and tube 5 (a♯ = −45 cents deviation) are 63 cents short of an octave. None of the other pitches, however, seems to create any tonometric consistency that can be compared with the pitches produced on the earlier Nasca panpipe. Not only do the octaves occur as imprecise intervals, but the interval of a fifth does not occur except between tubes 6 and 10. In fact, the interval of the fifth seems to be avoided between any other tubes. Finally, unlike the early Nasca instrument, this middle Nasca panpipe produces a foundation interval of a major third.

While no concrete musical conclusions can be made from the study of only two panpipes from two different phases of the same culture, numerous panpipes have undergone scientific studies by Haeberli in which he indicates that Nasca instruments were made in sets with very precise tuning in mind: "about one-third of the samples covered in two investigations were labeled twins, or pairs" (1979, 57). In describing thirteen instruments discovered in a tomb excavated by Julio C. Tello in 1929, Bolaños provides strong physical and acoustic evidence that Nasca panpipes were played in groups: "The important conclusion of the study of the panpipes from this tomb is that all their sounds were interrelated. It is as if all the panpipes had pertained to an instrumental ensemble very similar to the present Aymara sicuri groups of today, who are accustomed to organizing their cane instruments . . . in groups of two or more pairs of players, sometimes forming large ensembles in which each person, with his siku, has only a portion of the pitches of the musical scale" (1981, 24).[2] Likewise, Américo Valencia Chacón (1989a, 16) has photographed sets of Nasca panpipes that show several of the instruments to be exactly half as large as the others.

4.3. Nasca ceramic artifact depicting a procession with a man playing panpipes and a woman carrying two panpipes. National Museum of Anthropology and Archaeology Collection, Lima.

While this evidence points to a collective use of panpipes by Nasca musicians, the instruments' tunings suggest that the performance techniques were probably in groups of single-unit instruments at the octave, rather than double-unit panpipes that would have alternated the notes of their instruments in an interlocking fashion (like the siku panpipes of the present Aymara). This use of collectivity in ensemble playing at the octave has been studied carefully by Bolaños, who writes: "In these [complementary] ensembles [at the octave], more long panpipes were used than short ones. It is also possible that these instrumental groups played with other panpipes using a complex harmonic and melodic structure, although nothing is known about this" (1988b, 29).

Paracas or Nasca iconography showing collective performance, however, is rare, although one modeled Nasca figurine may suggest ensemble playing with several people (fig. 4.3). Helaine Silverman's recent analysis of this figurine, however, refutes group performance: "A unique Nasca modeled scene . . . depicts what appears to be a family going to/coming from some possibly special place to judge from the individuals' fine clothing. The father plays a panpipe and the mother carries two more, one in each hand. Parrots perch on the shoulders of the mother and daughter. . . . I suggest that the family is going to Cahuachi or another Nasca ceremonial center and that they are bringing parrots to sacrifice and/or deplume, panpipes to play [in ensemble], and a fancy ceramic bottle to sacrifice or exchange with other families or give in tribute to the priests of early Nasca society" (1993, 302). Hickmann (1990, 385) includes a drawing of this artifact, which she describes as two panpipe players. Clearly, however, only the man is playing, thus negating an ensemble context, at least during the particular moment represented in the iconography.

Paintings or drawings of panpipes in ensemble are also rare. Bolaños (1998a, cover) has reproduced a drawing from a Nasca ceramic vase that shows two men facing each another, each playing a panpipe. In what is fairly typical of Nasca painting, however, the depiction of the instruments lacks detail beyond showing three very thick-looking tubes per instrument. Nevertheless, the painting is of enormous value for providing contextualization. Additionally, an etching on an adobe plaster wall in the Room of the Posts in the Great Temple of Cahuachi includes eight panpipe designs along with other figures; Silverman (1993, 301) considers this room to be the center of a Nasca ancestor cult. Whether or not the multiple panpipe designs indicate ensemble playing, however, is unknown.

More common than iconography depicting ensemble panpipe performance are pots that show a single panpiper playing his instrument alone, or by himself with one hand while playing a drum with the other (see fig. 3.11). This performance technique, so common in the Peruvian and Bolivian highlands hundreds of miles east and southeast of the Nasca region, will be discussed under the subheading of ethnographic analogy. Other ceramic vessels show panpipe players shaking rattles while they blow their pipes.

Where and in what context have the Paracas and Nasca panpipes been excavated? Among the first to be excavated legitimately (rather than by grave robbers) were those by the German archaeologist Max Uhle in 1901 and 1905, and later by the Peruvian archaeologist Julio C. Tello in 1915, 1926, and 1927 (Silverman 1993). Others were excavated by the Americans William C. Farabee in 1922 and Alfred Louis Kroeber in 1926. The instruments found by these four scholars were deposited in such museums as the Peruvian Museum of Archaeology in Lima (today the National Museum of Anthropology and Archaeology), Field Museum in Chicago, Museum of the American Indian in New York, Peabody Museum in Philadelphia, and other museums in America, Europe, and Peru. Most of Tello's finds were placed in the Peruvian Museum of Archaeology, where he was director. In 1927 alone, he excavated 537 tombs in the Nasca region (Silverman 1993, 17), and the panpipes he found were studied by Bolaños in the 1970s and 1980s (1988a): "panpipes are known from tombs such as the famous cache of six matched Nasca 3 panpipes which were interred with an individual in the Copara cemetery in Las Trancas" (Silverman 1993, 241). Between 1952 and 1953 the American William Duncan Strong conducted major excavations that yielded panpipe fragments, which he documented as coming from the top of the Great Temple at Cahuachi; these were found "along with 'llama remains, bird plumage, and other apparently feasting and sacrificial materials.' Their association with Nasca ceremony, including funerary rites, is manifested in Nasca iconography as well as context" (Silverman 1993, 241). Beginning in 1983, Giuseppe Orefici, an Italian architect, excavated in the Nasca area and in 1992 made a great discovery for music archaeology, as Silverman explains: "In one of the lower rooms [at Cahuachi] on the northeast side of Strong's Great Temple (Unit 2), Orefici's team discovered a cache of hundreds of broken panpipes on the floor of the room: these are currently under study by the Peruvian musicologist Cesar Bolaños. . . . Orefici is now in agreement with me that there is often a ceremonial aspect to many of the construction fills we have excavated" (1993, 28).

Silverman (1993) has conducted the most recent excavations of Nasca sites that have produced panpipes, and she publishes detailed information about their site locations in the Great Temple at Cahuachi: "In my excavations, panpipes were found in Rooms 1, 4, 5, and 6 and the Lower Eastern Rooms of Unit 19 . . . ; in the fill between Walls 45 and 65 behind the Room of the Posts . . . ; at various levels in Test Pits 1 and 4; in the surface levels of Test Pits 7, 15, and 17 . . . ; and in various strata of Excavations 1 . . . and 7." The specifics of these sites are discussed in detail in her book, in which she concludes that Cahuachi was probably the most important Nasca ceremonial center. Her discoveries of hundreds of panpipe fragments, plus thousands more found by Strong and Orefici, corroborate her belief that panpipes were important ritual objects, probably associated with a Nasca ancestor cult. It was apparently a ritual act to break the panpipes, perhaps after their use, much as it was among the Aztec when sacrificial victims smashed their ceramic flutes on the temple steps before being sacrificed to their sun god (see picture from Florentine Codex of Bernardino Sahagún in Olsen 1998a, 17). Complete Nasca panpipes were most often found in individual tombs, such as those excavated by Tello.

Ancient Double-Unit Panpipes: Moche

The Moche of north coastal Peru, in the present department of La Libertad, produced panpipes made from cane and possibly ceramic, silver, and gold. What are believed to be double-unit panpipes are indicated iconographically in Moche pottery. Evidence of their possible use as interlocking halves of one instrument (a double-unit panpipe) is mostly based on iconology, suggested by three-dimensional figures on stirrup spout vessels, and both two-dimensional reliefs and one-dimensional fineline drawings on Moche pottery, where panpipers are either facing

4.4. Moche ceramic vessel depicting two skeletal panpipers in relief facing each other. Florida Museum of Natural History Collection, Gainesville.

4.5. Moche ceramic vessel depicting two panpipers with empty eye sockets standing side by side. National Museum of Anthropology and Archaeology Collection, Lima.

each other (fig. 4.4), standing side by side (fig. 4.5), or facing each other and playing instruments that are connected by a cord (fig. 4.9 bottom). In addition, the Gold Museum in Lima houses two Moche panpipes that are connected by a cord (according to César Bolaños, they had not been studied as of 1996, when I observed them).

Because of this evidence of dual collective use in some ancient Peruvian pottery examples (almost all from the Moche culture), some scholars are led to believe that all panpipes were played that way, in spite of the many examples of solo individual panpipe use as seen in most of the one-dimensional and three-dimensional representations in many pottery examples. Valencia Chacón (1989b, 85–93) makes conclusions about possible dualistic and collective uses for Moche and Nasca panpipes, and sees the musical practices in both cultures as prototypes for the present performance techniques of the Andean siku (double-unit panpipes), as did Izikowitz (1970, 396) many decades earlier (in the 1930s) for the Moche. Bolaños (1988a, 25), however, claims that there is no evidence among the Nasca for such dualistic panpipe use. Whether or not the ancient panpipes of the Moche were of the type like the siku, however, has not been determined acoustically, because none has been studied to my knowledge. Nevertheless, the pictures in figures 4.4, 4.5, and 4.9 suggest that in each Moche example the two front-to-front or side-by-side instruments are of slightly differing sizes, indicating either (1) a dualistic (perhaps interlocking technique), (2) an attempt by the artist to indicate perspective, or (3) simply artistic license. Furthermore, the pipers in figure 4.9 bottom are playing a six-tube larger instrument (left) and a five-tube smaller instrument (right). Some of the fineline drawings on Moche pots show two panpipes being played that are linked by a string (fig. 4.9 bottom). While the use of a cord would indicate pairing, it does not necessarily indicate interlocking of pitches, as among many present Andean panpipe ensembles in the central Andes. Nevertheless, these examples warrant an analogy with the present-day siku musicians of the Aymara people (to be explored further in this chapter), because there is no reason not to believe that an interlocking method of performing could have existed several thousand years ago, and that the practice has continued.

Iconology

Panpipes and Symbolic Transfiguration and Death

Moche iconography depicting panpipe musicians exists in three formats: (1) three-dimensional figures on top of stirrup spout pots; (2) two-dimensional figures in relief on the sides of pots; and (3) fineline drawings on the sides and top of pots. Possible dualistic use (i.e., double-unit performance style) of panpipes is strongly suggested by the second and third formats, while the majority of the instruments depicted in the first format show individual panpipe-playing humans. Benson (1997b, 43), however, explains that Moche pots may have been displayed or used together to create scenes, sequences, or narratives.

4.6. Moche ceramic
vessel depicting a caped
panpiper with deterio-
rated nose. Photograph
courtesy of the Moche
Archive, UCLA.

Some Moche pots depict two nearly identical skeletal or emaciated
humans playing panpipes. In the three-dimensional format, the panpipe
figures are always seated or standing side by side, rather than facing one
another. Moche fineline drawings, however, show realistic, skeletal, or
emaciated panpipe players facing each other as they provide accompaniment or lead other skeletal or emaciated men (or both), who are interpreted as dancers by Donnan. Many of the Moche ceramic pots of panpipe musicians in three-dimensional form feature altered physical human
characteristics, especially of the face (figs. 4.5, 4.6, 4.7), but often including skeletal or extremely emaciated bodies as well (figs. 4.4, 4.8). About
Moche death musicians Donnan writes: "Musicians appear in most of the

dance scenes, but their number, placement and the instruments that they play vary considerably. . . . Death figures constitute an important group in Moche iconography. They are normally engaged in erotic activity, playing musical instruments or involved in dances. . . . Quenas, drums and panpipes are found in dance scenes with death figures, just as they are in dance scenes with normal human figures. However, there is a much greater frequency of panpipes in the death figure scenes. They are normally played by two figures who stand facing one another" (1982a, 99–100).

4.7. Moche ceramic vessel depicting a caped and hooded panpiper figure with empty eye sockets. National Museum of Anthropology and Archaeology Collection, Lima.

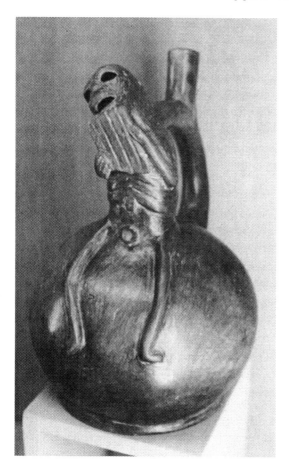

4.8. Moche ceramic vessel depicting a skeletal panpiper with empty eye sockets. National Museum of Anthropology and Archaeology Collection, Lima.

Both Benson (1975) and Donnan (1982a) have referred to many of these performers as "death musicians," "death dancers," or "death figures," while Jiménez Borja (1951) argues that many are representative of physical mutilation of living humans. Donnan explains that Alan Sawyer also put this latter theory forth: "Alan Sawyer (ms.) has suggested that many of the death figures are not truly dead, but rather are 'living dead,' a condition resulting from having their facial skin flayed. The emaciated condition of their bodies, according to Sawyer, 'would subsequently result from severe weight loss due to the extreme difficulty of ingesting adequate nourishment' (ms. p. 4). Sawyer's argument is very plausible when one considers the way death figures are depicted" (1982a, 102).

A third hypothesis is that many of the ceramic pots depict musicians suffering from leishmaniasis or verruga (Benson 1975, 113), diseases similar to leprosy because of body deterioration, especially of the face. In all cases, however, the musicians are probably representing musical performance as a symbolic act, since the absence of lips would make panpipe playing (or that of any wind instrument) impossible.

What, then, do these (often) grotesque figures symbolize? Benson offers the most detailed interpretive analysis of these musicians, dancers, and many similar figures:

> All of these figures depicted on the modeled pots have some physical disability: blindness, lameness, old age, or traces of disease, such as leishmaniasis or verruga—a disease with symptoms similar to leishmaniasis. . . . It seems evident that the priests were chosen for their office—which I presume had to do with death—because they had a physical deformity. They were associated with the dead by a sympathetic magic. Faces which have been affected by leishmaniasis or verruga look like mummified faces: blind faces have the blank look of the dead.
>
> Sometimes these figures are dead. A globular pot of a person, with a headdress tied on top, a cape, a white shift with lines, badge, and S's on the sleeves, has a skeletal face and holds panpipes. (1975, 113–14)

Earlier in the same article, Benson says that the way the Moche represented the dead "was to show socket eyes (if not a skeletal head) and, in some cases, a skeletal ribcage, but an otherwise normal body. Certainly sex organs never died" (1975, 106).

Some of these death characteristics can be seen in the figures of Moche panpipers, placed here on a continuum from "sickly," "dying," to "dead": (1) sickly—figure 4.6, showing nose deterioration; (2) dying—figures 4.5 and 4.7, depicting empty eye sockets and the deterioration of nose and lips, but otherwise full torso, covered with a cape and hood; and (3) dead—figures 4.4 and 4.8, where definite skeletonization is evident, or is about to begin. These figures, placed on such a continuum, suggest the theme of transfiguration and death, the former term referring to a stage in the process of bodily transformation. Mary Glowacki (pers. comm., 1999) suggests that the physical abnormalities of these Moche figures may indicate they are shamans or potential shamans who are experiencing a supernatural (and even physiological) ritual skeletonization, perhaps

4.9. Fineline roll-out drawings from two Moche ceramic vessels depicting (*top*) climbing, processing, or dancing warriors, accompanied and led by drummers and panpipe players (drawing by Donna McClelland), and (*bottom*) processing or dancing figures, accompanied by panpipe players whose instruments are joined by a cord (from Benson 1975, 115; permission to use from Dumbarton Oaks Research Library and Collection, Washington, D.C.).

as a stage of their initiation process. Additionally, in many parts of the world, potential shamans often receive a calling (vision, dream, etc.) if they have a physical abnormality or sickness. Disease can also be a part of the sickness-initiation concept of becoming a shaman, according to Eliade (1972, 33).

Benson (1975, 109) refers to a similar continuum with the themes "preparation-for-death and afterlife scenes," and also discusses characteristics that represent sacrifice and the funerary complex, such as the use of rope and tied objects, which can also include the tied-on cape and hood, later described as a priest's garment (Benson 1975, 112–13). If the use of rope and tied objects refers to the funerary complex and the afterlife, then the "double-unit" panpipes connected by a cord would possibly have a different reason for being depicted that way than to indicate interlocking musical pitches. Perhaps the connecting cord or string is symbolic of the funerary complex and the afterlife, rather than of the two instruments being connected as one. Of course, the cord connection between the two panpipes (or two panpipe halves) could symbolize both of the above.

Recalling the numerous examples of climbing, processing, dancing, or upward spiraling Moche warriors, priests, or others who are accompanied or led by drummers and notch flute players (depicted on fineline drawings from Moche stirrup spout vessels and discussed in chapter 3), Donna McClelland produces another drawing of numerous climbing men, accompanied or led (or both) by drummers in deer masks and two panpipe players whose instruments are joined by a cord (fig. 4.9 top). While I interpreted the contexts of the drawings in chapter 3 (with notch flutists) as life-giving situations, perhaps of transcendence or striving toward life-giving power, the climbers accompanied by panpipers are climbing within (and perhaps out of) the confines of a tunnel or cave, as symbolized by the rocks or bricks below and above them (notice how several of the anguished climbers peer out of the holes above their heads, as they continue their trek). Perhaps they are climbing out of the underworld as part of an act of transformation.

The figures and panpipe players in the fineline drawing shown in figure 4.9 bottom are clearly related to the stages of transformation and death described above for the three-dimensional representations of panpipers. Because they are without noses, but have eyeballs (no eyelids) and torsos, they relate to those classified above as sickly. The others with facial scarification perhaps also symbolize transformation and death.

Bolaños very poignantly summarizes the Moche culture's apparent preoccupation with sex, life, and death: "It is probable that for the Moche sex signified creation, multiplication of living beings, and source of life, not solely as sensuality and much less as pornography. Perhaps the Moche intended in their own way and with their abundant imagination to express their preoccupation with those themes. Also we can surmise that sex, life, and death were an inseparable triad for the Moche, and because of that, they placed them [sex, life, and death] in constant dialogue through their [ceramic] figurines" (1988b, 24).[3] Given the possible preoccupation with death among the Moche and possibly other coastal Peruvians, and their related interest in disease, scarification, possible mutilation, and most likely the curing of disease, is it possible that the use of the panpipe also existed for magical protection against dangers, both physical and spiritual?

Panpipes for Magical Protection

The coastal cultures of Peru (like most littoral cultures) have many activities and beliefs that include the sea, and have developed many ways to use it and sustain themselves from it, both physically and spiritually. The Moche, for example, were great fishermen who fabricated small totora reed *tule* boats that they would mount individually like a horse and ride into the surf, powered by a single paddle like a canoeist (their descendants still do this) (Cordy-Collins 1977b, 434). Farther south, the Ica culture in Peru's south-central coast (ca. A.D. 900–1550) fabricated larger water crafts that could accommodate numerous people. Stevenson wrote about a Spanish encounter with a native Peruvian raft on the high seas that had twenty men on board: "The first European ship entered Peruvian waters in September, 1526. The oceanic raft captured by the Spanish pilot Ruiz hoisted 'as fine cotton sails as ours'" (1968, 267). These were indeed blue-water sailing crafts, keelless rafts with several sails, according to a German drawing from the 1700s, now in the Dahlen Museum, Berlin. To provide lateral resistance for tacking, it is believed that the native sailors inserted three or more leeboards between the balsa logs. These boards (fig. 4.10), which can measure up to four feet long, have been referred to as carved ceremonial digging boards by Dorothy Menzel (1977, iv), ceremonial staves by Diane Olsen (1978, 107), and paddles by others. That they were leeboards for ocean sailing vessels, however, seems logical because of their many carved iconographic references to sea life and water, such as cormorants, pelicans, geometric symbols for waves, and so on; such carved three-dimensional figures would make the object difficult to grip as a paddle. Furthermore, they are similar in construction to the leeboards for rafts, as depicted by a German chronicler whose sketch is displayed in the Dahlen Museum.

The longest leeboard of the set in the Dahlen Museum, seen at the far left in figure 4.10, contains iconography depicting water fowl along the vertical plane of its shaft, and also iconography that may assist in the contextualization of panpipe ensembles. As the detailed photograph of that leeboard shows (fig. 4.11), a row of eight panpipers stand at attention on top of the board's blade (the lower half of the entire leeboard). Eleven more stand atop the shaft (not shown in the detail). Although we are dealing here with a culture that thrived several hundred miles south of the Moche, the Nasca and Moche were fairly contemporaneous, and it seems

4.10. Ica leeboards for use on a balsa raft. Dahlen Museum Collection, Berlin.

logical to look at the former's use of panpipes with the interpretation of the latter. These musician figures could be representative of well-dressed, panpipe-playing, warrior-priests, who performed to achieve magical protection for the seafarers aboard their ocean rafts. Or they could represent warrior-priest panpipers who participated in a supernatural oceanic journey to the afterlife.

Among the Moche on the north coast of Peru is another type of important personage, also perhaps a warrior-priest, who is often depicted as a panpipe player on stirrup spout ceramic pots (fig. 4.12). This design (reproduced as a roll-out drawing from a pot in the Museum für Völkerkunde, Berlin, and published in Benson 1975, 117) includes two men seen facing each other as they play their instruments, one man flanked by two trumpeters; this design is often presented as proof for Moche double-unit panpipes, whose musical notes are alternated between two players. These two musicians are also significant actors in the transfiguration and death theme presented below. About them, Benson provides the following description and analysis: "A status order in the instruments seems to be indicated in these scenes. . . . panpipers in general tend to be bigger than other musicians. . . . The panpipers are not only larger, but

4.11. Detail of an Ica leeboard with iconography depicting waterfowl and a row of eight panpipers standing at attention. Dahlen Museum Collection, Berlin.

more elaborately dressed. They have jaguar and bird headdresses . . . probably emulating the deity and his lizard helper who wear jaguar and bird headdresses, respectively. . . . The vertically striped shirt is sometimes worn by the deity in scenes where he is . . . attacking sea creatures . . . although it is one of his least frequently worn garments. It occasionally appears on the death-priest figures . . . and it sometimes appears on dead men in erotic scenes" (1975, 116–17). I suggest that the animals in these headdresses are a sea otter and a cormorant, animals that are seaworthy, sea-wise, and natural hunters. They are, perhaps, protectors against malevolent sea creatures (spirits) that could disrupt a Moche person's spiritual travels into and through (or across) the sea to the afterlife; therefore, they are protective psychopomps that function as guides to the afterlife. Again, Benson offers a descriptive interpretation: "I believe that there was a Mochica other world or afterlife that was probably entered through the sea, but was on the other side of it; that many Mochica pottery representations have to do with sacrifice, funeral rites, passage to—and life in—the afterworld; and that these themes are related to concepts of fertility, the rebirth of the sun, and the continuation of Mochica power" (1975, 105).

These well-dressed panpipers, then, are perhaps at the beginning of the transfiguration stage of the continuum explained above, as they prepare for a supernatural journey to the afterlife. About the rather elaborate panpipes played by these Moche priest-warriors and the unusual extension attached to the proximal ends, Benson says, "Panpipes are sometimes shown with a head or hand on the end, possibly suggesting ceremonial amputation and decapitation" (1975, 105). That these elaborate panpipes seem different from those played by normal, sickly, dying, or dead musicians can perhaps be explained by analogy with the ancient Greek culture's use of two different types of lyres: the citarra or elaborate box-lyre played by the elite, and the simpler spike-lyre played by commoners and satyrs. Many world cultures have musical instruments of a similar category or classification type, but which differ by degrees of ornamentation or shape or both, and are performed by different classes of musicians (the fancy ones are usually played by persons of higher class; the plain ones by musicians of a lower class). This difference may explain why the elaborately dressed and headdressed Moche warrior-priests play the elaborate instruments, while (as we will see below) caped and hooded death-musicians play a less elaborate kind of panpipe.

4.12. A roll-out drawing from a Moche ceramic vessel of two warrior-priest panpipers facing each other and flanked by two trumpeters. From the Museum für Völkerkunde, Berlin, and published in Benson 1975, 117. Permission to use from Dumbarton Oaks Research Library and Collection, Washington, D.C.

Why are panpipes so important in the suggested themes of transfiguration and death and of magical protection with the Moche? Benson (1975, 119) postulates that "their shape naturally forms a step motif," and that the step formation may be a symbol for mountains, the powerful cosmological world (where the sun rises). The step is a simplified and angular version of the Andes mountains. The step motif, she maintains, is paralleled by the other (conjectured) powerful cosmological region in Moche belief: the sea (where the sun sets). The sea, it is surmised, is symbolized by the scroll motif, a partial spiral that resembles the curvature of a wave. These two symbols, the step and the scroll, are prominent in Moche iconography (this combination may also be why conch shells were apparently venerated by the Moche and others, because the bumps on the outside of a conch symbolize the mountains, while the internal spiral symbolizes the sea). Regarding the panpipes, this dualism might be further symbolized by the alternation of notes and sharing of interlocking pitches by two players, as suggested by the iconography of the Moche.

Benson concludes her hypothesis: "If the step motif does signify something like 'mountains' and all that that implies, it is possible that people so marked, who have gone through the sea to the afterlife, are still stamped as 'mountain people,' inheritors of the importance or divinity of the mountains" (1975, 119). The fact that the mountains along coastal Peru, from north to south, seem to rise abruptly from the sea, helps explain this possible cosmological dichotomy.

With these studies of Tiwanaku, Nasca, and Moche panpipes, their musicians, and their suggested cultural contexts in mind, a survey of similar instruments, their performers, and known cultural contexts in the central Andes of today may assist in our ethnoarchaeomusicological pursuits.

Ethnographic Analogy

While today's Andean highland cultures in Ayacucho and Puno departments in Peru, and in La Paz and Potosí departments of Bolivia, are somewhat removed geographically and historically from the Paracas, Nasca, and Moche, they provide some of the best archaeological analogies available. Since analogies between ancient coastal Peruvian panpipes and their historical and not-too-distant relatives are often made by scholars (Bolaños 1981, 24; Valencia Chacón 1983, 37), it is worthwhile to examine present central Andean panpipes in some detail. First, however, some chronological background is necessary.

Some scholars believe that the Chimú culture (A.D. 1100–1470 [Lumbreras 1974, 179]) was essentially a continuation of the Moche, which would make a Moche/Chimú complex that was not significantly removed in time from the apogee of the Inca empire (late fifteenth, early sixteenth century). However, also according to Luis Lumbreras (1974, 151), between the two cultures was the Wari occupation (A.D. 700–1100), part of the Wari empire, which stretched from Lambayeque, in the north of Peru, to a region just north of Lake Titicaca in the south (including the south coastal region of Peru). Thus, one can perhaps think of a Moche/Wari/Chimú complex, which could have possibly been a factor in linking northern with southern Peru. The Wari occupation of the Nasca culture would also have possibly created a link between that region and the southern highlands of Peru. Lumbreras believes that "The great conquests of Wari II . . . subjugated almost the entire Central Andes from

Lambayeque and Cajamarca in the north to Camaná and Siscuani in the south, including the Moche, Cajamarca, Recuay, Lima, and Nazca territories" (1974, 165). He later makes the following conclusion about cultural cross-fertilization: "A conquest state initiates a process of bilateral acculturation through which the conquerors adopt customs of the areas they incorporate and the conquered tend to accept new ingredients that are compatible with their pre-conquest culture" (1974, 177). Rafael Larco Hoyle (1966, 147–48) suggests this theory even earlier than Lumbreras, when he calls the entire time period of Wari expansion the Epoch of Fusion. Based on these conclusions by two eminent Peruvian archaeologists, one could hypothesize that either (1) the highlands of southern Peru and north-central Bolivia (basically the area of Aymara dominance today, including some Quechua regions) were influenced by Moche and Nasca panpipe musical traditions through the Wari occupation of the entire region, or (2) the present panpipe traditions of the highlands of southern Peru and north-central Bolivia appeared on their own. Paradoxically, both are probably true, although concrete evidence for either possibility is scant. About the archaeological record in Bolivia, Stobart writes: "Archaeological evidence of musical activity in the Andean highlands of Bolivia is poorly preserved in comparison with the wealth from early Peruvian coastal cultures. The earliest finds, said to date from 900 B.C. to A.D. 300, include clay panpipes, vessel flutes, and three-holed bone notch flutes. These are on deposit in the university museum at Cochabamba" (1998, 282). The recent find of a cache of bone tubes in an archaeological site near Tiwanaku, believed to be that of a panpipe factory (Janusek 1999), may eventually offer evidence about the origin of panpipes in the southern Peruvian and northern Bolivian regions of the central Andean highlands.

Single-Unit Panpipes

Antara is a general Quechua word for a single-unit panpipe. More specific terms are also used in the central Andes, including *kanchis sipas* among the Quechua-speaking Q'ero of southern Peru and *rondador* in Ecuador. The most prevalent term for the single-unit instruments, however, is *antara*.

The antara was an important instrument of the Inca, who often made it from human bones, according to Huamán Poma, who explained that an Incan warrior, upon killing an enemy, made a "drum from his skin, a chicha drinking bowl from his skull, and an antara from his bones" (cited in Jiménez Borja 1951, 39).[4] Human parts invested musical instruments with great power, as Jiménez Borja writes: "These [antara] flutes from human bones, just like the drums from human skin, were not meant to be ordinary musical instruments. Instead, considering the joining of the parts: bones, skin, etc. for their essences, their voices should have been something alive" (1951, 39).[5]

Today the descendants of the Inca make their antara panpipes from the common American reed (*Phragmetis communis*), known as *carrizo* in Spanish. These instruments are found in and near Trujillo, on the north coast, and in the vicinity of Cuzco, in the southern Andes. The single-unit panpipe on the north coast is a pentatonic instrument, and it primarily functions as an instrument for entertainment, often played by beggars. In southern Peru, however, its use can be more ceremonial and associated with the communal aspects of peasant society:

> The antara coming from Sallaq Urcos, . . . is composed of four tubes, 28, 27, 25, and 24 cm. in length. The tubes are joined by agave fiber and pitch, forming a single very rigid row. One of the tubes, the longest, has various turns of a white woolen thread around its bottom end, and also has an engraving of a cross in the cane. This tube is not played because it would bring bad luck to the community; therefore, the antara has only three useful tubes. The "cañari" functionary in charge of playing this antara walks around the roads and streets of the village from the early morning. The voice of the flute calls the peasants together to harvest the wheat. This is the mission of the antara.[6] (Jiménez Borja 1951, 39)

Because of the white color and the cross on one of the tubes, this panpipe tradition could signify a purification ritual associated with the wheat harvest. The instrument's individual processional use is somewhat reminiscent of the scene depicted in the Nasca ceramic procession figurine described above, where one musician is seen playing a single-unit panpipe, accompanied by other people and birds.

Nowhere in the Andes is the use of the single-unit panpipe so well preserved as an instrument with supernatural power as among the Q'ero, isolated Quechua speakers who live high in the southern Peruvian Andes, at altitudes up to 16,000 feet above sea level. Some musical research has been done among the Q'ero, and all of it to date has been published by

Cohen (1966, 1998) and Holzmann (1986). Cohen, who has visited and lived among the Q'ero on numerous occasions, writes: "Panpipes are also used by the Q'eros. This instrument consists of a double row of seven tubes of reed, roughly one inch in diameter, ranging from 6 to 14 inches long. . . . The Q'eros name for these pipes is Kan chi si pas which means 'Seven years an unmarried woman.'" Holzmann elaborates: "Qanchis: seven; sipas: unmarried girls. This antara has seven reed tubes, in a double row" (1986, 219). The kanchis sipas (also written *canchis sipas*), however, has only one row of tubes that is playable; a second row consists of open tubes that function as resonators that are never directly played because of taboos attached to them (Cohen 1966, 5). Cohen writes that each playable tube "represents luck in a different area of life" (1966, 8). The kanchis sipas are so imbued with supernatural qualities that they had not been recorded, and probably had not even been heard by outsiders, until Cohen's investigations in 1964. No further information is known about them except that they are "played only during the fiesta of Santiago [on the Nativity of Saint John the Baptist on June 24], which is closely concerned with fertility rites and marking of the animals. There are only three melodies played on the pipes and these have verses about the alpacas, the cows, and the sheep" (Cohen 1966, 8). The Santiago festival occurs during the dry season in the southern Andes of Peru.

Much further north, among the Quichua and mestizo people of highland Ecuador, the rondador single-unit panpipe is the most important traditional Andean musical instrument; it is considered to be Ecuador's national instrument (see Schechter 1998, 417, fig. 1). The rondador is distinct because of its seemingly irregular arrangement of tubes and because it is played by one person who can play harmony with himself (two notes at a time, another dualistic technique). While the origin of this Ecuadorian panpipe is said to be pre-Columbian, the name *rondador* is Spanish, meaning "one who makes rounds," referring to a practice during the colonial period in Quito, Ecuador's capital, when a night watchman used the panpipe to announce his presence as he made his nightly rounds. The name has continued, even though the rondador is presently used by many rural and urban men to provide music for rituals, festivals, begging, and entertainment.

Although many types of rondador panpipes are found in Ecuador, the main ones include the following.

1. Rondador made from condor feather quills of diverse lengths. The

feathers at the ends of the quills are maintained, and serve as ornamentation (*Artesanía folclórica* 1970–71, n.p.). Coba Andrade (1981, 1:99) mentions the feathers of *buitre* (vulture) as a material, but other sources do not mention a feather quill rondador, suggesting a discontinuation of the instrument's use.

2. Rondador made from five small cane tubes, used in religious rituals (*Artesanía folclórica* 1970–71, n.p.). Carvalho-Neto explains that this small instrument is found only in the province of Imbabura, Ecuador, and is played but once a year: "it is a ritual instrument . . . only used in the festivals in homage to the sun, during the equinox of September" (Carvalho-Neto 1964, 367, citing Moreno Andrade).

3. A double rondador with forty-four (or more) tubes played in a dualistic manner for religious rituals and festivals (*Artesanía folclórica* 1970–71, n.p.). This instrument is not mentioned in other sources.

4. Rondador with from eight to more than thirty tubes, using a natural minor scale and played during festivals and for popular entertainment. This is the most common panpipe in Ecuador today, and the one that is most identified with Ecuadorian patrimony. However, it is no longer imbued with symbolism, as its pre-Columbian ancestors and its variants (numbers 1–3 listed above) surely were. Therefore, little information about its significance is useful for understanding more about ancient single-unit panpipes in the Andes.

Double-Unit Panpipes

The most important distinguishing feature of the current double-unit panpipe is the instrument's division into two halves. Among the Aymara of southern Peru and Bolivia, who refer to their double-unit panpipe as *siku*, the two parts are most commonly called *ira* (leader) for the half with six tubes and *arca* (follower) for the half with seven tubes. In cipher notation, the ira has pitches 1 3 5 7 2 4 (beginning with the longest tube, which is lowest in pitch), while the arca has pitches 7 2 4 6 1 3 5 (beginning with the longest tube, which is lowest in pitch). Ira and arca are meant to be played by two people (traditionally two men) in a musically interlocking fashion called in Aymara *jjaktasina irampi arcampi,* or "agreement between the ira and the arca" (Valencia Chacón 1989b, 34). To comprise the whole of the melody, the two halves of the instrument must be played together by alternating their pitches (this technique is often called hocket—from the Latin *hoketus*—by American scholars, after the medieval European vocal technique of alternating notes in vocal parts). This alternation, and the use of two halves, is a type of dualistic musical behavior.

The most common double-unit panpipe is composed of two rafts of closed tubes, with the tubes of each half of the set placed in a stepped arrangement, as organ pipes. Garcilaso de la Vega wrote about this among the Colla in ca. 1609: "The Colla Indians and all those in their district had a certain knowledge of music. They played reed or cane instruments, made by joining four or five tubes together, each one of which furnished a higher or lower note than the preceding one, as in the case of organ pipes" (1966, 79).[7] The end of each closed tube is the natural node of the cane, and because the pitches are arranged from low to high, each raft has a stepped form. In some regions the cane tubes are all cut the same length (with the internal nodes left intact) and rafted together in a rectangular form. Because the nodes are not opened, the instrument still consists of closed tubes with internal steps; the rectangular arrangement makes the instruments stronger when lashed together. In its stepped form the Aymara call the instrument *ch'aka siku*, and in its rectangular construction it is called *tabla siku* (García 1979, 12). The pipes are placed within several split pieces of cane that are either perpendicularly affixed parallel to each other on both sides of the tubes or wrapped around the tubes several times, then lashed with string. This stabilizing mechanism is called a ligature by Izikowitz (1970, 388–90), who provides several informative drawings of the most common varieties.

Double-unit panpipes can be constructed in either single rows of closed tubes or double rows, with the second, or back, row producing a nearly inaudible pitch an octave higher than the first or front row. The second row, which is lashed exactly parallel to the closed row, can be either closed or open (see Buchner 1972, fig. 114). In either case, the second row of tubes always produces a resonated octave, because air is not blown directly into the tubes; instead, the musician's air merely passes across the second row of tubes as he produces notes on the first row. When the flutist blows across the closed tube of his choice, the adjacent parallel tube (open or closed) resonates slightly, giving the instrument its characteristic timbre.

Double-unit panpipes are often constructed in groups that correspond to several pitch levels, as explained by Garcilaso de la Vega, again writing about the Colla: "There existed four such instruments, each one keyed to a higher or lower scale, in the same way as the four human voices: soprano, tenor, contralto, and bass. When one Indian played, a second answered him, shall we say, in fifths, then the third on another harmony, and the fourth on still another, each one in time" (1966, 79). Garcilaso de la Vega, of course, was not referring to harmony as currently conceived of in European-derived music, but was trying to describe particular pitches or pitch level. He continues: "These were professional musicians, who practiced in order to give concerts for the king and nobles of the Empire" (ibid.). While he is certainly describing ensemble performance technique, it is not clear whether he means alternation of pitches as understood by jjaktasina irampi arcampi, or just performance at different pitch levels, such as in parallel fourths, fifths, octaves, or other intervals.

In the southern Peruvian department of Ayacucho, double-unit panpipes are played by the Chuncho (also called Antecc). Their instruments, generally called antara in Quechua, are specifically called *tarawilla* or *jashua* for the largest panpipe pair, *jarawi* or *malta* for the middle pair, and *chipli* or *chiple* for the smallest pair (Instituto Nacional de Cultura 1978, 202). These three sizes are in the relationship of octaves between the largest and smallest sets of instruments, while the middle size is a fifth higher than the largest and a fourth lower than the smallest pair.

Farther south in the central Andean highlands (southern Peru, northern Chile, northwestern Argentina, and Bolivia), the most common name for the double-unit panpipe is the Aymara word *siku*, although the Spanish term *zampoña* is often used in Chile. The siku has a wide distribution in the central Andes, however, and is known by a variety of regional names (see also Gutiérrez Condori 1991, 135). Among the people of Aymara heritage in northern Chile, for example, it is known as *pusa* or *laca* (Dannemann 1977, 106; Yévenez 1980, 54); Spanish speakers of northern Chile, however, call it zampoña. The Peruvian Aymara in Huancané use the term *chiriwano* for their double-unit panpipe and their panpipe tradition during the Festival of the Cross every third of May (Turino, in Romero 1987, 20). In Paratía, Peru, the Quechua use the term *phuko* for a ceremonial music known as *ayarachi* (Valencia Chacón 1989b, 70–71), while the Bolivian Kallawaya, east of Lake Titicaca, call their panpipe *phukuna* (Baumann 1985, 148).

The widest dispersion of the siku today is in a region known as the Collao altiplano, a high plateau with "an approximate area of 200,000 square kilometers (77,220 square miles) at an altitude of about 3,500 meters above sea level (11,483 feet), and . . . situated within the present countries of Peru, Bolivia, Chile, and Argentina" (Valencia Chacón 1989b, 19). In the north-central part of this high plain, and at the heart of the cosmological world of the Aymara and Quechua native people, is Lake Titicaca, the highest navigable lake in the world. This lake is also at the center of the largest dispersion of the siku in Peru; however, Lima, the capital of Peru, is rapidly replacing the Lake Titicaca region as the center of Peruvian siku activity because of the large number of migrants from the altiplano. It is not uncommon today, for example, to see and hear siku ensembles performing in the streets of downtown Lima and in various folkloric nightclubs in the capital (Turino 1988; 1993).

Today, Andean double-unit panpipes are most often made from the giant reed (*Arundo donax*), known as *chocclla* (Vargas 1928, 6) or *chuqui* (Jiménez Borja 1951, 40), which grows on the eastern slopes of the Andes. The French scholars Raoúl and Marguerite d'Harcourt (1925, 49), however, write that the cane comes from the region of Lake Titicaca and is "exceptional for its dimensions." Since the dispersion of the double-unit panpipe is wide, a variety of natural tubes can be used to construct them in addition to cane, such as certain types of bamboo found in northern Chile.

In the traditional Aymara manner, siku are constructed and performed in families of different sizes, whose ranges commonly correspond (by way of analogy only) to the Western soprano, alto, and tenor, with the occasional addition of the bass range (Bustillos, Oporto, and Fernández 1981, 5). Many scholars (Bolaños 1988a, 114–16; Turino 1989, 10–11; Valencia Chacón 1989b, 44, 48–53, 58–59, 65–66, 70–72, 78–79) have studied the acoustic properties of the three-member siku families, and siku group characteristics depend on the particular tradition using them. Generally, the siku panpipe family members are an octave apart. Within each of the family member groups, however, can be three additional divisions of siku at intervals of major and minor thirds, totaling nine siku (eighteen halves) that play in parallel texture (Turino 1989, 10). Additionally, some siku are ordered in such a way as to perform in parallel fourths or fifths, referred to as *contra* (García 1979, 12).

A group of siku instruments, and the musician-dancers who play them, are sometimes called *sikuri* or *sikura* (Baumann 1982), and the most common type of music performed on them is *sikuriada* (lit., music for sikuri). There are also numerous religious or ceremonial and secular ensembles, however, that are known by different names. Several of the most common traditions in Peru are the Aymara sikuri, the Quechua sikuri from Taquile Island in Lake Titicaca, the Aymara *chiriwano* (Spanish: *chiriguano*) from Huancané, the Quechua ayarachi from Paratía, and the mestizo (mixed Aymara and Spanish) *pusamoreno* or *sikumoreno* style (Valencia Chacón 1983, 63–77; 1989b, 74–80). In Bolivia are the Aymara, Quechua, Chipaya, and Kallawaya (known as the *kantu* ensemble) traditions (Baumann 1981, 189–92, 1985). Within the Aymara siku tradition are many varieties of nomenclature for the instrument families, as Valencia Chacón attests: "The different ensembles in the Aymara sikuri tradition are actually complex orchestras with specific and distinctive structures. The ensembles are composed of different groups according to the sizes of the sikus" (1989b, 48). Table 4.1 lists the most common names for the family members of siku in use today.

When siku panpipes perform together for festivals, their numbers are greatly increased, but usually the middle or alto voice (the malta, for example) is given prominence by increasing their number (Turino 1989, 11). Likewise, an ensemble may use a disproportionately large number of tenor siku so the other stronger-voiced instruments will not overpower their weak sound.

As the names of the instruments often vary within the major traditions, so do the scales employed in the music. The following observations generally pertain: Peruvian Aymara siku music is pentatonic, hexatonic (1 ♭3 4 5 ♭6 ♭7 i), or heptatonic (1 2 ♭3 4 5 ♭6 ♭7 i); Quechua siku music from Taquile Island in Lake Titicaca is heptatonic (1 2 ♭3 4 5 ♭6 ♭7 i); Aymara chiriwano music from Huancané is hexatonic (1 2 4 5 ♭6 ♭7 i) and heptatonic; Quechua ayarachi music from Paratía is pentatonic (1 2 4 5 6 i); and the mestizo pusamoreno or sikumoreno music is heptatonic (1 2 ♭3 4 5 6 ♭7 i) (analyses from transcriptions in Valencia Chacón 1989b). The Bolivian Chipaya siku tradition has borrowed greatly from the neighboring Aymara (Baumann 1981, 190–91), although Chipaya music also makes use of a (major) heptatonic scale (1 2 3 4 5 6 7 i).

These details of instrument etymology, classification, voicing, and tuning reveal a great panpipe diversity and complexity in the greater Andes today. Because the panpipe is essentially an indigenous tradition, equal diversity and complexity must have existed in pre-Columbian times. It is important to understand this fact to help us appreciate how music has value in human lives in all time periods.

Table 4.1. Siku family names within documented Andean traditions

Name of tradition	Region	Soprano	Alto	Tenor	Bass
Aymara sikuri (Turino 1989, 10)	Conima, Peru	suli bajosuli contrasuli	malta bajomalta contramalta	sanja bajosanja contrasanja	
Aymara sikuri (Bolaños 1988b, 115)	Peru	chili (suli)	malta (ankuta)	sanja (bajo, basto)	
Aymara sikuri (Valencia Chacón 1989b, 50)	Rosaspata, Peru	suli sulfa	ankuta ankuta dúo barretón	tayka tayka dúo	
Quechua sikuri (Valencia Chacón 1989b, 58)	Taquile, Peru	cantante auca (chuli)	licu	maltona	mama
Aymara chiriwano (Valencia Chacón 1989b, 65)	Huancané, Peru	chili	ankuta	ayka	
Quechua ayarachi (Valencia Chacón 1989b, 71)	Paratía, Peru	suli	wala	lama	mama
Mestizo pusamoreno (Valencia Chacón 1989b, 78)	Peru	ñaño (chili, requinto)	cantante (chaupi, maltona)	bajo (bastón)	
Chipaya siku (Baumann 1981, 189)	Bolivia	sanja	taipi (malta)		
Aymara sikuri (Bellenger 1983)	Bolivia	chehuli	likhu	malta	taika
Aymara sikuri (Díaz Gainza 1962, 186)	Bolivia	chchulis	licus	malta	taika
Aymara sikuri (Paredes 1936, 80)	Bolivia	chuli	mahala	tayca	
Aymara sikuri (Paredes 1936, 80)	Bolivia	tuto	chuli	licu	mahalta
Quechua antara[a] (Bellenger 1983)	Bolivia	chilu	iskay	mamay	altu mamay

a. *Antara* is the Quechua term for panpipe. The Bolivian tradition is referred to here because it follows closely the Aymara performance practice of interlocking parts, called *kkatik* for the follower and *pussak* for the leader. Notice that Valencia Chacón uses *siku* rather than *antara* for the Táquili Quechua. This interchange of nomenclature is presently common among Collao altiplano cultures that live in close proximity with one another.

Other aspects of diversity and complexity include size of ensemble, choreography, performance mode, musical occasion or cultural context, and symbolism. The largest ensemble size of the present traditions is the chiriwano, which has been documented as having as many as 500 performers on special occasions (Bellenger 1983; Valencia Chacón 1989b, 64). Usually, however, ensembles *(tropas)* have fewer performers, ranging from about twelve to over fifty musicians. Siku performers are dancers as well as musicians, and they dance while they play their instruments. Among the sikuri of the Taquile Island, women join in the dancing, forming couples with the men (Valencia Chacón 1989b, 57). Some siku groups, such as the pusamoreno, also parade down streets during patronal festivals, breaking into a circle dance at street corners, whirling while playing. In several of the traditions, such as some of the Aymara sikuri and the Quechua ayarachi, the sikuri musicians play drums while blowing their panpipes, a tradition spanning over a thousand years. Similar playing techniques are depicted on ceramic pottery of several pre-Columbian cultures. On the other hand, the chiriwano use no percussion instruments whatsoever (Valencia Chacón 1989b, 64).

Another playing technique that also requires careful ensemble attention is the method of blowing the two halves (the ira and arca) as a single unit. Turino (1989, 12; 1993) explains that the Aymara musicians themselves express how important it is to play as one, or to sound like one instrument: "no individual's instrument should ever stand out . . . from the integrated fabric of the ensemble's sound." The style should be legato and slightly overlapping, and never should the musician blow so hard that an overtone is produced (Turino 1989, 13). Other panpipe traditions in the highlands, such as the *julajula* in Potosí, Bolivia, however, are loud and musicians produce overtones by blowing their instruments hard.

Many of the Andean siku traditions are imbued with symbolism, as expressed in particular musical occasions that are replete with elaborate costumes for the musician-dancers. One of the most symbolic is the ayarachi, which is performed by Quechua musicians in the southern Peruvian village of Paratía, a name meaning "rain place" (Bellenger 1983), from *parac-tiana*, the "seat of the rain" (Valencia Chacón 1989b, 68). Bellenger (1983) writes the following in his recording notes: "*Ayarachi* stems from the word *Ayar* (death) and means roughly: 'letting the deceased rest and leading him to the Hanac Pacha (the land of the death)': since it is a sad and almost gloomy music, it may well have been played under special circumstances such as funerals or ceremonies commemorating late Inca dignitaries. It is a pre-columbian tradition and *Ayarachi* groups in Cuzco have been reported by B. Cobo as early as the sixteenth century." Likewise, Valencia Chacón elaborates on the role of the ayarachi panpipe orchestras during death rituals: "Ayarachi can also mean 'soul that weeps,' a definition that probably comes from *ayarachic*, meaning 'to accompany the dead,' a name, according to the chronicler Bernabe Cobo (1653), which was given to the panpipes during the Inca period. Ayarachi, therefore, also refers to the pain and music associated with death" (1989b, 69). Some of the death rituals outlined by Valencia Chacón include performances in Cuzco for important royal funerals. "At the death of an Inca lord, or other persons of noble rank, a cortège would leave Cuzco carrying the cadaver to the snowpeak of Pachutusan (where the body would remain one month), accompanied by the funeral music of the ayarachi ensembles" (ibid.).

In addition, ayarachi "is related to the cult of the condor, considered a totemic bird among Andean cultures. The garments of ayarachis and a ceremony alluding to this bird are indications of this character" (Valencia Chacón 1989b, 69). The Andean condor (*Vultur gryphus*) symbolizes death in the Andes. It preys on animals and will fly off with live as well as dead ones. Because of its eating habits, the huge bird has "a natural connection with the world of the dead, and they sometimes play dead when injured or cornered. Vulture remains were placed in elite Pre-Columbian burials and caches. . . . Vulture burials have . . . been found at the Moche site of Pacatnamu" (Benson 1997a, 88). Ayarachi musicians (who also dance) wear elaborate feathered headdresses to represent the condor. The ayarachi musician-dancers, the funeral setting, and the instruments themselves symbolically bridge life and death.

Not all the symbolism associated with Andean panpipes and panpipe traditions, however, is mythological or cosmological. It can also be sociological:

According to the Aymara, a group of chiriguanos is considered complete only when it is composed of two subgroups, each one of which represents a distinct neighboring community. The two subgroups play while they parade together within the same extensive group. Both subgroups play their particular melodies simultaneously in a type of counterpoint. . . . The interaction between the two subgroups within the ensemble takes the form of a musical competition, in which each community unit tries to play its melody at a louder volume than the other, in order to dominate. . . . This explicit binary organization of the chiriguano group, and the musical competition manifested between the two halves is related to the organized leaders [*patrones*] of the Andean society: i.e., comparing the traits of the binary opposites with the fact that the two halves are structurally necessary to complete the whole. (Turino, cited in Romero 1987, 20)

This dualism in performance once again reinforces a symbolic concept that is so important in Andean ideology (Grebe 1974, 47–50). When combined with the ancient system of *mita* (*minga*), or communal work effort, dualism helps us to understand the Andean musical expressions that are so steeped in ancient traditions.

How does all this relate to the suggested transfiguration and death theme of the Moche and perhaps other ancient Peruvian cultures? Several of the current contexts for panpipe ensembles as explained by Turino are perhaps most relevant: "Sikuri ensembles traditionally perform for Pascuas (Easter), Santa Cruz (May 3), San Isidro (May 15), La Virgen de la Asunción (August 15), San Miguel (mestizo patronal fiesta, August 29), and weddings and other life-cycle events such as the *primer corte de pelo* (child's first haircutting, a pre-Columbian tradition)" (1993, 46). It is significant that several of the calendric and patronal religious festivals, especially Easter and the Virgin of the Ascension, pertain to aspects of transfiguration, namely Christ's Resurrection and Virgin Mary's Ascension into Heaven. Likewise, a wedding can be interpreted as a rite of transfiguration as the bride and groom leave their parents and are joined together in marriage—the two uniting to become one. A child's first haircut is physically a change in form or appearance, a change for the better, as the child is no longer recognized as an infant. These are all aspects of transfiguration to a degree: the religious festivals a change *from* life, the wedding and first haircut changes *in* life. The seemingly modern layer of Christianity should not be assumed to be an invalidation or illogical application of the ethnographic analogy mode of inquiry. Because of the anthropological analytical concept of Andean religious syncretism, which explains how ancient beliefs have continued under the disguise of Roman Catholicism, the present calendric and patronal religious festivals are perhaps but post-Conquest adaptations of pre-Columbian festivals of transfiguration, death, and life after death.

Perhaps the most profound ethnographic analogy can be made with the traditional and current performance of panpipes during the dry season in many parts of the central Andes. In Conima, Peru, for example, "panpipes are performed in the dry season (April-October) and duct flutes (pinkillus and tarkas) are associated with the rainy season" (Turino 1993, 41). Likewise, panpipes are played "in the kantu ensembles during the dry season . . . , i.e., in the period from Corpus Christi to the Fiesta de San Miguel (September 8)," explains Max Peter Baumann (1985, 1448–49) about the Bolivian Kallawaya, a Quechua-speaking people from the eastern slopes of the Andes near La Paz. In contrast, he also explains that transverse and duct flutes are played during the rainy season, "as it is the case throughout the Andean area." Respectively, the dry and wet seasons are symbolically associated with death and life in the Andes.

That panpipes are performed during living rituals of transfiguration in present highland Peru and Bolivia offers, by way of ethnographic analogy, important contextual evidence for similar modes of thought in pre-Columbian Peru. What the panpipes musically represent, however, has not been ascertained beyond the importance of dualism, male-female (ira-arca) dichotomy, and interlocking performance technique. These concepts are, nevertheless, symbols of opposition, just as life and death are opposites. The panpipes are joined together to represent a whole by the action of performance, just as a length of cord between two Moche panpipes physically joins them together as one. The performing act, like the cord, transfigures (changes for the better) the incomplete nonmusical panpipe halves into a complete musical whole. As such, panpipes are powerful symbols for bridging life and death, and the performing act is perhaps symbolic of the supernatural journey to the afterlife.

The next chapter looks at another air-sounding instrument, the globular flute, or ocarina, which bridges the mortal and immortal worlds by its power to call the spirits.

Ocarinas for Call and Communication

While life (or life giving) and death (or life taking) exist as concepts that pertain to a dialectic of polarity or opposition, both are directly related to the supernatural world. Humans must communicate with the supernatural to assure that life continues (thus, the curing of illness is a major occupation of the shaman), and immortal existence after death is often more important than life itself. Certain musical instruments seem inseparable from those concepts. Within the realm of theurgical communication (i.e., the persuasion of a spirit by a mortal), signaling or calling is often an important initial act. Priests, shamans, and other mortals often clap, sing, or whistle to call or summon the supernatural. Among ancient South Americans, small globular or vessel flutes (*ocarinas* in Italian and Spanish) were perhaps used as flutes of call or communication to bridge mortal and immortal realms. Sullivan writes, "A vessel frequently serves as an *axis mundi*, that is, as the symbol of communication between realms" (1988, 133). Although he elaborates on the fact that a vessel is a container that holds liquid, and therein lies its power, as "both a container of liquid and a vehicle through which liquid is carried," I shall interpret the vessel flute as a container of air and a vehicle through which air is carried. As a vessel flute, its voice (the music produced by blowing through the vessel) provides the physical manifestation of communication between realms.

The terms *whistle* and *ocarina* are European designations for globular or vessel flutes. In South America (as other places), such instruments can be ductless or with duct, although the latter is probably more common. Generally, common usage determines that the whistle and ocarina are the same except that a whistle is without fingerholes, while an ocarina has fingerholes. Because of the uncertain nature of that distinction, it is preferable to refer to them both as types of globular flutes.

The globular flutes from ancient South America that have survived the ravages of time are mostly made from fired clay. Other materials may also have been employed by early musicians, such as a mixture of beeswax and vegetable ashes, stone, or shell (Abadía Morales 1973, 131), but these musical instruments from those materials have disappeared. Globular flutes may have from zero to six fingerholes, and more than one chamber for those with duct mouthpieces. When a globular flute has multiple chambers and multiple ducts, or when it has a single chamber and multiple ducts, it produces multiphonics (multiple pitches that sound simultaneously).

In this chapter I will explore two broad topics relating to globular flutes: multichambers, multiducts, and multiphonics; and performance practice and calls and communication.

Music Archaeology: Multichambers, Multiducts, and Multiphonics

Numerous ancient cultures in the Andes manufactured globular flutes capable of emitting more than one pitch at a time (multiphonics). Multiphonic musical techniques occurred from the Tairona in northern Colombia to the Mapuche in southern Chile (Grebe 1974, 35–36), and they still exist today in Peru, as attested by multichamber or multiduct globular flute figurines from Ayacucho, often produced as caricatures of peasants. The most common pre-Columbian Andean exemplars come from the Tairona, Bahía, Nasca, and Moche cultures, and all are ceramic globular flutes with either multiple chambers and multiple duct mouthpieces, or single chambers with multiple duct mouthpieces. (Many other multichamber, multiduct, and even multitube musical instruments capable of producing multiphonics were fabricated by the Maya, Aztec, and other ancient cultures in Middle America; see Martí 1968; Stevenson 1968). The ancient Andean multiphonic musical instruments range in iconographic detail from two-headed snakes to human and jaguar- or cayman-faced bipeds with large biceps among the Tairona; brown and white chubby female figurines in the Ecuadorian Bahía culture; polychrome realistic birds and human heads among the Nasca; and small animal and plain globular and tubular flutes among the Moche.

I will examine two musical instruments from the Tairona (1a and 1b below), three from the Nasca (2a, 2b, and 2c below), and two from the Moche (3a and 3b below); then I will describe the multiphonic possibilities produced by them, and show how the ancient makers were aware of such acoustical phenomena as the concepts of beat frequency and difference frequency, also referred to as types of combination frequencies (Benade 1960, 81–82).[1] The greatest musical effect is in hearing the multiphonic globular flutes played, which my audio examples on the compact disc or Internet allow. The transcriptions in the notated musical examples offer an analytical view of the tones produced by giving the mathematical values of the pitches that help to explain the dissonances created by beat and difference frequency combinations. The following cross-cultural comparisons are based on the music technologies of the artifacts themselves and the sounds they produce.

Tairona Multiphonic Globular Flutes

The Tairona (see also chapter 10) were a coastal to highland rain forest culture at the northernmost part of the Andean chain that flourished from ca. A.D. 500 to 1550. Tairona pottery is mainly blackware, and it includes a multitude of zoomorphic, anthropomorphic, and abstract designs. A great number of Tairona artifacts are aerophonic musical instruments.

1a. The Tairona instrument in figure 5.1 is a two-headed, two-chamber, snake-shaped globular (nearly tubular) flute with a blackware finish. It has two mouthpiece ducts: the blowhole for each chamber is the mouth of each snake's head, and the two windows (the openings at the end of the duct, where the air stream is split when it strikes the sharp edges) are at each snake's throat. The snake's body has one fingerhole for each of its two chambers, and the pitches that can be produced are notated along with their cents deviation in musical example 5.1a. There are four combination frequency possibilities on this instrument, and they are beat-frequency types that vary from slow beats (produced between the G −18 cents and the G −23 cents, an imperceptible difference to the human ear until they are sounded together) to fast beats (produced between the F +48 cents and the G −23 cents). To appreciate the sounds of this type of ocarina, listen to audio track 11.

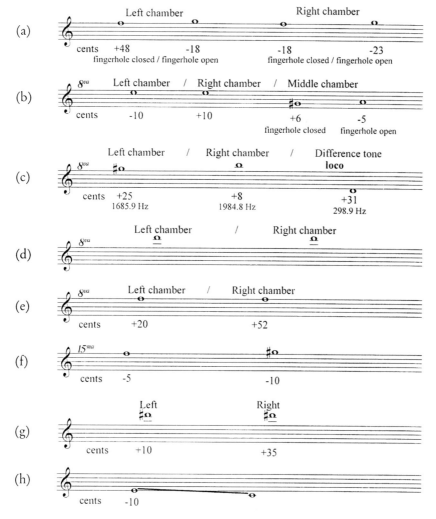

5.1. (a) Four pitches produced on a Tairona ceramic double globular/tubular duct flute in the shape of a two-headed snake, with two chambers (one fingerhole per chamber) and two mouthpieces (see fig. 5.1 and listen to audio track 11); (b) four pitches produced on a Tairona ceramic three-chambered globular duct flute in the shape of a jaguar god-man (see fig. 5.2 and listen to audio track 12); (c) two pitches and difference tone produced on a Nasca ceramic two-chambered globular duct flute in the shape of a seated bird (see fig. 5.3 and listen to audio track 14); (d) two pitches produced on a Nasca ceramic two-chambered globular duct flute in the shape of a human head (see fig. 5.4 and listen to audio track 15); (e) two pitches produced on a Nasca ceramic two-chambered globular duct flute in the shape of a human head (listen to audio track 16); (f) two pitches produced on a Moche ceramic two-chambered globular duct flute in the shape of two owls (listen to audio track 17); (g) two pitches produced on a Moche ceramic two-chambered globular (nearly tubular) duct flute (see fig. 5.5 and listen to audio track 18); (h) upper and lower pitches produced on a Chancay ceramic globular ductless flute in the shape of a dog, fox, or guinea pig (see fig. 5.9 and listen to audio track 19).

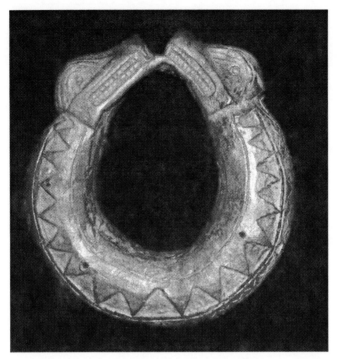

5.1. Tairona ceramic double globular (nearly tubular) duct flute in the shape of a two-headed snake, with two chambers (one fingerhole per chamber) and two mouthpieces (listen to audio track 11). Measurements: mouthpiece to the bottom or belly of the snake 10.8 cm, width 9.9 cm, circumference 9 cm. Guillermo Cano Collection, Bogotá.

1b. The artifact in figure 5.2 is a three-chamber globular flute, also with a blackware finish. It is fashioned as a jaguar- or cayman-faced biped (god-man?) in elaborate clothing with geometric patterns (iconographic details are discussed in chapter 10). The back of the figurine is plain, revealing how the three chambers are built, with the left and right biceps and the body each containing windows, and with the duct and blowhole in the creature's head. In addition, the creature's navel functions as a fingerhole for the middle chamber. The multiphonics produced by this musical instrument take full advantage of the beat and difference frequency phenomena, as seen in musical example 5.1b, notated with cents deviations. The two almost identical notes of the left and right chambers, which constitute the biped's biceps, work together to produce a slow beat frequency that creates extreme dissonance. Two individual pitches of the middle chamber (the belly of the biped) that are produced by its single fingerhole create even more dissonance because of numerous difference frequencies, as you can hear in audio track 12. This audio example has four parts: (a) and (b) are the middle chamber combined with the left and then the right chamber, respectively; (c) includes three improvisations showing the melodic and harmonic possibilities; and (d) includes another improvisation using varying air pressure.

1c. For audio comparison only (no picture is included), audio track 13 includes the sounds of another Tairona three-chamber globular flute, also with a blackware finish. Like the instrument in figure 5.2, it is also fashioned as a jaguar- or cayman-faced biped (god-man?) in elaborate clothing with geometric patterns. It is, however, smaller and, therefore, higher pitched.

5.2. Tairona ceramic three-chamber globular duct flute in the shape of a jaguar god-man (listen to audio track 12). Height 11.7 cm, width 8.8 cm, thickness 3.2 cm. Museo del Oro, Banco de la República, Bogotá.

Nasca Multiphonic Globular Flutes

The Nasca culture flourished from around 200 B.C. to A.D. 600 on the south-central Peruvian coast, an area well known because of the so-called Nasca lines. Nasca pottery is mostly polychrome, with an abundance of designs resembling stylized humans and animals, especially birds, cats, and fish. A few of the bird and human artifacts are ocarinas, and the majority of the musical instruments are panpipes (see chapter 4).

2a. The Nasca artifact in figure 5.3 is crafted as a double-chamber seated or standing realistic bird with a polychrome slip finish. By blowing into the bird's tail, two notes are sounded plus a difference tone (notated with their cents deviations in musical example 5.1c). A frequency counter indicates that the G-sharp is 1685.9 Hz and the B is 1984.8 Hz, resulting in a D difference tone of 298.9 Hz. These pitches are clearly heard in the recorded example (audio track 14).

2b. The Nasca artifact in figure 5.4 is in the shape of a human head with two ducts fused together that resemble a human neck. It also has a polychrome slip finish. The instrument produces the very high pitches notated in musical example 5.1d (they are too high to be measured with accuracy). The multiphonics in this example create a rather fast beat frequency (audio track 15).

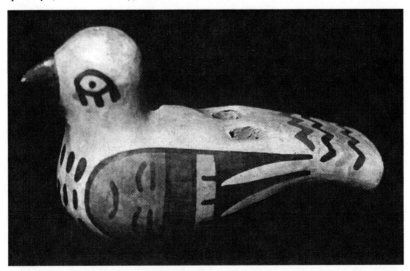

5.3. Nasca ceramic two-chamber globular duct flute in the shape of a seated bird (listen to audio track 14). Private collection. Photograph by Christopher B. Donnan.

5.4. Nasca ceramic two-chamber globular duct flute in the shape of a human head (listen to audio track 15). Private collection. Photograph by Christopher B. Donnan.

2c. A third Nasca musical instrument, an anthropomorphic head with a polychrome slip finish, is not pictured and is included for audio comparison only. Its two pitches are very close together, and the notation in musical example 5.1e shows a small cents deviation between them, which creates a slow beat frequency. When you compare the sound of this instrument with the previous one, you can hear the differences between the slow beats of this example and the fast beats of the previous example (listen to audio track 16).

Moche Multiphonic Globular Flutes

The Moche (see also chapter 8) was a northern Peruvian coastal culture that flourished from approximately 100 B.C. to A.D.700. Moche pottery is mostly brownware (fired in an oxidizing atmosphere) or blackware (fired in a smudging atmosphere), although later phases feature polychrome slip paint finishes. Moche pottery depicts nearly every aspect of Moche life, and only a few pieces are actual musical instruments (mostly ocarinas and trumpets). Donnan (1973, 96–97) discovered nine ocarinas and "whistle fragments" in the Santa Valley of north coastal Peru. "The whistles with a single resonator provide a single, uninterrupted note of high pitch when they are blown," he writes. "Those with double resonators generally sound a single note if blown softly, but when they are blown with force the second resonator begins to function and the two notes together provide a harmonic effect." While this quote lacks musical description, Donnan's later explanation that two of the "whistles" were found in graves provides important contextual data, although they have not been dated (1973, 97). More important, he continues, "Nevertheless, fragments of bugles, single and double note whistles, and drum shells were found at the site with Phase IV refuse," meaning a possible date of around A.D. 500. Ocarinas found in graves and/or grave refuse sites suggest a mortal-immortal nexus for them, as instruments for communication during a burial ritual or in life-after-death situations.

The Moche globular flutes I played and analyzed from Calderón's collection lack the type of documentation of provenience provided by Donnan. Nevertheless, Calderón's Moche ocarinas are musical instruments of great musical perfection, and were being used by him for his curing sessions (see chapter 8).

3a. The first of Calderón's collection selected for analysis (not pictured) is a small Moche globular flute with two chambers resembling two little owls sitting side by side (one owl face is broken off) and a long double-duct mouthpiece with two large circular windows at the bottom of the owls' backs. Its finish is a plain brownware. When I visited him in July 1996, Calderón was using this musical instrument on his curing *mesa,* or altar. The instrument produces two pitches (notated in musical example 5.1f) that are almost precisely at the interval of a minor third (295 cents, rather than the 300 cents of a tempered minor third), as heard in audio track 17, played by Calderón.

Calderón explained that the figure of the animal seen most in Moche iconography is the owl (most commonly the *paupaca*), and that sometimes owls are depicted in pairs, which he calls twins. Furthermore, explaining that the owl is the symbol of wisdom and magical science, he used this particular double owl globular flute to call the spirits of the dead, which help him in his curing ceremonies.

5.5. Moche ceramic two-chamber globular (nearly tubular) duct flute (listen to audio track 18). Scale in cm. Eduardo Calderón Collection, Las Delicias, Peru.

3b. The Moche instrument in figure 5.5 is a plain globular flute (actually approaching a double tubular flute) with two chambers, a double duct (which begins as a single duct), and two "wings" that house the two windows and two suspension holes. This beautifully crafted abstract musical instrument, also with a brownware finish, produces two very high pitches that are only 25 cents apart (notated in musical example 5.1g and heard in audio track 18). The instrument produces an acoustical beat reverberation that sounds like it is being played in an echo chamber. Calderón was also using this instrument on his curing mesa in 1996, and when he played it for me he blew it four times, each time facing and pointing the flute in a different direction. He explained that as a shaman he uses this instrument to call the negative and positive forces that enable him to cure. As a power tool, it is placed in the middle of his curing mesa (see chapter 8, fig. 8.1).

Observations

The manner in which the Tairona used the acoustical phenomena described above is all the more supported by the iconography of the artifacts; that is, the acoustically harsh qualities of their combination frequencies seem to give the ferocious demonlike creatures a terrifying supernatural voice (this observation will be discussed further in chapter

10). On the other hand, the rather realistic Nasca and realistic or abstract Moche exemplars produce combination frequencies that do not sound as harsh to the Western ear. It is, of course, impossible to know what the Tairona, Nasca, or Moche people considered harsh. The aesthetics of musical sound in archaeological cultures can only be speculated about.

Nevertheless, not only are the music technologies described here acoustically and perhaps metaphysically highly developed, they are also indicative of an extremely developed ceramic technology. That the Nasca, Moche, and other cultures fabricated figurines, ocarinas, whistling pots, and panpipes from molds is well known (Stevenson 1968, 246; Donnan 1992, 59), although it has not been determined whether or not the globular flutes of the Tairona were also constructed from molds. Nevertheless, the precision with which globular duct flutes must be made in order to produce a sound, and the additional precision needed to tune them to obtain multiple pitches that differ by only a few cents, implies complex musical and intellectual development.

The care with which the Tairona, Nasca, and Moche must have chosen the intervals for their multiphonic musical effigy figurines and other musical instruments suggests that the phenomena of multiphonics with combination frequencies were created for special effects to enhance the ambiance of particular occasions. The precise meaning of the multiphonics and the resultant combination frequencies, however, are unknown. Ethnographic analogy with the Kogi of Colombia provides no answer for their use among the Tairona; there are no direct historical ethnographic analogs to explain the use of multiphonics among the Nasca; and Calderón had no explanation of the Moche artifacts other than their ritual importance and significance to call the spirits that he employed in his curing séances (see chapter 8).

Music Archaeology, Iconology, and Ethnographic Analogy: Performance Practice, Calls, and Communication

Pre-Columbian globular flutes come in many shapes; most resemble animals (especially mammals, birds, and reptiles) and others have abstract shapes. While we have seen many multichamber and multiduct ocarinas capable of rich and dissonant multiphonics, there are also many single chamber artifacts capable of one or more pitches (although they do not sound simultaneously), depending on the number of fingerholes or playing techniques. Iconology and ethnographic analogy may provide some evidence about how they were used.

Performance Practice

Peruvian archaeologist Julio Castro Franco hypothesizes that certain ceramic globular flutes in Peru were performed by musicians who interlocked their individual pitches between several players: "Whistling-vases, oval zoomorphic, Chancay (Hacienda Lauri). These instruments were destined to collective musical interpretation. Each musician performed two or three notes of the melody on one vase, applying a musical technique [*juego mecánico;* lit., mechanical play] very similar to that which is today used by the panpipe ensembles [sikuris] of the altiplano" (1961, 28).[2] "Julio Castro Franco suggests that Mochica zoomorphic whistles formed consorts, each whistle player timing his pitch to succeed another's so that melodies could be performed," explains Stevenson (1968, 258).

However, there is no ancient iconographic evidence to suggest that globular flutes were performed in consort or in an interlocking manner in ancient Peru. To the contrary, they appear to have been played alone by single individuals. The Moche, for example, produced ceramic pots (figs. 5.6, 5.7) that depict globular flutes being played by a single male musician, suggesting a nongroup, individual use only. Moreover, there are no ethnographic analogies in Peru, and the closest analogy is with the distant Chipaya culture of Bolivia, where a collective performance technique using a globular flute is found among the Chipaya, as Baumann explains: "Then the clay vessel-pipe (wauqu) enters; its highest tone is played in the same hocket technique" (1981, 175). While Baumann discusses an interlocking technique for the Chipaya, it is not between several globular flutes in consort, but between one "vessel-pipe" and occasionally other (dissimilar) instruments (an example can be heard on Baumann 1982, C/2). Therefore, an ancient interlocking technique for an ensemble of globular flutes in the Andes seems highly unlikely.

The ocarinas represented in Moche ceramic pots are perhaps similar to small artifacts referred to as *silbatos* (whistles) by archaeologists and grave robbers who excavated them from Moche burial sites (Donnan 1973, 96–97). The instrument seen in figure 5.6 is shown played with one hand, which suggests that it does not have fingerholes. The instrument in figure 5.7, however, is shown played with two hands, meaning that it

5.6. Moche ceramic vessel depicting a human playing a globular flute. National Museum of Anthropology and Archaeology Collection, Lima.

probably does have fingerholes. A comparison of this figurine of a Moche ocarina player with a photograph of Calderón playing a Moche ocarina that he unearthed (fig. 5.8) shows similar physical performance postures, especially the fact that both hands are grasping the instrument. I will, therefore, use these two methods of performance practice to classify the ocarinas into two groups: those without fingerholes and those with fingerholes. Furthermore, it seems that the globular flutes without fingerholes all have duct mouthpieces, while those with fingerholes are all ductless, each with a cross-blown mouthpiece like the Western flute mouthpiece apparatus (i.e., an embouchure hole). Let us now look at these two types of ocarinas.

Ocarinas without Fingerholes and with Duct Mouthpieces

In 1972, I made a detailed study of a Chancay musical instrument (fig. 5.9) similar in shape and construction to the aerophone described by Castro Franco (1961, 28). It is a ductless zoomorphic globular flute in the shape of a dog, fox, or guinea pig (the latter animal suggested by Calderón). The instrument has a cross-blown mouthpiece in the middle of the animal's back and is without fingerholes.

In addition to its animal shape, painted designs on the animal's body resemble several rows of notch flutes with multiple fingerholes. While it

5.7. Moche ceramic vessel depicting a stylized human playing a globular flute. National Museum of Anthropology and Archaeology Collection, Lima.

5.8. Eduardo Calderón playing his Moche ovoid globular ductless flute in 1974 (listen to audio tracks 26–29).

is possible, however, that these designs could be simply rows of rounded spots (the fingerholes?) within horizontal lines that are closed at each end, some with notches (the tubes of the flutes?), the following Quechua folktale from the Peruvian coast, entitled "Big Mouth" in English, suggests a relationship between foxes and flutes: "Formerly Fox had a small, dainty mouth. One day he heard Wren singing and asked to borrow his flutelike bill. Wren gave it to him and sewed up his mouth to make it even smaller, so that the 'flute' would fit. To the sound of Fox's music, dancing skunks suddenly appeared, causing him to laugh so hard that the stitches broke and his mouth tore open to its present size" (Bierhorst 1988, 232).

In his discussion of this folktale, Bierhorst likens the fox in the Andes to a trickster figure that has ancient roots in the Americas. He also explains that the origin of the "Big Mouth" tale is unknown, and that although it did not appear in its Spanish form until the nineteenth century, scholars believe it to be pre-Columbian. While the relationship between the fox and the notched flute may be only coincidental, their appearance together in these two formats (ocarina and folktale) in coastal Peru suggests a significant relationship between animal and music.

The Chancay ocarina also contains a small piece of clay or stone inside its body, and can be made to sound as a concussion container idiophone (rattle) as well as an aerophone. When played as a cross-blown globular flute, one basic pitch is sounded (E −10 cents) that can easily be altered up or down by increasing or decreasing the air pressure or by altering the direction of the air stream (musical example 5.1h). As we hear in audio track 19, I played this instrument in a pattern that includes four melodic improvisations separated by four shakes of the instrument between each melodic improvisation. Since four is associated with shamanism in northern Peru (Calderón, pers. comm., 1974), I performed the globular flute in patterns emphasizing that number, as Calderón did in audio track 18.

I interpret this type of animal-shaped globular flute without fingerholes as a musical effigy figurine; as such, it was probably played by a single male individual by himself, perhaps as a part of a life cycle ritual. These conclusions are determined from the iconographic symbolism of

5.9. Chancay ceramic globular ductless flute/container rattle in the shape of a dog, fox, or guinea pig (cuy) (listen to audio track 19). Private collection. Photograph by Christopher B. Donnan.

the instrument and ethnological analogies with dogs and foxes in Peru. By using the direct historical approach of ethnographic analogy with the people of Moche (just up the coast from the Chancay site where the instrument pictured in figure 5.9 was excavated, according to Christopher Donnan), we learn that the dog is physically valued because of its ability to run fast and its "sense of smell and ability to track down lost or stolen objects and runaway people" (Sharon and Donnan 1974, 56). Moreover, it is metaphysically valued because of its ability "to smell the human shadow or soul . . . to smell out evil spirits who wish to do harm . . . [and] to see spirits" (Donnan 1976, 106). While explaining the spiritual quality of the dog, Calderón refers to two types: *alcosunca*, a spotted shorthaired dog, and the *alcocala*, a hairless dog (Sharon and Donnan 1974, 56). He also explains that when placed in the bed of a person with a fever, either of these dogs will remove the fever by absorbing it, a characteristic similar to that of the Mexican hairless dog known as Xoloytzcuintli among the Aztec. The body temperature of the Mexican hairless (105 degrees F) made it useful for reducing muscular aches and rheumatoid pains when placed in a patient's bed (Pferd 1987, 148–49). A map, drawn by William Pferd (1987, 158), places the distribution of the hairless dog (which was either plain colored or spotted) in Central America and the Pacific littoral, as far south as central Peru. The dog, then, is an important symbol for easing aches and pains and curing illness, especially that caused by the loss of one's soul (which causes illness, according to many shamanistic belief systems).

Likewise, the fox is an important animal associated with supernatural powers in Peru, as Gary Urton suggests: "Foxes are sometimes . . . called *Pascualito, hijo de la tierra* (son of the earth) and *perro de los machulas* (dog of the ancestor spirits). Foxes . . . are considered to be *paqos* (diviner-curers)" (1985, 260). As a diviner, the type of howling a fox does determines what kind of planting season the people will have and how abundant the harvest will be (Urton 1985, 261). The fox "would have been one of the most logical deity symbols of peoples living in the area," writes Alan Sawyer (1977, 383–85) about the importance of the fox motif in ancient coastal Peru. As a curer, the fox is a shamanic alter ego and, like the dog, has metaphysical significance.

Another attribute of the dog and fox among ancient Peruvians was an association with the moon, as William Hommel explains: "canines were considered the moon's messengers because of their night prowling habits.

... The dog['s] ... howlings at the moon were interpreted as conversations with the celestial master" (1969, 13). Playing the globular flute, a musician could perhaps symbolically reproduce the howling or yelping of the dog or fox and could metaphorically communicate with the supernatural.

Therefore, I suggest that the animal-shaped musical instrument represented in figure 5.9 was a tool to provide an individual with transcendent powers. It perhaps combined the special power of the dog or fox, as seen by its physical shape, with the power of the notch flute, as represented by the painted exterior designs of several kena flutes on the animal's body.

Bird-shaped globular flutes without fingerholes are also common in ancient coastal Peru. An example from Chancay that I studied at UCLA is a small brownware artifact that I also call a musical effigy figurine. Like the previous exemplar, this bird figurine also has only one pitch in theory (because it has no fingerholes). Inspired by its bird shape, however, I made it sound like a bird by using my imagination and varying my air pressure (audio track 20).

In 1996 Calderón showed me two Moche bird globular flutes without fingerholes in the shapes of a *pinto* bird (fig. 5.10) and a pelican (fig. 5.11) that he was using on his curing mesa (see chapter 8). The former artifact is

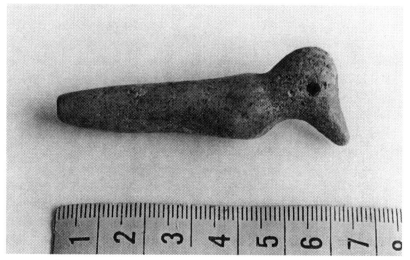

5.10. Moche ceramic globular duct flute (nearly tubular) in the shape of a *pinto* bird (like a hummingbird) (listen to audio track 21). Scale in cm. Eduardo Calderón Collection, Las Delicias, Peru.

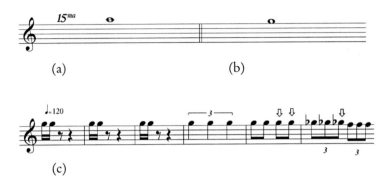

5.2. **(a)** Pitch produced by Dale A. Olsen on a Moche ceramic globular duct flute in the shape of a *pinto* bird (like a hummingbird) (see fig. 5.10); **(b)** pitch produced by Eduardo Calderón on a Moche ceramic globular duct flute in shape of a pinto bird; **(c)** melody played by Eduardo Calderón on a Moche ceramic globular duct flute in shape of a pinto bird.

a small brownware bird-shaped globular flute without fingerholes that has a single fundamental pitch. When I played it for him (audio track 21), imitating a bird by varying my air pressure (force of blowing), he was amused. Although Calderón did not play it in the manner of bird imitation, several factors hint that this and other bird ocarinas without fingerholes were perhaps played in this way. Why, for example, would they have no fingerholes, be shaped like birds, and have such high pitches? Calderón explained that his version of playing only repeated notes is how he calls his bird spirit helper, his little "pinto bird" ("like a hummingbird," he said), which flies all the way from Lake Ipacaraí in Paraguay to Lake Atitlán in Guatemala (and vice versa).

Calderón's other small bird whistle he was using in 1996 is in the shape of a sleeping pelican (fig. 5.11) and also has a single pitch that can be slightly varied (audio track 22). However, he explained that his playing is in a manner of the pelican's singing voice, used to awaken someone. "Nobody fishes until the pelican sings," he said (interview by author, 1996). While demonstrating how he plays the pelican flute during a curing séance, he repeated the sound four times and stressed the importance of four calls to give the sound power. When he performed the instrument

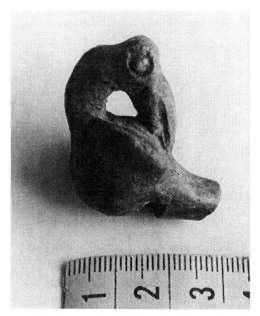

5.11. Moche ceramic globular duct flute in the shape of a sleeping pelican (listen to audio track 22). Scale in cm. Eduardo Calderón Collection, Las Delicias, Peru.

for my recording, however, he did not play it four times, perhaps negating its power during the noncontextual recording. In its role for curing illness, Calderón also explained how both the pelican and the pinto bird have long beaks that are symbolic of the sucking or removal of the poison (i.e., the illness) from a patient.

Ocarinas with Fingerholes

Based on a music archaeology study, other globular flutes that were used by the Moche and perhaps other ancient coastal Peruvians are cross-blown ductless instruments with two fingerholes and abstract shapes. Because of those traits, they are organologically in contrast to the globular flutes without fingerholes. Three Moche ocarinas of this type are in my sample: two from the UCLA collection and one from the Calderón collection (now in my collection).

The Moche abstract ocarina in figure 5.12 is crescent-shaped with a cross-blown embouchure hole in its convex top. I was able to produce four pitches (the alternation of the two fingerholes produces nearly iden-

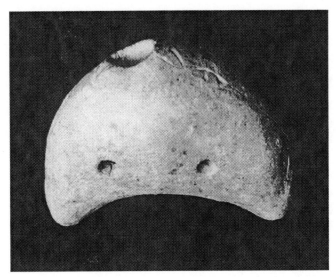

5.12. Moche globular ductless flute in crescent shape with embouchure hole in convex top (listen to audio track 23). Private collection. Photograph by Christopher B. Donnan.

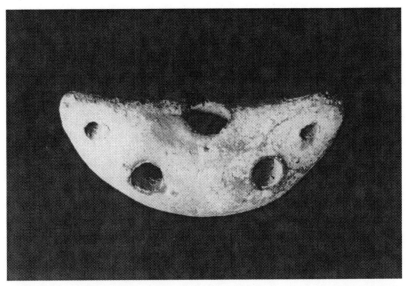

5.13. Moche globular ductless flute in crescent shape with embouchure hole in concave top (listen to audio track 24). Private collection. Photograph by Christopher B. Donnan.

tical pitches) with its two fingerholes during a recording session at UCLA in 1972, as heard in audio track 23. Except for its crescent shape, this globular flute seems to have no visual metaphoric or symbolic content.

The crescent-shaped Moche ocarina in figure 5.13 has its embouchure hole in its concave top; it also has two fingerholes. The placement of the embouchure hole on this cross-blown ocarina has no effect on its tone or tuning, and its four pitches (recorded at UCLA in 1972) are very similar to the previous example, as heard in audio track 24.

The ovoid Moche ocarina in figure 5.14 belonged to Calderón until he gave it to me in July 1974. Like the crescent-shaped globular flutes, this also has two fingerholes and is capable of producing four pitches when I play it (musical example 5.2a). I was intrigued by the manner in which Calderón played it, however, which was completely different than how I would have thought to play an instrument with fingerholes. The next few audio examples (audio tracks 25–29) include his performances, some within the context of my interview with him. When he played the ocarina for me in 1974 he lifted off only one finger (see fig. 5.8), creating only two basic notes. However, he varied his air pressure, creating many more

5.14. Moche ceramic globular ductless flute in ovoid shape (listen to audio tracks 25–29). Scale in cm. Dale A. Olsen Collection, gift from Eduardo Calderón.

microtonal pitches than I produced on it. He explained that this is how he plays it during a typical curing séance, shaking a rattle four times between his melodies (as heard in audio track 25). In an interview with me in 1974 he described its physical characteristics: "It is possible that this ocarina represents a tuber, a sweet potato, because you find that in the majority of the representations, the ocarinas are in the shapes of ears of corn, of *zapallos* (green like a watermelon, with yellow insides), of sweet potatoes, of fish, of seals."

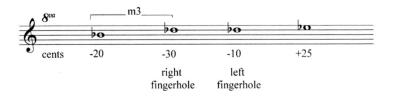

5.3. Pitches produced by Dale A. Olsen on a Moche ceramic globular ductless flute in ovoid shape (see fig. 5.14).

Today, globular flutes such as all of those discussed above are often found in and removed from pre-Columbian *huacas* (referring here to ruins, ancient shrines, dwelling places of ancestor spirits, and tombs) by Peruvian north-coastal curanderos who frequently use them during their curing séances. Huacas are elements of ancient power, explained by Stern as "sacred beings or powers materialized in hills, waters, caves, stones, ancestor mummies (*malquis*), and so forth" (1993, 14). Therefore, the term *huaca* can refer to a sacred object as well as a sacred place or structure. As a sacred structure, *huaca* today refers to either a temple or a tomb, although the original meaning of the term for the ancient Chimú in Trujillo was temple (Ramírez 1996, 139–48). Curanderos such as Calderón, José Paz, and Jorge Merino have described their use of musical instruments taken from huacas during nocturnal curing séances in studies by Gushiken (1977), Joralemon (1984), Sharon (1978), and Skillman (1990). According to them, the ancient globular flutes are always placed within the left field of the curandero's mesa (see chapter 8).

In the early 1970s, Calderón described all the objects of his mesa in detail to anthropologist José Gushiken (1977, 63), and had this to say about the globular flute from the left field of his mesa (see fig. 8.1, near lower left corner, third row from left; this is the same instrument pictured in fig. 5.14, which he gave to me as a gift in 1974): "[This is] a whistle from a grave, an ocarina to call the *huaca*: the *huaca chililí* [a place], the *huaca del sol* [sun], the *huaca de la luna* [moon], the *huaca boquerona* [wide opening], the *huaca prieta* [black], the *huaca del gallinazo* [vulture], the *huaca rajada* [cracked], and all the huacas that are in the north [can be called]. In other words, all the *gentiles* [ancestors] can be called with this ocarina. With its two tones, during the night, you can come to an agreement with them, you can speak to them, and the ancestors come."[3] According to Douglas Sharon, Calderón explained this very globular flute, which he called *pito para las huacas* (whistle for ancient shrines), this way: "This is an ancient ceramic ocarina from a tomb. It is used to invoke the spirits of the dead and of the pre-Columbian past. The spirit of the person with whom it was buried is believed to be captured inside it" (1978, 163).

In July 1974, Calderón and I also talked about his use of Moche globular flutes in the curing of illnesses (I had seen Douglas Sharon's photograph of Calderón's mesa containing the ocarina pictured in fig. 5.14). After explaining my interest in his musical knowledge, Calderón played his Moche globular flute for me (audio track 25). As you can hear once again, he played two pitches back and forth; then he raised the tuning of those pitches by changing the direction of his airstream against the mouthpiece. He played his two-pitched melodic patterns several times in the lowered and raised tunings, followed by shaking a rattle and then playing the melodic patterns again. When he finished playing, I interviewed him and he explained his melodic usage, the spirit-calling process, and how he learned the ocarina tradition as a part of the curing ritual (in several places during this interview he punctuated his explanations with short musical performances):

D.O.   You also play three sounds, as you told me before? And what are they?

[He plays again: audio track 26]

D.O.   You said before [the interview] that you play your ocarina for calling the huacas?

E.C.   Yes, this is the custom, because huacas are elements, let's say, materials or tools, possibly used by these people [Moche]. *Huaca* in Quechua means rock [peña]. Translated into Spanish it becomes cemetery or ancient structure, pertaining, for example, to Chimú, Mochica, or any other ancient archaeological culture. This is huaca. Thus, like inert work in the, let's say, esoteric plan of the mystical and magical realm, these instruments are precisely used to call the sense of, or let's say, within the entire dimension of the magic of the huaca, the spirits, the gentiles [spirits], the dead, those who inhabit the huacas.

D.O. There were only two melodies that you played first?

E.C. Yes.

D.O. And after that there was a third melody?

E.C. Yes.

D.O. How do you choose which melodic pattern to play? For example, is one melody unique for a particular spirit, or what?

E.C. Well, the call is in general, but it all depends, let's say, on the intention, or rather the mentality of the shaman. Sometimes in a moment of trance, when certain mechanisms, shall we say, of the manipulation come to you, and musical notes come out that have never come out before.

D.O. Yes. Thus, it depends?

E.C. It depends, yes, in the moment that one finds himself in. All of a sudden you get sounds that you have never thought of and they come out.

D.O. And you also play with both fingers off?

E.C. Yes. Like this [he plays, but only air comes out]. It is not responding. But in all cases you have to cover it [the fingerholes] like this [he plays again: audio track 27].

D.O. Where did you learn how to play the ocarina?

E.C. Well, this I heard from some curanderos in the north. Up there they find many [ocarinas] and use them, and they make them exactly like that: huacas, ocarinas, and a series of little things. And there I heard one of them play these instruments to call the huaca: whwhwhwhwhwh [he imitates the sound of an ocarina]. They have some large ones that give much different sounds than this one. This one is a little high, no? But good; it at least serves my purpose.

D.O. They taught you then?

E.C. I heard the sound, because they have their musical system for these things. They are not all equal, no? For one type of thing there is one type of music, of rhythmic patterns; and for others, other types. Just like that.

D.O. Each person then plays distinctly?

E.C. Each shaman is distinct. Each one, for example, is the absolute owner of his intention, no? Of his assimilation (whatever your spirit gets is what you play). For example, I have a different sense [than others]. One person works, for example, with his back to the north, while I work facing the north. Others work, for example, with their faces to the sea. Each person has his way of doing things, his form. For me it is a question of the sounds. For example, I have, a form . . . [he again plays the ocarina: audio track 28], let's say. There are others who call in a different way. Each person has his form. When there is much haste, I have to call loudly, no? Because there are things that are needed [he plays again: audio track 29].

D.O. Just like that?

E.C. Nothing more. It's like the policeman's whistle [laughs]. I will give this [ocarina] to you.

It is clear that Calderón uses particular melodic patterns to call particular spirits, or to do certain things during his curing séance. The spirits (the huacas) can come from the mountains or the sea, and each curandero has his particular way of making the calls; some melodies are played softly, others loudly, as Calderón's examples on the CD demonstrate.

After our 1974 interview, Calderón gave me his Moche ocarina as a gift. In return I gave him four metal Cherokee bells that I purchased in the United States at an intertribal powwow in 1973. He was very excited to receive the Native American bells, and when we again met in 1979, he told me that he cherished them and had been using them on his curing mesa.

Twenty-two years later, in 1996, Calderón was employing another ocarina on his mesa that was very similar to the instrument he gave me in 1974. This instrument (pictured in Olsen 1998b, 29) is another cross-blown globular flute with two fingerholes, although it is in the shape of a fox (or dog) rather than plain ovoid. The embouchure hole is in the animal's belly, requiring the animal to be upside down when played. This instrument, which produces four pitches, was used by Calderón to call the huacas and all the organs of mankind (interview by author, 1996).

According to Joralemon (1984), José Paz also employs ancient globular flutes, which he keeps just to the left of center of his mesa, the life-taking side. Nothing specifically is said of them other than the fact that they were found in archaeological sites (Joralemon 1984, 17). Joralemon does explain, however, that pre-Hispanic ceramics and stones from ancient ruins and tombs, items of the ancestors, "are 'dead' both because they are inert and because they are from places of the dead" (1984, 5). Many of the objects on the left field "also have strong associations with animals [such as] snakes, deer, monkeys, guinea pigs, owls, frogs, felines, foxes, and birds of prey" (1984, 3).

Globular flutes associated with or in the shapes of animals are also found on the left side of Jorge Merino's mesa, as Skillman explains: "This is a pre-Columbian ceramic whistle that was found in the vicinity of Cerro Aypate near Ayabaca (Píura). It makes the sound of a nightingale and is appropriately named *ruiseñor* (nightingale). Accompanied by another . . . pre-Columbian ceramic whistle [in the shape of a duck and therefore called *patito,* or little duck, both are] used to note and record *encantos* as they appear at the *mesa*" (1990, 18–19). Using ethnographic analogy and based on these comments by present curanderos and the ethnographers who have interviewed them, I suggest the following interpretation of the pre-Columbian ocarinas: ancient Peruvians used their globular flutes for calling and communicating with the supernatural, much like they are used today among northern-Peruvian shamans.

In this chapter I have described the high level of physical and acoustic construction of small musical objects that archaeologists often call whistles. More than mere whistles, the artifacts represent sophisticated musical instruments with great cultural significance. On the other hand, when we in the West think of whistles, the policeman's whistle or the Brazilian samba whistle come to mind—instruments of call and communication within their own cultures, to be sure. Calderón's ideas regarding his use of the ancient "whistles" as instruments of call and communication strongly suggest a similar use in ancient times. The next chapter explores another ancient Peruvian globular or vessel aerophone, the whistling bottle, which has also been interpreted by some scholars as a tool for communicating with the spirits.

6

~,~,~

Whistling Bottles

Treasures, Tools, or Tea Kettles?

So-called whistling bottles are unique archaeological globular or vessel duct aerophones. In this chapter I will describe their construction and present an explanation for their use (how they were sounded), rather than determine their significance (why they were sounded). The latter will probably forever remain a mystery, although people often make speculations, calling them treasured "government gifts for meritorious service [and] valued objects of the more distinguished members of [the] community" (Menzel 1977, 29), ritual tools for reaching ecstasy (Garrett and Stat 1977), means for making spiritual contact (Ransom 1998), or receptacles much like today's whistling tea kettles; others have perhaps wisely avoided the issue altogether (Donnan 1992, 23).

From ancient Mexico to Peru, a great variety of single- and double-chamber ceramic vessels that contain a small internal duct whistle at the top of the spout are known as whistling bottles (Garrett and Stat 1977), whistling jars (Izikowitz 1970, 369–72), whistling water jars (Ransom 1998), or whistling pots (Furst 1965) in English, and *vasos silbadores* (Martí 1968) or *botellas silbadoras* (Bolaños 1988b; Amaro 1996) in Spanish. Ransom (1998, 12) maintains that the single-chamber type is the older of the two, and that it must be blown into for a sound to be produced. The later double-chamber bottle can produce a sound both by being blown into and by passing a liquid from one chamber to the next.

Among the Moche, Donnan (Donnan and Mackey 1978, 103, 110–11) has excavated tombs that contained whistling pots, thus providing evidence that they were probably not used in temples or other sacred spaces, like the ceramic panpipes of the Nasca were (see chapter 4). One of his excavations in 1972 yielded two single-chamber whistling pots in a Moche IV tomb. This gravesite seemed to be for a high-ranking adult male, judging from the body's elaborate headdress and other items indicative of high status (Donnan 1978, 208). The tomb was located in what Donnan believes to be a cemetery on a desert plain between the Moche Pyramid of the Sun and Pyramid of the Moon.

Figures 6.1 and 6.2 are, respectively, two ancient double-chamber whistling bottles from the Moche and Chimú cultures (provenience unknown). Within the bird's head on the Moche pot and the bird's body on the Chimú pot are their sounding mechanisms, each consisting of a small duct and window, similar to a duct flute mouthpiece assembly. Figure 6.3 is a cross-section of a typical bird's head double-chamber whistling bottle showing the elaborate sounding mechanism within the bird's head (which cannot be seen from the outside of the vessel). As the drawing

6.1. Moche ceramic double-container stirrup spout whistling bottle with bird's head (listen to audio tracks 30 and 32). Private collection. Photograph by Christopher B. Donnan.

6.2. Chimú ceramic double-container stirrup spout whistling bottle with complete bird (listen to audio tracks 31 and 33). Private collection. Photograph by Christopher B. Donnan.

reveals, when a liquid within the bottle moves from the spouted intake chamber into the whistling chamber, caused by tilting the bottle, air is forced into the duct, producing a whistling sound when the air is split by the sharp edge of the window in the hollow sphere. The sound waves and the forced air escape through the beak or nose of the figure that encases the sounding apparatus.

Additionally, some whistling bottles contain one or more small holes at the base of the creature's head or body that, when covered by the handler's fingers, slightly alter the pitches of the whistling bottle when blown into. However, I interpret these holes as air vents rather than fin-

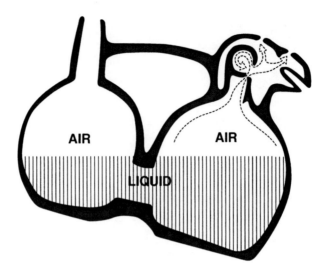

6.3. Cross-section of a typical double-chamber whistling bottle, showing the sounding apparatus within the bird's head and how the sound is made when the liquid displaces the air and forces it through the whistling apparatus. Drawing by Robert Burke.

gerholes, unlike Iván Amaro (1996), who measured the intervals produced by blowing into and fingering the vents of hundreds of pots from various northern Peruvian cultures (his study included 2,900 whistling bottles that were analyzed for iconographic content). Through his careful and extended study he has dispelled previous theories that particular intervals pertain to particular animals represented on the bottles, as he explains: "Very dissimilar figures such as, for example, human beings, felines, monkeys, ducks or parrots emit very similar sounds" (Amaro 1996, 133).[1]

In addition to Amaro's recent musical analysis of whistling bottles, the most noteworthy earlier studies that include sound production have been made by the team of Steven Garrett and Daniel Stat (1977) from UCLA and by Samuel Martí (1968) from Mexico. The former scholars conducted a detailed study of the sounds of seventy-three whistling bottles from nine ancient Peruvian cultures; they concluded that a standardized pitch was employed for the bottles in each of the nine cultures. To conduct their study they utilized a mechanical blowing machine for maintaining consistent air pressure, while the pitch results were recorded in an anechoic chamber that furnished optimum recording conditions. Based on their standardized pitch theory, Garrett and Stat speculate that the native Peruvians using the whistling bottles blew into them in order to achieve a trance state for religious purposes, and they were not used as containers for liquid (Alexander 1976). Their conclusions, however, are debatable since there are no examples in Peruvian iconography where such a practice of blowing (or even placing a whistling bottle to a person's mouth) is depicted. Had the pots been employed in such a manner, it is likely they would have been molded, drawn, or etched into ancient Peruvian (or Mexican) art, since nearly every aspect of religious or ceremonial activity was depicted in the iconography of ancient Americans, especially among the Moche. In spite of my misgivings about this type of performance technique, in 1972 at UCLA I recorded myself blowing into two ancient Peruvian whistling bottles (figs. 6.1, 6.2) in the manner described by Garrett and Stat (audio tracks 30 and 31). As you listen to these sounds, you can hear how increasing and decreasing air pressure causes the pitches to microtonally rise and fall.

In contrast to the theory of Garrett and Stat, Martí eloquently presents his theory about how double-chamber whistling bottles (in Mexico) were possibly used:

> Emulating the priest-astronomers and constructors, the priest-musicians had a profound knowledge of their art and of acoustical phenomena. The ingenious whistling bottles can be cited as examples that, besides being musical instruments, were desirable as ritual, magical, or exvotive objects to deities related to music. This artifact consists of two ceramic chambers united by a tube, one of which is closed with a zoomorphic or anthropomorphic ornament that functions as a whistle. The other chamber has a free opening into which water can be placed; upon moving or inclining the bottle, the water is forced into the closed chamber, and upon increasing the volume of the water, the air is compressed; this air is sent into the mouthpiece of the whistle producing a prolonged and suggestive sound that causes surprises because of its beauty and provenience. It is easy to imagine the impression that the "magic song" of the whistling bottle would have caused to the people in the dimness of a temple, whenever the priest moved or inclined the water inside it. (1968, 110)[2]

I would agree with Martí's theory that the double-chamber whistling bottle was sounded by water displacing the air within the chambers. I support this conclusion with experiments done by Christopher Donnan and myself in 1972, using two double-chamber whistling pots (figs. 6.1, 6.2) in the UCLA collection. Martí's conclusion is also supported by Brian Ransom (1998), who studied eighty-two whistling bottles by playing them (some with breath and others with water) and recording the results.

Ransom's eighty-two and my two whistling bottle samples are clearly sufficient to provide musical verification of the theories that such bottles are capable of holding liquid, that the liquid displaces the air as it is sloshed back and forth from one chamber to the next, and that sounds are produced. I believe that the ancient double-chamber whistling bottles were not intended to be blown into, as described by Garrett and Stat (and possibly Amaro), but rather were used in the manner described by Martí.

My experiments reveal that the whistling bottle's whistle apparatus produces innumerable pitches when water is transferred back and forth from one chamber to the next through the attached connecting tube (audio tracks 32 and 33). As the liquid displaces the air in the chamber containing the whistle, the air, which is unevenly forced into the whistle by the uneven entry of the water into that chamber, produces sounds in the whistle that are remarkably similar to the chirps of a bird. Conversely, the intake of air through the same whistle opening, produced as the water returns into the spouted chamber through the connecting channel, is similar to animal or human inhalation sounds. While water was the liquid chosen for my experiments, perhaps a different liquid was used by the ancient Peruvians, such as a ritual hallucinogenic brew similar to the San Pedro cactus (*Trichocereus pachanoi*) drink still used today by northern Peruvian shamans (Sharon 1972). Ransom, however, writes, "It is unlikely, though, that they were used as receptacles for hallucinogenic substances as no organic stains in the vessels have been found" (1998, 15). Although his point is well taken, the bottles could have been washed out after each use.

The sonic results of my experiments are all the more noteworthy considering the bird iconography into which the whistle apparatus is built. Birds, being important symbols of shamanic flight and power among native South Americans (Wilbert 1974, 33), are among the most frequent designs of the spouts that house the whistles of whistling bottles, as Ransom also notes: "An incredible variety of realistic as well as highly abstracted bird images are among the fluid-type whistling water vessels which I sampled" (1998, 13). Other whistling bottles exist, however, with iconographic representations of animals other than birds. Frequently depicted, for example, are sea lions or seals (Diane Olsen 1978, 110, fig. 21), monkeys, and humans, some of which are playing musical instruments (Diane Olsen 1978, 111). Amaro (1996) identifies dozens of animal (including human) types on Peruvian whistling bottles. He places their iconography within the funeral art complex found throughout the Andes.

While the whistling bottles I studied have double chambers, some have only one chamber, making the sloshing/whistling theory difficult (but perhaps not impossible) to validate (see Velo 1985). Although I have never tested it, it is possible that water sloshing within a single-chamber bottle may also cause a displacement of air, thus activating the whistle of a whistling bottle. Certainly steam activates the air within a single (or double) chamber as well. That the whistling bottles (single or double) were ever used with heat to create steam, however, is unknown. Christopher Donnan (pers. comm.) believes that heating to the point of producing steam from the liquid, as in a tea kettle, would probably cause a ceramic bottle to break. For practical reasons, therefore, I never conducted such an experiment.

While I do not consider the sound makers studied in this chapter to be flutes because their sounds were probably not produced by musicians blowing air directly into them (although Amaro, Garrett and Stat, and Ransom claim they *were* blown into), the next chapter returns to instruments that were undoubtedly air sounders activated by human breath. We now leave the category of globular edge sounders, and examine tubular flutes that were held horizontally (in a transverse manner) and cross-blown in a way similar to the Western orchestral flute.

Transverse Flutes and the Cult of the Dead

A transverse flute (also called horizontal flute, cross-blown flute, or cross flute), by virtue of how it is blown, is an instrument similar to the European fife or concert flute (without keys). Because of the lack of archaeological evidence until recently, and aided by its pervasive presence in Western civilization and use by Jesuit missionaries in Bolivia and Peru, the transverse flute in the Andes had been credited to Western influence. In the past several decades, however, archaeological evidence has revealed its presence in the Andes. It is the purpose of this chapter to provide additional concrete evidence for its existence in pre-Columbian Peru, and to suggest a possible context for its use.

Music Archaeology

Several early scholars of pre-Columbian Andean music have insisted that the transverse flute did *not* exist in ancient Peru, or at least its presence was in doubt. "The transverse flute is not conspicuous anywhere,"[1] write Raoúl and Marguerite d'Harcourt (1925, 62), and Jiménez Borja gingerly explains in 1951, "The use of transverse flutes among the ancient Peruvians has been placed in doubt" (1951, 44–45).[2] Stevenson, however, contradicts them: "During the Chimú period, last before the Incas subjugated the north coast, cross flutes came into vogue. Decisive evidence can be taken not only from the recovered flutes but also from the clay effigies astride Chimú stirrup jars" (1968, 256–57). Both Stevenson and Jiménez

Borja (the latter author was apparently not sure) mention a ceramic Chimú stirrup spout jar as evidence for the transverse flute in pre-Columbian Peru (pictured in Bolaños 1988b, 37, archive no. 3509, Museo de la Universidad de Trujillo).

The strongest evidence, however, comes from the instruments themselves. Coba Andrade (1992, 2:582), for example, cites several Ecuadorian scholars who provide lists of numerous pre-Columbian ceramic transverse flutes and their measurements. In addition, María Ester Grebe (1974, 35) describes two ancient transverse flutes made from cane or wood from the region of San Pedro de Atacama in northern Chile. More recently, Hickmann (1990, 254–57) describes transverse flutes from Ecuador and Peru, placing them into closed and open categories according to their distal ends. Thus, pre-Columbian South American transverse flutes did exist, and we have the ancient exemplars that are still playable.

In 1979, I photographed and recorded myself playing an archaeological Peruvian ceramic tubular transverse flute in the Cassinelli Museum Collection in Trujillo, Peru (fig. 7.1). Although the instrument was la-

7.1. Moche or Chimú ceramic tubular transverse ductless flute being played by Dale A. Olsen, 1974 (listen to audio track 34). Cassinelli Museum Collection, Trujillo, Peru.

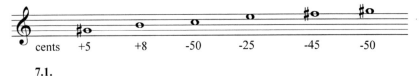

7.1.

7.1. Six pitches produced on a Moche or Chimú ceramic tubular ductless transverse flute (see fig. 7.1 and listen to audio track 34).

beled Moche, it is probably Chimú, a culture that replaced the Moche, according to analogical iconographic evidence. Approximately two feet long, this transverse flute has a cross-blown mouthpiece near its proximal end, two fingerholes near its distal end, and both ends are closed. When I played the flute, I was able to produce the fundamental pitches notated in musical example 7.1 and heard in audio track 34. Moreover, I was able to produce many other pitches by overblowing and producing overtones. By using a combination of fingering and overblowing, I was able to play scales in several octaves.

Because of the location of two fingerholes at the distal end of the tube, and the ease with which I could produce harmonics and a great number of overtone pitches to create scales, this archaeological transverse flute is acoustically very similar to the present flute of the pipe-and-tabor (one-person flute-and-drum) combination found almost directly east in the department of Cajamarca (where the flute is called *flauta*), southeast in the departments of La Libertád and in the Callejón de Huaylas in the department of Ancash (where this type of flute is called *roncador*), further north in Ecuador (where it is called *pingollo*), and in Moche itself (Calderón calls it *waraoria*). Pipe-and-tabor flutes, however, differ greatly from the Chimú transverse flute in the following ways: (1) each of the former has a duct mouthpiece like a recorder and is played vertically; (2) each is performed with one hand while the other plays a drum suspended from the musician's wrist, neck, or shoulder; and (3) each is open at the distal end. Therefore, an analogy of the Chimú transverse cross-blown flute with the current vertical duct flutes such as the flauta, roncador, pingollo, and waraoria will not be made, because they are physically different and their acoustical similarities of producing many pitches by overblowing and obtaining notes of the overtone series may be only coincidental to the ancient transverse flute. However, analogies will be made with other transverse cross flutes found in current usage throughout the Andes.

Uceda Castillo and other archaeologists from Trujillo, whose recent archaeological excavations have revealed interesting evidence for an ancient cult of the dead, have suggested a possible context for archaeological transverse flutes in the Chimú region.

Iconology

Contextualization: The Cult of the Dead

In 1993 a Chimú wooden model of a ceremonial plaza from the ancient city of Chan Chan was discovered in a section of the nearby Huaca de la Luna (Tomb of the Moon) in the Moche River Valley, near Trujillo, Peru (Uceda Castillo n.d.). The model contains a scene in which several individuals are interpreted as playing transverse flutes and are flanked by rattle players (or drummers) and other individuals. According to Santiago Uceda Castillo, the modeled musicians are possibly depicting a death or ancestor ritual. If the individuals holding tubes are indeed transverse flute players, then this is the first discovery of contextualized information involving horizontal or transverse tubular flutes. The relationship of the conjectured transverse flutes to the individuals' mouths suggests that each flute has its mouthpiece (embouchure hole or blowhole, which cannot be seen) in the center of the tube rather than the end. Therefore, the modeled Chan Chan flutes seem to differ slightly in their playing position from the actual Chimú transverse flute in the Cassinelli Museum Collection. This is perhaps because of the following factors: (1) the abstract representation and small size of the models, (2) artistic license, (3) they are completely different instruments, or (4) they are not flutes at all.

The context portrayed by the small Chimú wooden scene is interpreted by Uceda Castillo as a cult of the dead or cult of the ancestors, related, perhaps, to the Moche context suggested in chapter 4. Uceda Castillo describes certain personages, perhaps relatives, who are Chimú priests of the dead in charge of preparing the bodies of the ancestors, "feeding" them, and generally preparing them for their journey. This preparation, he explains, also included performing music on transverse flutes and drums (similar to the Moche who performed panpipes and possibly drums). Whether or not the musicians accompanied the dead into the afterlife is not known, although Uceda Castillo writes, "In this way, death had its own life, and the dead danced, celebrated, and 'reproduced,' in much the same manner as those from the living" (n.d., 5).[3]

They were also apparently serenaded by musicians, perhaps much like the elite buried in Etruscan and Greek tombs, who were provided music to accompany dancing and feasting in the afterlife (Olsen 1990).

Hickmann (1990, 258–59) has photographed two pottery vessels from Lambayeque-Chimú whose iconography resembles the Chimú transverse flute-playing figures described and drawn by Uceda Castillo, with one relevant difference: the flutes are held in a manner similar to how I played the Chimú instrument described above (i.e., the right hand covers the fingerholes at the distal end, rather than in the middle, as in Uceda Castillo's drawings). Contextually, the vessels verify a small ensemble situation because one depicts two musicians playing their transverse flutes side by side, while the other shows one musician playing a transverse flute while another plays a drum.

Beyond these pottery vessels and Uceda Castillo's suggested contextualization for ancient transverse flutes, nothing else is known about how they were played, by whom they were played, and for what purpose. Let us next consider analogies with living cultures.

Ethnographic Analogy

Some Current Contexts

Most ethnomusicologists who have written about the cultural contexts of transverse flutes in the Andes today associate them with Western-influenced festivals that celebrate Christian feasts or saints' days. John Schechter (1998, 419), for example, explains that in Cotacachi, Ecuador, the cane transverse flute with six fingerholes is used in groups of two or three during Holy Week, and especially on Palm Sunday. Among the Q'ero, high in the Andes near Cuzco, Peru, John Cohen (1998, 227) describes how the *pitu*, a transverse flute with six fingerholes, is used during the Corpus Christi festival, when the musicians imitate the music of the Ch'unchu (Chuncho) of the rainforest. A similar flute called flauta or *pífano* is used in ensembles in highland Bolivia to caricature the Ch'unchu Indians, according to Henry Stobart (1998, 286). In Conima, a village in southern Peru, the mestizo people play pito transverse flutes in ensembles to "accompany two different costumed fiesta dances: *achachk'umu* (or *auki auki*, hunchbacked old man) on May 3 for the Fiesta de la Cruz, and *pastorcitos* (shepherds) at Christmas" (Turino 1993, 48). Such ensembles of transverse flutes at one time performed during the festival of the Virgen de la Asunción (Virgin of the Ascension). These ethnographic analogies are relevant to the Chimú cult of the dead interpretation because all of them are either Roman Catholic fiestas directly related to death (Holy Week, Corpus Christi, the Ascension, and the Crucifixion), or other fiestas loosely related to death (old age with the hunchbacked old man and the birth of Jesus, whose death on The Cross completes His life).

It was widely believed that the Jesuits introduced the transverse flute in the Andes and adjacent rainforest areas during the seventeenth century. Indeed, in many regions of Peru, Bolivia, and Paraguay, the Jesuits taught the native inhabitants how to play innumerable European-derived instruments, such as the transverse flute, shawm (double-reed instrument like an oboe), violin, harp, and others. It is no wonder, then, that the transverse flute is still used for feast and saints' day celebrations. That it is more common than the shawm is perhaps due to the pre-Columbian foundation of the transverse flute in ancient death rituals.

Part III

≋

Musical Case Studies

8

~·~·~

Musical Enchantments of the Moche of Peru

The data used in this chapter are presented according to the four modes of
my methodological model for ethnoarchaeomusicological inquiry; however, iconology and ethnographic analogy are the predominant modes
employed. Unlike the musical topical studies of the earlier chapters, and
the musical case studies of archaeological cultures presented in chapters 9
and 10, in this chapter I consider iconology and ethnographic analogy
together. The musical knowledge I seek is the use and significance of
Moche ceramic pots that depict musicians, musical events, and dance.
The use of Moche musical instruments is determined through iconology,
while the significance is determined by ethnographic analogy.[1] Specifically, this chapter attempts to demonstrate that Moche pottery (especially
those ceramic vessels depicting musical instruments and their use) are
icons of and repositories of *encantos* (enchantments), powerful forces of
nature that the shaman must be able to control in order to maintain a
proper balance between life and death for a community. Therefore, I argue that the Moche artifacts such as the stirrup spout vessels (*huacas*)
were used to receive the encantos or spirits and functioned as receptors or
homes for the spirits when they arrived.

Moche Background

The Moche (also referred to in the literature as Mochica, Early Chimú,
Pre-Chimú, and Proto-Chimú) were a fairly diverse group of people in-
habiting numerous coastal river valleys in northern Peru between ap-

proximately 100 B.C. and A.D. 700 (although Lumbreras [1974, 99] dates the Moche from A.D. 100–800). The internal diversity of the Moche culture is due to the nearly 800 years of its existence and its breadth throughout north coastal Peru, as Lapiner writes: "Hills and mountains, occasionally rising to a height of 5,000 feet, and a network of rivers, the source for irrigation and agriculture, formed natural barriers between Mochica settlements. City-states or towns flourished in some forty river valleys, none more than twenty to forty miles from any other" (1976, 111).

Archaeologists have determined major differences between the northern and southern realms of the Moche. Like other ancient South American cultures, the Moche had no written language, although Rafael Larco Hoyle (1966: 103) claims they had a written language of ideograms, comparing it to the Maya's use of hieroglyphs. There are still people today who claim to speak Mochica, the name given to the language, but the Moche's use of ideograms has not been deciphered like the Mayan writing system.

Lumbreras (1974, 165) suggests the Chimú culture (A.D. 1100–1470) may have been a continuation of the Moche, with the Wari occupation (A.D. 550–900) perhaps partially bridging the gap between them. Such a Moche/Wari/Chimú complex could possibly have been a factor in linking north coastal Peru with southern highland Peru, since the Wari culture nearly reached the north shore of Lake Titicaca. This would have created an overlap with the apogee of the Inca empire (late fifteenth, early sixteenth century). There was also a relatively short time between that complex and the eve of the Spanish conquest of Peru. Therefore, while the Moche culture itself had disappeared, the north coastal Moche/Chimú complex, which was subsumed under the Inca, was not necessarily a dead culture by the early sixteenth century.

The Moche themselves left a rich legacy of detailed pottery buried in tombs—so rich that archaeologists, especially Elizabeth Benson (1972, 1975) and Christopher Donnan (1976, 1978), have been able to outline a rough ethnography of the Moche from iconographic remains. So numerous are Moche iconographic ceramic stirrup spout vessels that the UCLA Moche Archive contains over 7,000 different entries (Donnan 1976, 11) arranged into ninety categories. Although most of these categories have been carefully analyzed and interpreted, those containing musical themes have not been systematically studied. In this chapter I will provide ethnomusicological analyses and interpretations of many Moche stirrup spout vessels, from the Moche Archive and dozens of other collections, that depict musicians, musical events, and dance.

Today, while Moche descent is impossible to prove, many Peruvian north coastal shamans, known as curanderos, practice curing techniques that suggest possible Moche retention of basic elements. According to Donnan (1976, 92–108), Moche knowledge from an earlier time period has probably continued in fishing technologies, shamanism, and other specific areas of daily life. Present knowledge about northern coastal Peruvian curanderos, so thoroughly documented by Joralemon (1984), Sharon (1978), and Skillman (1990), can, by way of ethnographic analogy, provide plausible interpretations about the ancient Moche. That northern Peruvian coastal shamanism has been a continuing tradition is evidenced by a comparison of what are believed to be curing scenes depicted on Moche pottery with present ethnographic studies of curanderos from the northern Peruvian coastal states of La Libertád, Lambayeque, and Píura (Donnan 1976 and 1978). Sharon sums it up this way: "through a combination of archaeological, ethnohistorical, and ethnographic evidence, it has been possible to establish a continuum for curanderismo stretching from circa 1200 B.C. to the present" (1976b, 359). Ana María Hoyle writes, "the instruments that are frequently observed in [curing] contexts are shaken container rattle idiophones, with and without handles. Neither aerophones nor membranophones are found. . . . In the present practice [of shamanism], container rattles with handles and whistles are used. . . . If we are to consider that the present practices of traditional medicine [shamanism] are maintaining their origins from pre-Hispanic times, then the sense with which those [ancient] instruments are used would be, if not the same, at least similar" (1985, 371).[2] This chapter will reveal that, indeed, many of the instruments and techniques from ancient times are still used, while others exist that are very similar to those from the past.

Moche Musical Instruments and Ceramic Pots Depicting Music

Moche musical instrument taxonomy, based on music archaeology (actual instruments) and iconography (depicted in pottery), includes aerophones, idiophones, and membranophones. In the flute-type aerophone category are vertical tubular notch flutes (see chapter 3), panpipes (see chapter 4), and globular flutes (see chapter 5). The Moche also made use of trumpet-type aerophones, such as conch shell trumpets and their ceramic imitations, straight trumpets, and coiled trumpets. In the idiophone category are single-container rattles, double-container rattles, raft rattles, and bells. Moche membranophones included shallow-frame drums, kettle drums, and possibly hourglass-shaped drums. Because Moche notch flutes and panpipes have already been studied in earlier chapters, the present chapter does not repeat that information. Likewise, basic details about Moche globular flutes will not be repeated, although I will elaborate on their use and significance as explained by modern Peruvian shamans. Additionally, I will use ethnographic analogy to suggest the use and significance of Moche whistling, singing, container rattles, skin drums, conch shell trumpets, and stirrup spout vessels in general.

It is perhaps tempting to assume that the Moche played all the above instruments together, as Larco Hoyle suggested decades ago: "These Indians were also a musical people, using shells as instruments of percussion, playing flutes and Pan pipes, tambourines, and straight or curved trumpets made either of pottery or of shells. With these instruments they organized orchestras to accompany their theatrical performances" (1966, 103). The iconographic evidence, however, as presented in chapters 3 and 4, does not indicate large-ensemble use of those instruments by the Moche; only two or three melodic instruments playing together with one or two drums seems to be the norm. If by "theatrical performances" he includes curing rituals, then present-day examples of such ceremonies may provide us with suggestions about Moche musical instrument use and significance.

Curanderos, Mesas, and Music

The knowledge and interpretations of the following five Peruvian shamans or curanderos (the terms will be used interchangeably) are central to this chapter: (1) Eduardo Calderón, (2) José Paz Chapoñón, (3) Jorge Merino, (4) Masías Guerrero, and (5) Alberto Guerrero. The data they provide have been published in several ethnographies by American and Peruvian scholars. In addition, my work with Calderón spans several decades.

Eduardo Calderón, known as El Tuno, lived in Las Delicias, a small fishing village (actually a beach suburb of Moche) on the outskirts of Trujillo in the department of La Libertád. Calderón's fame, both for his ability to cure and willingness to lecture about his magical practices, has spread from Trujillo to Lima, Los Angeles, and Europe. Douglas Sharon's publications (1972, 1976a and b, 1978; Sharon and Donnan 1974), a case study by the Peruvian folklorist José Gushiken (1977), and my interviews (1974, 1979, and 1996) with Eduardo Calderón are invaluable to my study.

José Paz Chaponón, from a coastal village outside Trujillo, conducts curing rituals regularly in Huanchaco (department of La Libertád) and Lambayeque (department of Lambayeque). Donald Joralemon (1984) has worked extensively with Paz and has written a valuable analysis of his curing techniques.

Jorge Merino lives inland from Chiclayo in the department of Lambayeque. Donald Skillman's study (1990) of the curing practices of Merino is important for its interpretive analysis.

Finally, Masías Guerrero, who was born in 1910 in Ferreñafe, Peru, and his eldest son, Alberto, are an important team of curanderos. Both men have worked closely with Joralemon and Sharon (1993).

Calderón, Paz, Merino, and the Guerrero team are not familiar with each other's individual shamanistic techniques. All, nevertheless, practice a form of shamanism that includes several ancient techniques, tools, and practices, some traceable back to the Moche. The ingestion of a hallucinogenic drink made from San Pedro cactus, for example, was a practice common with Moche religious men, as suggested by Moche iconography (Sharon 1972, 115). Another may be the use of an altar referred to as a mesa (lit., table in Spanish, double field in Quechua) by the shamans (fig. 8.1), although Sharon and Donnan write, "In Moche art there is nothing depicted which closely resembles Eduardo's mesa. Nevertheless, certain objects and individuals that are commonly represented [on Moche pottery] correlate directly with items on the mesa" (1974, 52). Several of the objects on a curandero's mesa are musical instruments, including globular flutes and container rattles, the former studied in chapter 5 and the latter to be discussed below. First, however, let us observe some details about the curandero's mesa.

The shaman's mesa physically consists of a blanket or cloth spread on the ground onto which numerous objects are placed into two main zones called *campos* (fields) or *bancos* (benches); these are left- and right-hand areas separated by a neutral zone. Calderón's mesa includes the following fields and attributes: "The left and smaller side of the oblong mesa is called the *Campo Ganadero* (Field of the Sly Dealer, Satan). . . . The right

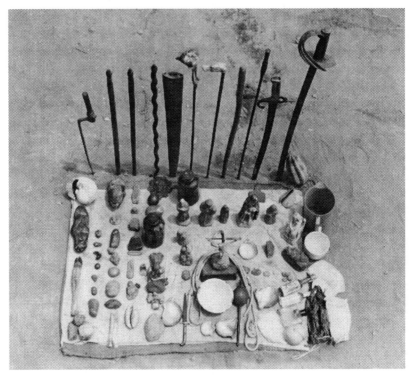

8.1. Eduardo Calderón's mesa or altar. Photograph by Douglas Sharon.

and larger side of the mesa [is] called *Campo Justiciero* (Field of the Divine Judge or Divine Justice). . . . The neutral field (*Campo Medio*) [is where] the forces of good and evil are evenly balanced" (Sharon 1972, 125). Joralemon, however, speaking about the mesa of José Paz, interprets the fields in a less Christian sense (he explains, in fact, that Calderón trained for the seminary) when he writes the following: "I think a more useful interpretation of the underlying message of the *mesa* can be offered, one that has greater explanatory power and is more consistent with what have been seen as shared traditions among Peruvian shamans . . . a contrast that permits mediation, namely, Life-Taking (Sorcery) vs. Life-Giving (Curing)" (1984, 3–4). Skillman (1990, 11) seems to concur when he discusses the divisions of Jorge Merino's mesa by introducing the term "balanced dualism." Merino refers to the zones of his mesa as the *mesa negra gentileña incaica* (black zone of ancient Inca inhabitants from the area) on the left, *mesa blanca curandera* (white curing zone) on the right, and *mesa de centro* (center zone) as the mediating area. Sharon defines *gentiles*, derived from Merino's term *gentileña incaica*, as follows: "the former *gentiles* [are the] ancient inhabitants of the areas, who now reside in the lower portions of the earth (*Uku Pacha*) and cause a large number of the diseases that attack the Indians" (1978, 76). Thus, the shaman's mesa becomes the abode of many types of spirit helpers and supernatural forces.

The most important aspect of the mesas of these five curanderos, and a very relevant point about shamanism in general, is that the shaman is one who mediates between the two opposite forces of life taking and life giving. Like most shamans around the world, they do this by employing forms of nonspeech communication, physical paraphernalia, and trance. The forms of nonspeech communication employed by Peruvian curanderos include whistles, songs, prayers, proverbs, and other types of supplications. The physical paraphernalia are material objects laid out on their mesas or stuck in the earth in front of them. Their trance states are induced by ingesting a brew made from boiling slices of San Pedro cactus in water, with or without other additives, depending on the type of illness being cured (Sharon 1972, 120). In addition, dance may be used, although dancing by shamans is more common in the highlands than on the coast, as Calderón explained: "Dance is not used generally in the coastal region, only the highlands; however, I have occasionally danced" (interview by author, 1996). Let us now observe if and how these attributes are found among the Moche, as depicted in their iconography.

Whistling, Singing, and the Power of Music

Numerous Moche ceramic pots depict in three dimensions people who are making facial contortions that suggest whistling and singing. The individual depicted in figure 8.2 is called a "spirit curer" by Menzel (1977, 135, fig. 149), who gives a detailed description of it, including references to whistling: "We see an ancient individual with a deeply lined face, his lips pursed in whistling position. . . . The form of the eyes and the pursed whistling mouth show this personage to be a mythical being. The eyes are the lidless, round, staring eyes characteristic of some classes of mythical beings. Mythical individuals similar to the one shown here are often shown whistling, an act that evidently had mythical significance. At the present time, curers of the north coast, who combine physicians' skills

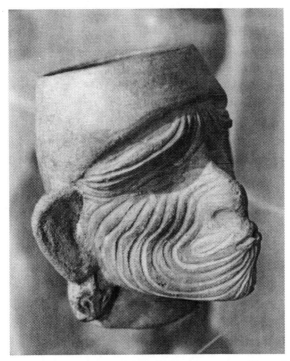

8.2. Moche ceramic vessel depicting a human making a facial formation that suggests whistling. Minneapolis Institute of Art Collection, Minneapolis, Minnesota.

with religious powers, use whistling at various times during rituals to invoke guardian spirits" (1977, 66).

Indeed, an important part of the curandero's curing technique includes whistling and singing songs known as *tarjos*, as Calderón explains:

> Each shaman or, better said, each school of shamanism, has its whistle. In the northern school of Ferreñafe (from Punto Cuatro, Salas, Penachí, and Chontalí), the shamans have their special whistles that they call *tarjos* or songs. There are songs for each activity: a specific song and whistle for love, for example, and also specific whistles for war or fighting, for curing, for investigating; there is, actually, an entire series of whistles and songs.
>
> In reality, the whistle or song is used for the act of meditation and concentration, to project oneself afterward into the problem with which one is trying to encounter or whose solution is being sought.

It is for when one has to believe a series of things with the mind and arrive at the point being sought; one has to use the proper whistle and mental force that occur at a precise moment during the act of meditation. This is traditional; all the curers have to whistle in order to make contact, in trance. (in Gushiken 1977, 115–16)[3]

When I read this passage to Calderón in 1996, he commented:

E.C.   There are whistles for calling and for preparation, for the conduction of rhythm for special moments of the shaman. [He whistles a tune for preparation.] This is a call. Then there is a whistle like this [he whistles another tune].
D.O.   That is a huayno.
E.C.   Yes, it is a huayno from Huaylas.

The huayno [*wayno*] is a fast dancelike musical genre in duple meter; it is the most common rhythm of the Andean highlands of Peru, so common that even the curing songs, with their rhythm established by the shaman's rattle, are in huayno form. Calderón continued to explain the tarjo: "The tarjo is a song that is sung over some object, about the history or legend of an object. It is sung, not whistled, although a whistle can accompany a tarjo."

Why are these musical forms significant? In his own words, Calderón elaborates in detail about the power of music, and how and why it is so important in shamanistic curing: "Music plays an important role in shamanism. The octaves of sound are important, and tone color is also important. The tone color of the octave is the sequence within which its intensity is perceived, as much by ear as by sight, in order to harmonize the human chakras. Color comes into play and depends on the temperament of each octave. There are those that are yellow, some are green, and others blue. It depends on the astral [spiritual refinement] of each one. This is what is important" (in Gushiken 1977, 114–15).[4] Calderón explained to me (interview by author, 1996) that "the colors depend on the quantity of hallucinogens that the shaman takes, and each color represents the particular cause of the illness. The color is the aura of the person it reflects. This is logical."

E.C.   Each sound has its color, and these are obvious when one is in trance.
D.O.   Which color is the most powerful?

E.C.   Most powerful is *lila,* or violet.

D.O.   Which tone do you sing for violet?

E.C.   It depends on the sound [he sings].

D.O.   Do you see the colors when you sing?

E.C.   Yes, of course. You arrive at that point. It is just a question of concentration.

D.O.   Does each color represent a spirit?

E.C.   No. It represents the position or energy of the person's organic makeup.

D.O.   Of the shaman?

E.C.   Of anybody. The shaman has to know this.

D.O.   Which color is the most dangerous?

E.C.   Black. "Whoom" it sounds, from below.

D.O.   And yellow?

E.C.   Yellow relates to the stomach.

D.O.   Blue?

E.C.   Blue is tranquility. Green is number five; it is nature.

D.O.   Red is hot?

E.C.   Red is blood. White is not seen; however, someone who is partially crazy can produce it. Yes, the crazy person produces white.

D.O.   And each color has its song, or its tone?

E.C.   It is the tone quality rather than the song itself. But I don't sing like that when I cure. The people wouldn't understand it.[5]

Such use of synesthesia by Calderón, in which the visualization of colors is related to the tone quality of singing and particular spiritual attributes, is similar to experiences of shamans documented by Katz and Dobkin de Rios (1971) in the Amazon region of Peru. It is probably quite universal among cultures where the ingestion of hallucinogens affects perception. Because of the iconographic evidence of San Pedro use by the Moche, it is highly probable that Moche shamans experienced similar synesthetic characteristics when they sang. However, because synesthesia is purely performance based (Sullivan 1986, 6), its occurrence among the Moche can only remain a plausible possibility.

Calderón continues to explain to Gushiken about sound and why it is important to cure at night: "The mesa has to be set up during the night. Night is the most important time, because then the fleshly spirits are resting. In the moment of rest one opens the door of his subconscious, because of the principal of transitoriness. In other words, one opens one's frequency with which he can capture and emit his waves, his vibrations. And precisely in the night when resting, one operates this way because the octaves of sound play an important role. There are sounds that man cannot perceive when he is in an alert state of consciousness; but at the moment of sleep, yes, then they can be perceived. This is the reason why the mesas are done at night" (in Gushiken 1977, 124).[6]

These comments by Calderón properly set the stage for music, which for him and most other coastal curanderos from northern Peru plays a principal role within the esoteric practice of curing illnesses. According to Sharon and Donnan, whistling and songs attract guardian spirits, and with the rattle the shaman activates "all of the supernatural forces concentrated by the mesa" (1974, 52). Calderón sings during his curing rituals, often making references in his song texts to the act of singing and calling the powers and encantos, as in the following excerpt of a song: "I go singing. With my good herbalists I go calling. All the powers and the enchantments. So that my good remedy comes now. Looking, justifying, raising, standing up. With their good enchantments" (Calderón et al. 1982, 57). Sometimes Calderón cups his ear as he sings, similar to a human representation depicted in a Moche pot I showed him a picture of in 1996. About this particular icon he commented, "This man is cupping his ear when he whistles, to give him better resonance. Singers do this too. This is probably a call [llamada] or a signal [aviso], at least." "Are these people shamans?" I asked. "One cannot know," he replied. "They are probably just people whistling, or positions of people whistling" (interview by author).

Not all Peruvian coastal curanderos use music, according to Skillman: "Merino does not sing songs (tarjos) as other coastal curers do. Instead, he employs prayer, proverbs, anecdotes, and advice to accomplish the same end" (1990, 9). Unfortunately, one can only speculate about what the mouth positions on the Moche ceramic portrait figurines mean. Whether open mouths or puckers depict whistling, singing, blowing, yawning, praying, speaking, or yelling, will never be known. There is little question, however, about the musical instruments depicted in Moche iconography, and little question about the importance of certain musical instruments by north coastal curanderos.

Musical Instruments and Curanderos

Common Moche musical instruments such as the notch flute and panpipe are not a part of the present northern coastal curandero's curing paraphernalia. The instruments employed by today's shamans, or remembered by them as being used at one time, are the globular flute, container rattle, skin drum, and conch shell trumpet.

Globular Flutes

We have already seen that several Moche ceramic pots show men playing globular flutes or ocarinas (see chapter 5, figs. 5.6, 5.7), and northern coastal Peruvian curanderos still play them. The concepts of encanto and its counterpart, *desencanto* or *daño* (harm), however, are crucial to an understanding of the role of the Moche ocarinas used by present-day curanderos. According to Merino, "Encantos are forces of nature that exist independent of and uncontrolled by other powers. It is the role of the curer to call forth and dominate the *encantos*. Then they are brought in and deposited as companions to the *mesa*. This is the case with many artifacts of the different *mesa* sections that compose the whole. For most of the artifacts there is a companion *encanto* that is brought under control" (in Skillman 1990, 10).

Skillman uses the term *calicanto* for the negative concept (the opposite of encanto), which he also explains as a force of nature: "More specifically, [the *calicanto* or *desencanto*] is composed of all the shadows or spirits that are called to a power spot and delivered there. It, too, must be dominated by the curer before it can be of any use to him. The *calicanto*, once dominated and assigned to a particular place, stays put. It is then available to receive the *encanto*" (1990, 10).

Calderón gave me a different explanation, insisting that the "calicanto is a mixture of *cal* [lime] and sand, a paste [*algamasa*]. Donald Skillman has either misunderstood, or Merino gave him the wrong information" (interview by author, 1996). Calderón explained that the correct term for the negative force or opposite of encanto is *desencanto* or *daño* (damage).

Calderón continued to explain the concept of encanto to me: "Encantos are those geographic points in valleys that coincide by their coordinates, for example, with the jungle. You climb a very high mountain, and then suddenly you encounter a valley and you find in this valley below monkeys, parrots, and important jungle plants. Suddenly a coldness of the devils is emitted and 'bam,' they die; only llamas can exist. These are the famous encantos. Even though you have never seen them; enchantments they're called. And why are they this way? It's because of the geographic problems" (interview by author, 1996). Shamans must learn to control these intangible forces of nature and weather, in addition to the ancestor spirits. All are types of encantos that the shaman learns to call to his side, aided by globular flutes into which they may take their abode. These concepts are consistent with Calderón's explanation to Sharon, cited above, that the globular flute contains the soul of the person within the tomb where it was found.

Even more consistent with the encanto concept are Calderón's explanations to me (interviews by author, 1974, 1996), that with his globular flute he calls the spirits of the mountains and ocean. According to Calderón, these ancient powers are called up by globular flutes; their presence is made known ("noted and recorded," according to Merino) by the music of the globular flutes; their powers reside on the mesa within the globular flutes themselves and within the shaman himself during the curing séance; and they enable the shaman to identify particular evil forces, control them, and defend against them. Skillman suggests the same: "Thus alerted, the maestro who is under attack—with the aid of San Pedro and his own power of *vista* [seeing]—is able to ascertain who is attacking him and from which direction the attack is being mounted. He can then take appropriate defensive measures" (1990, 10).

Let us again consider the Moche ceramic stirrup spout vessels that depict individuals playing globular flutes. These may be representations of ancient musicians, flute-playing curanderos, or their invocations (i.e., what they want or what they are looking for through their musical calls) (Calderón, interview by author, 1996). More important, perhaps, they are possibly representations of the powers within the globular flutes themselves. That is, they are the icons of the encantos, the powerful enchanting forces of nature, and the spirits themselves dwell within them (ibid.).

Container Rattles

Another musical instrument type often depicted by Moche potters is the container rattle idiophone. Moche container rattles in iconography generally have double chambers (figs. 8.3, 8.4). Actual Moche rattles also include ceramic instruments with two chambers (fig. 8.5), although single-chamber rattles are also found (fig. 8.6). Single-chamber rattles made

Above: 8.3. Moche ceramic vessel
depicting a human playing a double-
chamber container rattle. Photograph courtesy of the Moche
Archive, UCLA.

Right: 8.4. Moche ceramic vessel depicting a human playing a double-
chamber container rattle. Photograph courtesy of the Moche
Archive, UCLA.

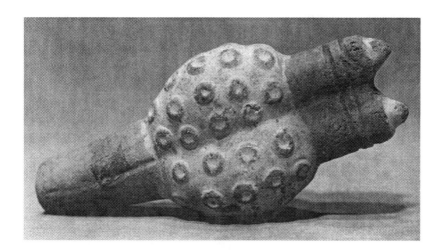

Above: 8.5. Moche ceramic double-chamber container rattle. Photograph courtesy of the Moche Archive, UCLA.

Left: 8.6. Moche ceramic single-chamber container rattle. Private collection. Photograph by Christopher B. Donnan.

from bronze or copper are also common. In addition to playing a rattle, the musician in figure 8.3 also holds a strap to which small shells are attached. This strap, which is connected to the double rattle, was possibly shaken to produce a noise or rhythm, according to Calderón (interview by author, 1996).

The typical present-day northern coastal Peruvian curandero employs a modern-made gourd rattle or, in rare cases, an ancient Moche-made ceramic or copper rattle, as a shamanic tool that he strategically places on his mesa and often shakes as an accompaniment for his songs. Sharon explains this phenomenon: "Present day folk healing practices consist of all-night curing sessions involving elaborate ritual, chants sung to the beat of a gourd rattle, ingestion of potions derived from a hallucinogenic cactus, and invocation of supernatural powers" (Sharon and Donnan 1972, 51–52). About the shaman's rattle as used by Calderón, he adds: "This instrument—used today in conjunction with whistling and songs to attract guardian spirits—activates all of the supernatural forces concentrated by the mesa. It also has a defensive function [significance] in warding off evil spirits, and is used by the shaman in a purification ritual that involves rubbing the bodies of all those present at the curing ceremony" (Sharon and Donnan 1974, 52). Calderón describes his rattle, which he calls *chungana, maraca, macana,* or *sonaja*: "[It is made from] a calabash [*tutuma*] that is pierced in its center with a stick of *chonta* [a hardwood palm] wood, and around the entirety of the rattle there are incisions that are esoteric and mystic designs, and holes to give it sound. Inside the rattle are *chira* [a fruit?] seeds and pieces of lapis lazuli, *pedernal* [flint], and turquoise, so it has a sound during the night, and so that sparks of fire come out of it. This sound is used in order to heighten the rhythm of the song of the whistle, which has its influence, its power of abstraction of a person" (in Gushiken 1977, 58).[7]

In 1996 I asked Calderón why he used a rattle, why there are different names for it, and how and why it produces sparks:

D.O. Why do you use the chungana?

E.C. The chungana is used to provide the rhythm of the song, to give it more energy. Because it is used for rhythm, it is logical that it will attract spirits or, better said, to make connections. *Macana* means club, and it is used to combat the evil forces [he made clubbing motions in the air].

D.O.   Explain about how and why the chungana produces fire.

E.C.   The chungana uses *chira* seeds, and in order for it to produce fire, little *pedernal* [flint] stones are used. When the stones strike together, sparks of fire come out.

D.O.   Who sees this?

E.C.   Everybody sees it. This is to impress, more than anything else.

D.O.   Do you know the work by [Johannes] Wilbert about the Warao and their rattle, the *hebu mataro*?

E.C.   No. But the North American Indians use a rattle that also produces sparks when they are in their sweat lodges. When the shaman shakes his rattle, fire comes out of it and a white buffalo appears, running. And not only does one person see this—they all see it. This happens when one's body loses water and salt. (Interview by author, 1996)

The spark-producing parallel between Calderón's rattle, the *wisiratu* shaman's *hebu mataro* rattle among the Warao Indians of Venezuela (see Olsen 1996, 64–66), and some North American indigenous cultures, may be coincidental, or it may reinforce a fundamental shamanistic concept. The use of exterior designs, however, is probably universal for shamanic rattles. Moreover, it can be seen as a continuation of ancient Moche custom. Donnan, for example, describes a large number of Moche copper rattles acquired by the American Museum of Natural History in 1961, including "several rattles with long narrow handles. The chamber portion of one of these rattles has a design incised on each of the four sides and on the top. Each design is distinct, but taken as a group they clearly relate to the Presentation Theme" (1976, 125). Whether the Presentation Theme (which Donnan later calls Sacrifice Ceremony [Benson 1997b, 47]) as interpreted by Donnan is related to shamanistic curing is purely conjectural. Nevertheless, one of the panels of the Moche rattle he analyzed depicts an anthropomorphized bird figure, and perhaps Calderón depicts an owl on his rattle for similar reasons:

Traditionally [the rattles are adorned] with figures or designs of owls, serpents, genies, gods, or *auquis* [Quechua term for spirits]. The animal figure that is seen the most is the owl; sometimes there are two, double owls, twins. The owl is the symbol of wisdom, of magical science [*Ciencia Hermética*]. The figures on the rattles are not used traditionally now. At least I have not seen them. . . . On mine I have put figures, incised symbols such as the cross, the symbol of the spiral, the signature of the three angels of the light, the sun and the moon, the Holy Spirit, the triptych of the triangle, and so on. And I proceed this way because I have studied it, and, fittingly, I believe it. No other shaman that I have seen uses these things; that is to say, like those that I have drawn and made. Actually, it is my mode, my manner of proceeding. (In Gushiken 1977, 113–14)[8]

He also explained to me about the power of the owl, and about the placement of the rattle on his mesa:

D.O. Can you tell me something about the power of the owl that you have drawn on your rattle?

E.C. Yes, the owl (I also have an eagle), the owl is a symbol of wisdom and the dominion of the night. These include the *lechuzón* (large owl), the *lechuza* (medium owl), and the *lechucita* (little owl) or *paupaca*. They all have their myths. When the lechucita sings, it is for a particular reason.

D.O. In which part of the mesa is the chungana placed?

E.C. In the center of the mesa, no, to the right side as well; either in the center or to the right. You can also put it in the campo ganadero, or left side. You can put one in the left side and another in the general [middle] zone.

D.O. Is this for a balance of power?

E.C. Yes, but it is more to make the proper connections, the links.

D.O. The modern calabash rattle is for calling and the ancient Moche metal one is for receiving the powers?

E.C. More than anything, they are used to prepare and call, or awaken the spirits. (Interview by author, 1996)

Calderón emphasizes his originality with regard to his choice of drawings, unlike the designs on other rattles belonging to other shamans. His syncretistic juxtaposition of Christian symbols with the traditional Peruvian north coastal shamanistic rattle is similar to the iconographic syncretism found on some rattles of the Native American Church (a peyote cult) in the United States. A Native American Church rattle in the Field Museum of Natural History in Chicago, for example, contains a drawing of

Jesus Christ on its gourd resonator. Indeed, the joining of power symbols on the religious tools of shamans often is believed to increase their power.

José Paz also employs a rattle for his curing rituals; however, it is kept on the curative side of his mesa, rather than in the center (Joralemon 1984, 20), and no description of it has been made. Jorge Merino, on the other hand, keeps two rattles on his mesa: one an ancient bronze rattle with a wooden handle, kept in the left field, the black zone of Inca belief; and the other a modern rattle made from calabash with a wooden handle, simple in construction and kept in the center field. Skillman describes Merino's two rattles: "*Chungana de bronce* (bronze rattle). This is a pre-Columbian rattle that was found . . . in a grave in the vicinity of Batangrande in Lambayeque. It belongs exclusively to the *mesa negra gentileña incaica* and serves no other purpose than to work with this [field of the] *mesa*. . . . *Chungana de mesa de centro* (rattle of the central mesa). This rattle . . . is a simple affair consisting of nothing more than a small gourd stuck on a stick with a few seeds inside. It belongs to the *mesa de centro* and does not function outside of this context. Merino uses it primarily to summon *encantos*" (1990, 19, 23). Like the other artifacts on Merino's mesa, his rattles function within the concepts of encanto and desencanto. The modern rattle summons the encantos, while the pre-Columbian rattle, like some of the other ancient artifacts on his mesa, functions to summon and receive the desencantos.

Skin Drums

During lengthy interviews given to Peruvian folklorist Gushiken, Calderón spoke about skin drums as tools infrequently used by northern Peruvian curanderos: "Those who are very traditional use a small drum; this is the general usage in the mountains; not on the coast. Here, only the maraca is used, the chungana made from bronze, taken from the ruins; also used are chunganas made from tutuma or ceramic" (1977, 115).[9] This is all any of the curanderos had to say of skin drums, and Calderón does not specify what type of drum is used.

In spite of their apparent disuse in the present north coast of Peru, membranophones seemed to have had great importance to the Moche, because so many are depicted in numerous ceramic stirrup spout vessels. The drums shown in Moche pottery are of three types: (1) double-headed frame drum (*tinya* type), (2) single-headed horizontal kettle drum, and

(3) double-headed hourglass drum (from the Vicus culture, related to and perhaps the same as early Moche).[10] The Moche also constructed actual skin drums from fired clay and wood, and some have survived, although without their membranes.

According to Moche iconography, anthropomorphic and birdlike figures consistently play the frame-type drum with a single stick. The anthropomorphic representations include realistic humans (fig. 8.7), grimacing humans, deformed humans (fig. 8.8, perhaps an *uta*, or leper, according to Calderón; but see chapter 4 for facial deformation and music), dead humans (fig. 8.9), and the fanged deity (fig. 8.10). The large number of birdlike creatures performing the frame-type drums on Moche vessels suggest metamorphosis from humans to birds—some perhaps in the process of change with both human and bird features (fig. 8.11), and others as complete birds (fig. 8.12), which are probably ducks according to Calderón (interview by author, 1996). Birds are among the most magical of animals because they can traverse heaven and earth. It is

8.7. Moche ceramic vessel depicting a human playing a frame drum. American Museum of Natural History Collection, New York.

Above: 8.8. Moche ceramic vessel depicting a deformed human playing a frame drum. National Museum of Anthropology and Archaeology Collection, Lima.

Right: 8.9. Moche ceramic vessel depicting a death figure playing a frame drum. Museo de La Plata Collection, La Plata, Argentina.

Above: 8.10. Moche ceramic vessel depicting the fanged deity playing a frame drum. Cassinelli Museum Collection, Trujillo, Peru.

Above right: 8.11. Moche ceramic vessel depicting a human-bird creature playing a frame drum. National Museum of Anthropology and Archaeology Collection, Lima.

Right: 8.12. Moche ceramic vessel depicting a birdlike creature playing a frame drum. National Museum of Anthropology and Archaeology Collection, Lima.

8.13. Moche ceramic vessel depicting the fanged deity or fanged animal (jaguar) playing a kettle-shaped drum with one stick, one hand, or both. Photograph courtesy of the Moche Archive, UCLA.

the quest of shamans throughout the world to adopt the alter ego of birds because of their relationship with the cosmos and their role as messengers of the gods (Olsen 1981, 368).

Moche iconography also indicates that the kettle-type (the bottom is not visible) drum is played with one stick, one hand, or both, by humans, the fanged deity or seals (fig. 8.13), and foxes or dogs (fig. 8.14). This instrument, which appears to be a single-headed membranophone closed at its bottom, is perhaps a water drum, according to Calderón, who said it is similar to an extant Moche water drum in the Archaeology Museum of the National University of Trujillo.

D.O. Tell me something about the water drum, which you explained when viewing the Moche kettle-shaped drums in my figures [8.13 and 8.14].

E.C.   Nobody uses this today, but it was used. There is one in the Archaeology Museum of the National University of Trujillo.

D.O.   What power does the water have?

E.C.   The water affects the sound, giving it a special low quality. It also
changes the pitch of the instrument when moving it while striking
it. There is nothing else about it that is important. (Interview by
author, 1996)

According to Moche (or perhaps Vicus) iconography, an hourglass
drum existed that is shown being played exclusively by a human with a
pointed chin or beard (perhaps a goatee) and long hair arranged into a
fancy coiffure; he plays his instrument under his arm in the manner of the
West African pressure drum (fig. 8.15). In addition, a complete stirrup
spout vessel in the shape of an hourglass drum exists (fig. 8.16). Moche
pottery, including representations of hourglass drums, is also found farther

8.14. Moche ceramic ves-
sel depicting a foxlike
creature playing a kettle-
shaped drum with one
stick, one hand, or both.
National Museum of An-
thropology and Archae-
ology Collection, Lima.

Above: 8.15. Moche (or Vicus) ceramic vessel depicting an hourglass-shaped drum played by a human with long hair, arranged into a fancy coiffure, and a pointed chin, perhaps a goatee; he plays his instrument under his arm in the manner of the West African pressure drum. Photograph courtesy of the Moche Archive, UCLA.

Right: 8.16. Moche (or Vicus) ceramic stirrup spout vessel resembling an hourglass-shaped drum. Photograph courtesy of the Moche Archive, UCLA.

north in the Píura Valley among the Vicus culture, as Donnan writes, "Along with ceramics in the Vicús style, the [Vicús] cemeteries yielded hundreds of superbly sculpted Moche vessels, many with stirrup spouts similar to those of the early Moche style. These Moche vessels were probably imported from the Jequetepeque Valley where nearly identical Moche ceramics have been excavated" (1992, 70). Calderón explained that the pot drummers I showed him probably represented particular individuals (interview by author, 1996).

Many of the zoomorphic drumming figures are perhaps encantos associated with the sea and the mountains because of the seabird, seal, fox, and other zoomorphic realism. This suggestion is substantiated by the curanderos' teachings about animal symbolism. Joralemon, for example, describes ancient animal iconographic artifacts that occur on the left side of the mesa belonging to José Paz: "There are stone and wooden images of owls, monkeys, frogs, snakes, lions, and bears on the left side of the altar. No such wild animal symbolism is found in any other field. The same association of wild animal symbols and the left side of the curing mesa can also be found on Eduardo's altar" (1984, 6).

Donnan provides the following details about Calderón's interpretation of the fox (see also chapter 5): "The fox is another important animal. It is symbolized on the mesa by the Fox Ceramic, a pre-Columbian pottery fragment modeled in the form of a fox head. . . . To Eduardo the fox symbolizes misfortune and danger caused by guile and deception. At the same time, it represents the ability to overcome setbacks and obstacles with the astuteness of the fox. Eduardo also associates it with the moon. The fox, in either natural or anthropomorphic form, is the most frequently depicted animal in Moche art, including scenes with possible lunar symbolism" (1976, 106). Because these animal icons are situated on the left side of the shaman's mesa, they are associated with negative, or death-receiving, forces. They actually function, however, as protective figures, such as animal guardian spirits. Ethnographic analogy also suggests the animal guardian hypothesis for these Moche artifacts mentioned by Joralemon and used by Calderón. Calderón, for example, explained that the animal figurines receive the encantos because "they are protectors. Snakes, jaguars especially—these are totems. The eagle is also important. These are guardians" (interview by author, 1996).

Joralemon, however, writes, "There are some very strong indications that mesa symbols [e.g., the animals] are concrete representations of hal-

lucinatory imagery" (1984, 8). That is, they are the material manifestations of the encanto spirits that arrive during the shaman's trance. José
Paz also refers to these forces (encantos) as poisons, and to receive them
he often erects a secondary altar (*mesa de afuera*, "outside altar") placed
some ten yards in front of the main altar, as Joralemon explains: "José
associates the mesa de afuera with the left, negative side of his central
altar. During this phase of the ritual, ancestor spirits (i.e., of the dead)
arrive, the mesa de afuera turns cold, sorcerers may attack, and José visu-
alizes in the form of animals the poisons that his patients have been given.
For José, the goal of this part of the session is to dominate the negative
forces that have been called into play" (1984, 10). The wild animals are
used as symbols of poison, meaning they can also be the causes of illness.
They are the life-taking encanto forces of nature that must be controlled
by the shaman in order for him to effect a cure. As they come to the
shaman's altar, their presence is made known (sometimes by sounds produced by the curandero on the Moche animal-shaped globular flutes kept
on the left side of his mesa), and they reside within the animal-shaped
artifacts that function as desencantos or receivers. The Moche ceramic
vessels depicting anthropomorphic as well as zoomorphic drummers are
perhaps additional icons of the encantos, the powerful forces of nature.

Yet another interpretation for bird drummer iconography can be pos-
ited with ethnographic analogy. Sharon and Donnan, for example, give
this account of Calderón's belief: "Another bird given supernatural significance by Eduardo is the hummingbird, which finds expression in a
Hummingbird Staff. Because of the sucking ability of the hummingbird,
this artifact is associated with the removal of foreign objects inflicted by
sorcerers. . . . Hummingbirds, both natural and anthropomorphic, find
frequent expression in Moche art." Calderón explained it to me this way:
"the hummingbird, or *pajarito pinto* [little painted bird], is important
because it sucks out the poison within a patient" (interview by author,
1996; see chapter 5). He also interpreted the bird in figure 8.11 as a possible hummingbird: "This could be a hummingbird, although its beak is
rather short. These are all masks, of course—people with masks. Masks
like this, however, have not been found."

A song performed by Calderón during his curing ritual empowers the
various staffs on his altar, and the importance of the encanto is evident as
the hummingbird and other birds are named: "Account my Hummingbird Staff! Playing in their great herb gardens, The hummingbirds gather,

All the bad pains and sicknesses, They play with their enchantments. The speckled [painted] bird, Working from Paraguay to Guatemala, And with its song in its time, Flowering my enchantment, It plays with my account" (Calderón et al. 1982, 61). This song and its symbolic hummingbird power reinforce Calderón's belief in the power of his little hummingbird ocarina, discussed earlier in this chapter and in chapter 5.

Conch Shell Trumpets

Of the musical instruments employed by north coastal Peruvian curanderos, the conch shell trumpet, a lip concussion aerophone, is the least used. Among the shamans whose ethnographic stories have been consulted, only José Paz uses the instrument, although Calderón explained to me that he used to use one (interview by author, 1974). Before I present Paz's views about the conch shell trumpet and shells in general, the Moche's use of the conch shell trumpet warrants study.

Peter Kvietok (1989) has carefully researched three types of Moche trumpets—conch shell, straight, and coiled—and interpreted the uses of conch shell trumpets by analyzing information from site excavations and comparing them with Donnan's thematic analyses (Donnan 1975, 1976, 1978; Donnan and McClelland 1979). Through iconographic analyses Kvietok suggests that Moche conch shell trumpets and their ceramic copies were primarily used in the Presentation Theme (Sacrifice Ceremony) and the Mountain Offering or Sacrifice Scene, while straight and coiled trumpets (and whistles) were used in the Presentation Theme and the Bloodletting of War Captives (see Donnan 1975 for an explanation of these Moche themes). Indeed, there are many examples of its use in the Presentation Theme, and one of the most telling is an actual Moche conch shell trumpet with an etching of the Presentation Theme close to the opening of the shell (fig. 8.17). Additionally, numerous Moche vessels depict normal-looking humans (fig. 8.18) and deformed or death figures holding or playing conch shell trumpets, as well as the fanged god either holding a shell trumpet, emerging from one (fig. 8.19), or transformed into a conch shell. Some uses and significance of Moche conch shell trumpets are suggested here from analyses of the teachings of Calderón, Paz, Merino, and the Guerreros. Among these curanderos, only Alberto Guerrero uses a conch shell trumpet on his mesa as a musical instrument.

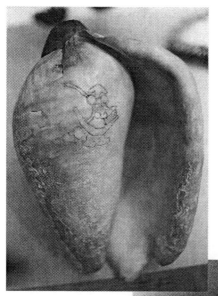

Left: 8.17. Moche conch shell trumpet with an etching of the Presentation Theme or Sacrifice Ceremony on it. American Museum of Natural History Collection, New York.

Below: 8.18. Moche ceramic vessel depicting a human holding a conch shell trumpet. Museo de La Plata Collection, La Plata, Argentina.

8.19. Moche ceramic vessel depicting the fanged deity emerging from a conch shell trumpet. Photograph courtesy of the Moche Archive, UCLA.

All of the shamans, however, consider conch shells and other shells to be of extreme importance in north coastal Peruvian shamanism.

Various types of shells are found on both the right life-giving field and the left life-taking field of the curanderos' mesas. Joralemon relates the life-giving aspect of shells: "Shells, long associated in Peruvian religion with fertility, are symbols of life-giving 'stones,' especially in their capacity as divining tools for determining curative prescriptions. . . . At the end of José's ritual, a divinatory shell-tossing is performed to confirm the identification of the curative herb he has visualized as the proper treatment for each patient. . . . Here mesa artifacts—shells—are used to authenticate or verify a message that the shaman has gleaned from visions" (1984, 5, 9). Joralemon continues with a discussion of the life-taking aspect of several shells that are found just left of center (the banco ganadero, or life-taking side) on José's mesa: "[they are] called 'caracoles' with no further elaboration. These, and most other shells were not distinguished by type or significance" (1984, 17).

Calderón provides the most enlightening information about the power of shells. First, he speaks about the white magic of his mesa, or the curative side, and of several shells that are placed just to the right of a crucifix: "After this we have this conch, which is related to the story of St. John the Baptist, or rather, a conch for baptism with holy water. And here there is a small conch that is related to the Virgin of the Rosary; it is a little plate for giving the offering" (in Gushiken 1977, 57).[11] He then elaborates about the shells in the center of his mesa: "In the middle we have a small fan-shaped seashell called Hand to Serve, joined with another seashell, a mollusk, which only I use as the master. Just to the right of this is a rattle" (58).[12] Calderón continues with a description of the left side of his mesa: "Now the negative side, the ganadero, that of black magic. Let's begin, as always, from the left. A large shell like a triton signifies a special role for the work of receiving, from the abstraction and unfolding of a certain problem, from some aspect of a sequence" (60).[13] Calderón's emphasis on receiving, as the use of the conch shell, is consistent with Donnan's interpretation of the role of conch shells among the Moche, as depicted on Moche pottery: "The third activity shown on each of the six bottles in our sample involves the transfer of conch shells. . . . Kneeler is consistently shown reaching forward with one hand, which often holds a conch shell. . . . It is not clear whether Kneeler is giving the conch shells or receiving them. . . . Conch shells are obviously the focus of activity in conch-shell transfer, and may be related to those seen as part of the grave goods in the burial activity" (1979, 8–9).

The action of receiving conch shells in Moche iconography, however, was possibly a physical one if the figures are interpreted as representations of real people. In the context of Calderón's mesa, however, the receiving action is a supernatural one, "from the abstraction and unfolding of a certain problem, from some aspect of a sequence," as he explained to Gushiken (1977, 60).[14] This explanation seems to suggest that the triton shell's significance is similar to that of the globular flute, also on the left side of the shamans' mesas; that is, it is a receiver for its appropriate encanto. After I read this interpretation to Calderón, he responded:

D.O. Let's talk about the power of conch shells.

E.C. Only the sound is important, like the sound of the ocarina.

D.O. But it is found on the left side of your mesa.

E.C. [It's found] on the left, the right, the center, wherever you place it, or wherever you need to place it.

D.O. Are conch shells also used to receive the encantos?

E.C. They are used to open, to receive, to reflect. (Interview by author, 1996)

Donnan's description of what he calls the *Strombus galeatus* monster as "an important supernatural creature in Moche art" perhaps suggests the physical manifestation of an encanto force: "[the *Strombus galeatus* monster is] a combination of a conch shell, an eared serpent head, and a feline body with claws and feline spots" (1978, 63). The fusion of these physical attributes, however, perhaps characterizes a protective force against negative powers, which the receiving object or calicanto is, as the curandero's dominating abode for the encanto. This is substantiated by folk evaluation of the three aspects that constitute the *Strombus galeatus* monster (conch shell, serpent, feline), as derived from the beliefs of present-day curanderos:

> *Conch shell*—Shells, long associated in Peruvian religion with fertility, are symbols of life-giving "stones," especially in their capacity as divining tools for determining curative prescriptions. (Joralemon 1984, 5)
>
> *Serpent*—[Calderón] sees the serpent as the mediator of opposing forces (e.g., good and evil, light and dark, male and female, death and rebirth), which are activated by the mesa. It also unites the sun and ocean. (Sharon and Donnan 1974, 56)
>
> *Feline*—Felines are important in the ideology of present day folk healing . . . the cat is valued because of its sharp eyesight, symbolic of visionary insight. . . . it is important because of its swiftness and agility, which are used to chase off supernatural dangers. Finally, the force and valor of the cat are considered indispensable to Eduardo's success as a shaman. . . . they help him attack and defend against evil spirits. (Sharon and Donnan 1974, 55–56)

Among the Moche iconography that depicts conch shell trumpets, various performers or personages associated closely with the instrument can be seen. Most frequently the fanged god (with his feline teeth and serpent belt) is modeled into ceramic stirrup spout jars as a conch shell trumpeter. Accompanied by a serpent and feline, such a vessel is perhaps an iconic physical manifestation of an encanto associated with regeneration, rebirth, and curative powers. This would also explain why the fanged god is also seen emerging from a conch shell trumpet (fig. 8.19), and even transformed into a conch shell himself, perhaps as a modeled form of the *Strombus galeatus* monster described by Donnan.

Alberto Guerrero, the son of Masías, is the only one of the five northern Peruvian shamans (whose ethnographic accounts have been consulted) who uses the conch shell trumpet as a musical instrument. Joralemon and Sharon, who consider the father and son to be a single unit, reflecting a Guerrero family tradition, describe the Guerreros' use of the conch shell trumpet: "In general, bivalves are used for raising *tabaco* to 'throw away' sickness and evil while spiral conches are for blowing them away" (1993, 58). Earlier they describe the placement and use of shells on Masías Guerrero's mesa: "Besides two small bivalves for serving the tobacco in counterattacks against sorcerers and spirits, the Ganadero has three large conch shells used to rub patients for their defense as well as a cluster of bivalves stacked on their sides in the lower left-hand corner" (1993, 55). While these uses of conch shells are not further explained or analyzed, both the blowing or rubbing of them are indicative of their supernatural significance as objects of power.

Alberto Guerrero's use of the conch shell as a trumpet is the only available documentation of a present musical contextualization for that instrument in the northern coast of Peru. Because it is a ritualistic musical function performed by a single person, I offer it as a direct analogy of the single Moche conch shell trumpeter depicted so many times in Moche iconography. Whether the ancient personage is a priest or the fanged deity, as a trumpeter he is perhaps also blowing away the evil essences that pervaded his spiritual world.

Dualism and the Power to Cure

All the north coastal Peruvian curanderos classify their powers and power actions, their ritual space and ritual time, within a dualistic framework. Not only are their mesas organized into zones of opposite powers, but the chosen sequence of events also has a dualistic makeup that is related to the zones themselves. The first part of the curandero's séance involves the left fields of the mesa, while the second part involves the right fields. Moreover, as Joralemon writes, this balance signifies curative power: "Taken together, the left-to-right connotations of both *mesa* symbols and the ritual sequence are entirely appropriate to the therapeutic object of the event; for the patient, a healing ritual *is* a passage from life-taking to life-giving forces, from sickness to health, from left to right in the language of the shaman's ritual" (1984, 10; emphasis Joralemon's). The dualism, however, is a "balanced dualism" (Sharon 1978, 62). The shaman is the mediator, the fulcrum who maintains the proper balance between the opposing forces.

Joralemon summarizes the curandero's mesa and its meaning this way: "What, then, does the *mesa* mean? . . . the *mesa*, as it is understood by the shaman, is a gameboard, a symbolic paradigm against which the ritual is played. It represents the struggle between life-taking and life-giving forces, between left and right. But this struggle, this opposition, becomes a passage, a resolution, by the shaman's re-affirmation of mastery over *both* the left and the right. . . . [He] is a balancer in the contest between opposing forces . . . [and] the game of the ritual, which the *mesa* presents in concrete symbols, is a balancing act performed by an individual who stands above the contest by mastering both sides. It is thus that struggle—opposition—becomes passage, and cures are accomplished" (1984, 10; emphasis Joralemon's).

When I returned to Peru in 1996 to verify information with Calderón, his explanations about dualism were particularly enlightening. I was searching for the verification of a possible musical parallel to the dualism of the shaman's altar, as suggested by Lévi-Strauss (1973, 331–36), who describes an analogous balance of opposites within an aural taxonomy whereby whistle sound (female symbolism) is balanced by buzz sound (male symbolism), while rattle sound (staccato of realization) is the mediator. This is how Calderón responded to my questions that were based on my prior conclusions:

D.O. Please explain about the importance of dualism.

E.C. We receive something from the left and give it from the right. These are formulas.

D.O. Lévi-Strauss has explained about a balance of opposites. Is such a balance of opposites important in your concept of shamanism?

E.C. Oh yes. There always has to be a balance. Without it there would be only one point, and that would be dangerous.

D.O. Do you conceive of song and whistle as opposites?

E.C.   Of course, they are two different things.

D.O.   Do you see the chungana as in the middle, as mediator between the two?

E.C.   It could be, but the chungana has its function. (Interview by author, 1996)

While the balance of sound opposites does not occur instrumentally within the present curandero complex because the conch shell trumpet is not blown, such a balanced musical dualism seems to have existed in ancient times in Moche culture. Even within the present realm of north coastal Peruvian shamanism, globular flute and human whistle sounds balance with human song (buzzing of the vocal chords), while the staccato of the curandero's rattle is the mediator. This way the shaman is the ultimate musical conductor of the curing concert, while the ancient ceramic Moche vessels are the soundless but often musical enchantments of the past, silently sitting and perhaps listening as repositories of ancient power.

The Soundless Enchantments of the Past

Because my goal in writing this chapter was to demonstrate that Moche pottery (especially those ceramic vessels depicting musical instruments and their use) are icons of and repositories for encantos, I continued to share my ideas with Calderón, seeking his opinions:

D.O.   My hypothesis is that the Moche artifacts such as the stirrup spout vessels (huacas) were used to receive the encantos or spirits, to be as receptors or homes for the spirits when they come.

E.C.   Yes, this is very possible, like the icons or saints in the Catholic Church. They are the receptacles of the powers, the ideas, the thoughts, the intentions; it could be.

D.O.   Do you think they were representations of real people, like portraits of real individuals?

E.C.   Some of them are in ecstasy, like when a shaman sings. They may be representations of people, or perhaps of invocations or petitions.

D.O.   Could they be ancestors?

E.C.   They could be ancestors; but they could also be from the present, or from the future. (Interview by author, 1996)

Indeed, as Donnan writes, "Very little is known about the function of elaborate ceramics in ancient Peru" (1992, 119). Calderón, who was highly skilled and trained by his father as a potter, told the following to Sharon: "the famous Mochicas [and] the Chimú are introducing something from mysticism in their plastic manifestations, in their symbology. . . . Those individuals always related art with mysticism, with the esoteric, with the mysteries" (1976a, 370). Likewise, Lapiner suggests that the ceramic pots of the Moche were possibly used for more than simply portraits of people, depictions of animals, and accounts of daily life: "But does the presence of visual reference justify us in taking these depictions to be illustrations of Mochica daily life? Surely we must recognize that these vivid images may have served as the symbolic terms in which the Mochica cast their theology, science, and history. An effigy vessel in the shape of a cormorant (pl. 310), for example, appears to be an isolated naturalistic bird. But placed in a panoramic context (pls. 291, 311, 312), one can deduce social relationships and religious significance even though the meaning may not be clear. Thus, we see that when dealing with visual materials the forms of life are often inseparable from the forms of thought" (1976, 115). In one of the illustrations to which Lapiner is referring (pl. 312), a running man can be seen carrying a stirrup spout vessel in the shape of a cormorant. He follows a dignitary (a priest or shaman?) wearing a cormorant mask who is being carried on a litter by another figure wearing a cormorant mask. In addition, another running man wearing a cormorant mask follows the stirrup spout vessel carrier. The scene includes several clumps of vegetation that could be San Pedro cactus. The stirrup spout vessel in question, therefore, seems to be relegated to some role in a Moche life-giving or life-taking ritual, perhaps even a curing ceremony that is about to take place.

Calderón explained the following to me about Moche stirrup spout vessels: "The Moche, after using a bottle, would [possibly] throw it away and break it. There are places, tombs, where there are a large quantity of those objects that are broken. They were probably once used for water in earlier times, but there came a time when they were used for burial, for the dead" (interview by author, 1996). That the stirrup-spout vessels were repositories for supernatural life-taking or life-giving forces that were invoked by music is speculation. Nevertheless, when I discussed the possibility with Calderón and asked his opinion about it, he answered in his usual wise manner, as a man of great knowledge. "It is logical."

9

Magical Flutes of the Sinú of Colombia

Among the hundreds of ancient Colombian flutes that have been deposited in Colombian and American museums and private collections, most without significant documentation, a small number are designated as Sinú (ca. A.D. 1000–1550) from northern Colombia. During field research in Bogotá in 1974, I played, photographed, and measured forty-four ceramic tubular duct flutes that were labeled Sinú, ten others of similar construction that were called Tairona, and two others labeled Dibuya, for a total of fifty-six instruments that I have classified together because of physical similarities. Because nearly four-fifths of these ceramic musical instruments have been designated as Sinú, I will assume that the Sinú region is indeed their place of origin, although I will discuss other theories about their provenience.

My two objectives in this chapter are to determine whether or not there is a relationship between the Sinú flutes' tone system possibilities and their iconographic design (animal or other exterior motif), and to explore the use and significance of the flutes to support my interpretation that the Sinú ceramic flutes were used as musical instruments for personal religious purposes, perhaps as symbols of water ideology, fertility, or male sexual aggression versus female sexual invitation.

Sinú Background

Very little is known about the Sinú culture, or about the various cultures that existed in the Sinú River basin of northern Colombia. The large area known as the Sinú archaeological region of Colombia includes the basins of the Sinú, San Jorge, and Nechí Rivers (*El Dorado* 1974, 117), the basins of the lower Magdalena and lower Cauca Rivers (Legast 1980, 10), and the hills of San Jacinto and San Lucas (ibid.) in the departments of Córdoba, Sucre, Bolívar, and northern Antioquia. The outstanding features of the first three river basins are many swamps, or *ciénagas,* as well as "shallow depressions seasonally covered with water and permanent backwater lakes" (Gordon 1957, 4). One of the largest swamps, which is also the site of the greatest archaeological discoveries, is Betancí in the Sinú River flood plain.

The inhabitants of this large area were generally known as Cenú or Zenú, while specific names may have included Calamari, Mocana, Tulú, Urabá (Enslow 1990, 55–56), and Malibú (Falchetti 1998, 172). At various times many of these diverse peoples congregated into three regions, the most important perhaps in and around a city called Finzenú, the apparent capital of the Sinú Valley, located at the edge of the Ciénaga Betancí (Gordon 1957, 33). East of Finzenú, near the San Jorge River, was Panzenú, known by its inhabitants as Ayapel; to the southeast was the third region, Zenúfana, near the Nechí River in the present department of Antioquia. These ancient cities were spacious, with central squares, streets, houses for dwelling and storage, temples, and burial grounds. Gordon writes that the temple of Finzenú "was of imposing dimensions, with lodging space for more than a thousand persons. Inside stood twenty-four tall wooden idols carved in human form, their surfaces covered with little plaques of gold foil, each figure wearing a tiara fashioned of gold. Two such wooden giants stood face to face, bearing a staff across their shoulders from which a hammock was suspended to receive offerings of gold" (1957, 34). It was the cemetery at Finzenú, however, that covered the most territory, as Gordon explains: "From the Río Betancí, down its northern and higher bank almost to the Río Sinú, stretched one vast cemetery, tumulus after tumulus, small and large, cubical, pyramidal, or cone-shaped, laid out, like the buildings in the Zenú cities, in neat rows" (ibid.). Beyond these descriptions, little else has been written of the Sinú territory and its complex of ancient structures.

Although the Spanish made contact with the coastal regions of the Sinú area as early as 1501, it was not until 1510 that Alonso de Ojeda began the conquest (Hernández de Alba 1948, 329). Interested primarily in gold, the conquistadores looted graves, sacked and destroyed the cities, and enslaved, drove out, or killed the native populations (Gordon 1957, 39). Warwick Bray writes, "In 1536–37 Francisco César defeated the tribes of the upper Sinú and plundered their graves; he obtained 20,000 pesos of gold (183 lbs.) from a single tomb" (1974, 41). Indeed, the amount of gold taken from this area was among the largest in the New World, and within forty years the great necropolis of Finzenú was depleted and forgotten about, not to be discovered again until the beginning of the twentieth century (Parsons 1952, 72). Because of the rapid destruction and scattering of the native populations in the Sinú Valley, and the disappearance of most of their cities because of neglect and the rapid growth of vegetation, much of the area has still not been studied by archaeologists. As Parsons explains, "It is not even certain who the Cenúes were" (ibid.). One of the great early American archaeologists, Wendell Bennett, writes, "The archeology of the region of the Sinú River . . . is virtually unknown in spite of the fact that it was one of the first regions explored by the Spaniards" (1944, 78). Yet, "The density of the population in pre-Columbian times is evidenced by the traces of an almost unbelievable profusion of burial mounds, which stretched for at least 15 miles along the margin of the ciénaga [Betancí] and its meandering overflow channel to the Río Sinú" (Parsons 1952, 71). Beginning in the 1950s, archaeological explorations were undertaken in this region by Gerardo Reichel-Dolmatoff (1957), Gerardo and Alicia Reichel-Dolmatoff (1957, 1964), and others.

Some of the early ceramic periods in northern Colombia have been dated to the third millennium B.C. (Bischof 1964, 483), while later ceramics have been dated to the late thirteenth century A.D. (Reichel-Dolmatoff 1965, 129) and even as late as 1700 for ceramics in the Malibú style (Labbé 1998, 87, fig. 65). About the last Sinú culture, the so-called Malibú, Ana María Falchetti writes: "After the tenth century, the Zenúes progressively left the floodplains of the Lower San Jorge River and the surrounding areas, allowing the entry of groups related to the Malibúes around the fourteenth century" (1998, 172). Archaeologists Falchetti and Luís Antonio Escobar (1985) call the types of flutes studied in this chapter "Malibú flutes," although I will refer to them consistently as Sinú flutes for reasons given below (see note 1) and already mentioned above.

Music Archaeology

Many of the Sinú ceramic artifacts, and especially the tubular flutes, reveal an advanced technology suggesting that the later Sinú period possibly had close ties with the Quimbaya to the south (Reichel-Dolmatoff 1965, 127), the Chorotega and Choclé in Central America, and the Tairona to the northeast. Most of the musical artifacts, however, have been unearthed by grave robbers who have not provided documentation beyond general location for the flutes or the thousands of other ceramic artifacts that have turned up in museums, private collections, and stores in Colombia and elsewhere. The only published archaeological locations for Sinú tubular flutes have been given by Anne Legast (1980, 33–34, 108–9, figs. 100, 101), who calls them "fish-shaped" and attributes them to sites in Ovejas (northeastern Sucre department) and El Anclar (near Villa Fátima in southeastern Córdoba department) (see map in Legast 1980, 37, fig. 21).

None of the early-published descriptions or photographs of Sinú artifacts includes tubular duct flutes. Therefore, I have not been able to make direct comparisons of the musical instruments I studied with similar artifacts excavated by archaeologists who have published their findings prior to 1980. Only Reichel-Dolmatoff makes reference to Sinú ceramic aerophones: "Thirty-eight fragments of whistles, the majority ornithomorphic, correspond to the description given for the excavation. Two whistles in the form of cayman were found near the surface, the same with a whistle in the form of a turtle. . . . It is observed that all the whistles have only one pitch" (1957, 100). With those last seven words Reichel-Dolmatoff is clearly referring to musical instruments that differ from the four-fingerhole tubular duct flutes I studied. More recent publications (Legast 1980; Labbé 1998), however, make brief references to similar musical instruments (see also note 1). I will make the assumption, therefore, that probably all the Sinú tubular duct flutes I studied were originally discovered by grave robbers, who had no interest in documentation beyond noting the general area where the artifacts were found. Hence, my archaeomusicological conclusions are based completely on my analysis of the instruments themselves.

The Sinú ceramic duct flutes described in this chapter are fashioned from two elongated cones (or variants of that shape) with the cones adjoined at their widest points. Because this rather unusual shape produces a chamber that is more tubular than globular, I will consistently refer to this instrument as a tubular flute.

Each Sinú tubular flute has an air duct or fipple mouthpiece assembly and is therefore similar in mouthpiece construction to the Western recorder. A suspension hole often found near the proximal end of most of the flutes perhaps allowed an individual instrument to be worn around the neck of the performer.

In 1974, I photographed, measured, and recorded myself playing a total of fifty-six Sinú ceramic tubular duct flutes from a number of collections in Bogotá. Twenty-four were from five antiquities stores: Almacén Taironaca (1), Estampillas y Monedas Arqueología (6), Galería Alonso (5), Galería Cano (2), and Precolombinos San Diego (10). Two flutes were from the Museo del Oro (Gold Museum) of the Banco de la República, and thirty were from the Guillermo Cano private collection (in his home).[1] Fifty-four of the instruments have four fingerholes and only two have three fingerholes, although one of the latter appears to have had a fourth fingerhole plugged during a repair process. A remaining single instrument with three fingerholes is unique for its exterior motif, which includes a superimposed (bas-relief) anteater on the proximal end.

I have classified these fifty-six Sinú flutes into three general categories according to exterior motif: (1) plain, (2) superimposed animal on the proximal end (fig. 9.1), and (3) entire instrument in the shape of a fish (fig. 9.2). The second category is further divided into type of animal (see Legast 1980 for a study of animal types represented in Sinú art), including anteater, turtle, and cayman. The pitches of one flute have not been considered because the instrument's distal end is broken, and another was inadvertently not recorded. Therefore, I analyzed and compared the tone systems of fifty-two flutes with four fingerholes, based on two musical relationships: *foundation interval* (from the principal tone to the next highest pitch) and *overall span interval* (the distance from the lowest to the highest pitch of the entire gamut).

How do the Sinú ceramic duct flutes compare with others in ancient South America and elsewhere? Ceramic tubular duct flutes are rare in South America outside northern Colombia, and most of the ceramic aerophones are either globular or ocarina-type flutes (throughout Colombia, Ecuador, and Peru), notch flutes (Peru), or panpipes (Bolivia, Chile, Ecuador, and Peru). Only eastward among the ancient Tairona (with whom the Sinú had contact) in the present department of Mag-

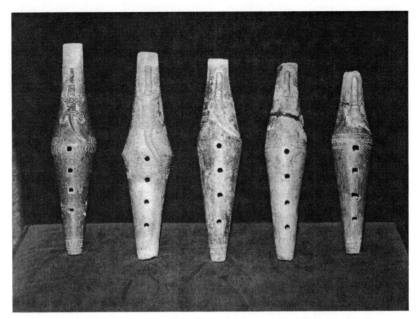

9.1. Five Sinú ceramic tubular duct flutes with cayman iconography (listen to audio track 36). Guillermo Cano Collection, Bogotá.

dalena, are ceramic tubular duct flutes also found, and these are generally anthropomorphic or abstract (i.e., without zoomorphic or anthropomorphic designs). To the northwest of the Sinú region, among the ancient Chorotega and Nicoya cultures of present Nicaragua and Costa Rica, ceramic tubular duct flutes are found that are generally zoomorphic. Likewise, further north among the ancient Maya and Aztec, similar tubular duct flutes were common (Martí 1968).

Several scholars (Reichel-Dolmatoff 1984; Wilbert 1975; Stone 1966, 19, 55) have pointed to ethnographic similarities between ancient Mesoamerica, Central America, and northern South America, and indeed, diffusion via land and sea could easily have occurred over such short distances. However, comparative studies of ceramic musical instruments between the Sinú and other ancient cultures to the north have not been done, and only superficial similarities can be noted.

I began my systematic analysis of Sinú tubular flutes by measuring each instrument, photographing its four sides, and recording myself playing its pitches. Based on my photographs of the fifty-four flutes, I placed the instruments into four categories according to a taxonomy determined by their number of fingerholes and exterior design.

In the first category, *plain,* only three flutes are included, and all have a foundation interval of a major second (M2) and an overall span of a perfect fifth (P5). The second category, *superimposed cayman* (fig. 9.1), includes forty-one flutes. As for the foundation intervals produced on these flutes, twenty-one produce a major second (M2) (audio track 35), fifteen produce a minor third (m3) (audio track 36), four produce a minor second (m2), and one produces a major third (M3). Of the overall span intervals, sixteen produce a minor sixth (m6), thirteen produce a major sixth (M6), eight produce a perfect fifth (P5), three produce an augmented fourth (+4), and one produces a minor seventh (m7). The third category, *superimposed turtle,* includes only one flute; it has a foundation interval of a major second (M2) and an overall span of a minor sixth (m6). The fourth category, *entire instrument in shape of a fish* (fig. 9.2), includes seven flutes, of which six have the foundation interval of a major second (M2) (audio track 37), while the seventh has a minor third (m3) foundation interval. The overall span intervals include the minor sixth (m6) (four

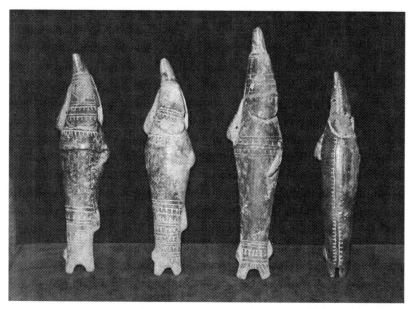

9.2. Four Sinú ceramic tubular duct flutes in the shape of fish (side views). Guillermo Cano Collection, Bogotá.

instruments), the perfect fifth (P5) (two instruments), and the minor seventh (m7) (one instrument).

From the data in category two (the largest sample), I am able to make the following conclusion: *there is no particular tone system that pertains to a particular animal or to exterior design.* In addition, all the categories feature the major second (M2) as the most common foundation interval, a fact that strengthens the above conclusion.

Iconology

There is little Sinú iconographic evidence available (instances of painting, sculpture, and other plastic arts) that depicts musical instruments. I have found only two examples, and both are from secondary sources.

The first example, photographed by and pictured in Falchetti (1998, 186, fig. 10), is a small ceramic figurine from the Museo Sergio Restrepo S.J., in Tierralta, Córdoba, Colombia: "This man with musical instruments and woman with receptacle once decorated a Betancí vessel from the middle reaches of the Sinú River. . . . Music, which as ritual language must have been an essential part of ceremonies, and ritual beverages are alluded to in some Betancí vessels and in gold objects. Musicians may hold wind instruments and *maracas* in their hands while women carry a vessel (fig. 10), possibly the gourd bowl known as *totuma,* filled with *chicha,* a fermented beverage made of corn" (Falchetti 1998, 186, 197). While it is impossible to tell which of the objects in each of the man's hands is a wind instrument or a maraca, because neither is placed to the man's mouth, the object in his right hand is shaped like a double cone and could be either a double-cone tubular flute similar to what I have described or a poorly represented maraca. The object in his left hand, however, is cylindrical, resembling a short staff. Because neither object is held to the figure's mouth, it is doubtful either one is a flute, unless the figurine is a representation of a pipe-and-tabor (here a pipe-and-rattle) musician holding his instruments but not playing them. Indeed, pipe-and-tabor and pipe-and-rattle musician figurines existed in pre-Columbian times farther north in Central America and Mexico, and the female member of the present *gaita* duo in the Sinú region plays a tubular flute with one hand and a rattle with the other (discussed below).

The second example is from a secondary source written in the "seventeenth century": "Some years past at the Villa de Tolú a great guayacán trunk drifted up on the beach which is washed by waters of the Río Zenú. It seemed to be from one of their sanctuaries since carved upon it in half-relief, and not badly fashioned, were many figures of Indians; some were drinking holding totumos [calabashes] in their hands, some playing instruments and others dancing with serpents" (Gordon 1957, 44; original credited to Pedro Simón, who published his five volumes between 1882 and 1892). Although Simón does not detail the types of musical instruments, his account is useful for placing Sinú music within a ritual context. Because of the nearly universal application of the serpent as a fertility symbol (Wilbert 1974, 91–92), Simón's reference to "dancing with serpents" is a relevant piece of descriptive data because of the similarity between serpents and caymans in native American cosmology.

A more direct application of the iconology mode of inquiry for Sinú flutes is an analysis of the exterior motifs on the instruments themselves. Although this type of analysis produces little cultural information, the motifs themselves, such as the cayman, fish, and turtle, suggest possible religious significance for the flutes. It is perhaps no coincidence that these animals are aquatic, suggesting an ideological connection to water.

Since flutes with cayman iconography comprise the largest number of Sinú musical artifacts, I asked myself the following questions: What is the significance of the cayman in northern Colombia? What is its relationship to the reptilian images superimposed on Sinú flutes? Many of the superimposed caymans depicted on the distal ends of the Sinú flutes bear little resemblance to the *caimán* or *caimán de agua* (Gordon 1957, 73) found today in Colombia. This reptile, also referred to as the crocodile by Gordon, "is distinguished by its larger size, shorter neck, and more pointed nose from the true caiman, *babilla* (*Caiman sclerops*), which is plentiful and harmless" (ibid.). Legast gives a slightly different interpretation, however: "These [ceramic and gold] figures are generally realistic because they capture the determining characteristics of the [crocodile's] classification. In the Sinú region only two species of that order exist: the *Crocodylus acutus* (caimán de agua or water cayman) of very large size, and the *Caimán fuscus* (babilla), which is smaller" (1980, 94). Although Legast (1980, 98) presents color photographs of these two Colombian reptiles as part of her comparison, I am not completely convinced that the reptiles on the Sinú flutes are intended to be those found in Colombian waters; most of the reptiles depicted on Sinú flutes have longer and flatter jaws with smaller bodies than current Colombian crocodiles. Whether or not this indicates an extinct reptile or artistic license is unknown. In addition, numerous types of skin or hide are depicted by various methods of incising. Are these representations of actual caymans or supernatural aquatic creatures associated with some aspect of an ancient religion?

Perhaps the extremely long and pointed heads of the reptiles are the most important characteristics of these iconographic representations. Speaking about the gold figurines of the Sinú, Estanislao Gostautas explains that they "are almost always zoomorphic and ornithomorphic. . . . The . . . forms are lizards, birds, and other classes of undetermined animals. The birds are characterized by their long and wide beak, and the lizards or caimans by their realism" (1960, 142),[2] by which he possibly means their long heads or jaws. Situated within the long jaws of the cayman are hundreds of sharp teeth that can often be harmful, as Bachiller Martín Fernández de Enciso, a Spanish chronicler, wrote in 1519: "what I did see as I crossed a river in those parts were lizards of huge size. These lizards lie about the banks, and if an animal or an incautious Christian passes by, they rush and seize him, carrying him off below the surface of the stream to make a meal of him" (in Cunninghame Graham 1922, 36). Hernández de Alba, however, writes, "In addition to other wild animals, the Cenú ate caymans" (1948, 332). While such mutual consumption (i.e., the Sinú eating caymans and the caymans eating Sinú) is notable, this fact in itself may not be important enough to have prompted the depiction of caymans on so many Sinú ceramic flutes. Rather, I suggest that the Sinú desired to capture the power of the cayman, both by eating them and by playing music on flutes that captured their essence by virtue of the cayman representation on the instrument itself. The cayman was probably appreciated as powerful and imbued with supernatural power because of its aquatic and amphibious nature. Sherbondy, for example, writes, "cayman images on stone carvings and pottery reveal a religion in which water was important as a vehicle for the movement of the ancestors, concepts that may have originated with Amazonian peoples" (1992, 53). Furthermore, the cayman is possibly even more powerful than other animals because its long nose may have been a phallic symbol, much like the flutes themselves.

Fish iconography is another important category for Sinú flutes. Fish were apparently important to the Sinú, as attested by their flutes and also by flying fish that they crafted in gold (*El Dorado* 1974, 116). Fish may have had significance for the Sinú as religious symbols involving a water ideology or fertility. Legast has identified one type of fish represented in a Sinú ceramic flute: "Besides having the form of a fish, because of its plain mouth region and the angle formed at the level of the representation of the dorsal fin, it is possible to deduce that the fish is a bagre of the Pimelodedae family. The gills are visible and the scales or colorations of the skin are represented. While the genre and species of this figure are not identifiable, it can be noted that the species *Sorubin lima*, a large fish whose general form is very similar to this representation, is frequently found in the Sinú River" (1980, 108).[3] She is able to identify the precise type of fish represented because of the great iconographic detail. Indeed, there is so much detail that it is possible to count individual scales on the animals' bodies (see note 1). Such identification, however, still tells us nothing about the significance of the bagre or any other particular fish among the Sinú.

The single Sinú flute example featuring a superimposed turtle also suggests a relationship with water, which, as with the cayman and fish flutes, may have religious significance. About the importance of water in native Colombian mythology, Labbé writes: "In the esoteric lore of many native groups, life results from the union of the female and male aspects of the life force, said to manifest itself in the real world by permeating the medium of water, resulting in protoplasm, blood, and chlorophyll. In pre-Columbian iconography, the serpent is the symbol par excellence of the life force" (1998, 87).

A comparison of the exterior designs or motifs of the Sinú flutes with artifacts from neighboring cultures may provide clues to their symbolism. The ancient Quimbaya in the present Colombian department of Quindio (south of the Sinú region), for example, produced numerous ancient artifacts with lizard designs that resemble the reptiles depicted on the Sinú flutes (*El Dorado* 1974, 84). Reichel-Dolmatoff, in fact, also noticed a possible connection between the Sinú and the Quimbaya, as he writes about the former, comparing them with the latter: "Hollow-cast twin-figurines of birds, reptiles, or fantastic animals are typical. . . . It is evident that here we have a new culture which has no local precedents in the coastal lowlands and which must have penetrated from the south, probably from the Cauca valley. The physical type depicted on the figurines and anthropomorphic vessels, the excised decorations, the spindle whorls, the bar-shaped stamps, and also the gold-work show close similarities with the so-called Quimbaya area and the regions lying north of it, in the mountains of the district of Antioquia" (1965, 127). The presence of reptile and fish motifs among the Sinú and the Quimbaya, and the words of Labbé quoted above, suggest a water ideology complex for certain regions of northern Colombia.

History

Gregorio Hernández de Alba has researched the history of the native peoples of the Sinú River basin. About Sinú musical instruments he states (1948, 337): "Heredia [a Spanish chronicler] observed among the *Calamari* and *Turbado* [just to the north of the Sinú River mouth] . . . [that] fighting was accompanied by cries and the sound of trumpets and other musical instruments." "Musical instruments," he continues, "included drums, conch-shell trumpets (caracoles), trumpets, and whistles" (1965, 127). Beyond this, no descriptions of musical instruments from the Sinú region and adjacent areas are found. While the term *whistle* could have referred to ceramic flutes similar to those used in this study, present usage of the term in music archaeology generally refers to an instrument without fingerholes and capable of only one pitch, rather than one with multiple fingerholes and therefore capable of multiple pitches.

Ethnographic Analogy

Unlike the circumstances of north coastal Peru, it is difficult to establish a relationship between the ancient cultures of the Sinú River basin and present societies that may be their descendants. Precise descent cannot be established, as Gordon writes: "Zenú descendants survive by the thousands, but they have lost their identity as a people; with the exception of a few place names, scarcely a word of their language can be recovered. Thus, if the Zenú were not exterminated, aside from a few fragments their culture was" (1957, 45).

Also unlike in Peru, precise musical analogs do not exist, and it is possible that the ceramic flutes of the type presented in this chapter were among the exterminated aspects of autochthonous Sinú culture. The only musical instrument analogy based on shape can be found with a ceramic flute of the Amazonian Tukano, who inhabit regions of the Colombian rainforest, a great distance and across the Andes from the Sinú. Reichel-Dolmatoff describes a Tukano ceramic flute as being "shaped like two cones joined at their bases and open at one end" (1971, 115). He does not describe the mouthpiece apparatus of the Tukano flute, however, making a comparison of it with the Sinú flute impossible, beyond comparing their double-cone shapes. In 1974, I photographed several double-cone Colombian Amazon ceramic flutes in the National Anthropology Museum in Bogotá, and they are cross-blown, with the embouchure hole in the very center where the two cones are joined. Therefore, they (and by deduction, the Tukano flute) are dissimilar to the Sinú duct flutes, even though both types are made from clay and are double-cone-shaped.

Today the only type of duct flute found among the inhabitants of the Sinú region of northern Colombia is the *gaita,* a bamboo flute with an external duct made from the quill of a bird feather encased in a beeswax mass resembling an ax head. Played in pairs known as *macho* and *hembra* (male and female), the former, with four fingerholes and a thumb hole, provides melodies while the latter, with only two fingerholes, plays static counter melodies produced by overtones. The performer of the female flute, however, also simultaneously plays a rattle with one hand while he plays his flute with the other. List (1983, 65–71), writing about the gaitas, claims they are indigenous to (northern) South and Central America because they have no prototypes in Europe or Africa. However, there are also no clear prototypes among the ancient cultures of Colombia and Panama, except for the Sinú ceramic duct flutes. The indigenous gaitas and rattle are used for entertainment, often accompanying dance and song. In addition, African-type drums sometimes accompany the gaitas, and when singing is included, the texts demonstrate Spanish characteristics (List n.d.). Such blending of three heritages (native American, African, and Spanish) is obviously common in the Sinú region today, as revealed by the gaita ensemble and its cultural and musical context. Because there are few physical and no known contextual relationships between the modern gaitas and the ancient Sinú ceramic flutes, however, ethnographic analogy provides little information about the use and significance of the Sinú instruments under study.

Conclusion: Symbols of Water Ideology, Fertility, or Male Sexual Aggression versus Female Sexual Invitation

In spite of the lack of information about the Sinú ceramic duct flutes and the unlikelihood that any modern instruments exist that are descended from them, my interpretation that they were symbols of water ideology, fertility, or male sexual aggression versus female sexual invitation, is supported by a broad application of ethnographic analogy with several native American cultures that have retained ancient beliefs. The evidence for comparison is based on a symbolic analysis of fish and crocodile motifs as researched by Lathrap (1977), Roe (1982), Wilbert (1974, 86–92), and others.

Wilbert discusses the symbolism of fish: "As a fertility symbol the fish is widely distributed throughout the tropical forest area of South America. It occurs in ritual song, in narratives, as masks, costumes, body paint, and amulets. It decorates baskets, boats, and paraphernalia. . . . However, no matter how varied the shapes and forms in which the fish symbol occurs, it carries one basic message—that of fertility" (1974, 86). Likewise, he describes the symbolism of reptiles, "especially snakes, iguanas, and crocodiles" (91), as fitting well "into the symbolic syntax of the 'fertility cult' complex" of South American, Mexican, and Central American ideology (92). And, as I mentioned before, the phallic shapes of the tubular ceramic Sinú flutes themselves could have been symbolic of fertility.

Peter Roe, citing Jules Henry, explains the fertility symbolism of the cayman: "The cayman's 'principal occupation is to seduce women when they come to fetch water' (Henry 1964:72, on the Kaingang) as it was for the anaconda and the dolphin" (1982, 200). Donald Lathrap, however, describes the cayman iconography among the Chavín, a very early culture from northern Peru: "a cayman, the tropical crocodilian of the Amazon and Orinoco Basins, . . . was originally worshipped as the master of fish. This prime entity, who was in a real sense the whole universe, was transformed into a sky deity and a deity of the water and underworld. The Sky Cayman became the basic rain god and the Water and Underworld Cayman the source of fecundity. Both were celebrated as donors of the major cultivated plants and of these gifts the most important was manioc" (1977, 741–42). Roe and Lathrap describe two aspects of the cayman as a fertility symbol: human fertility and vegetable fertility. Combined with Lathrap's interpretation of the relationship between cayman and fish, both animals are powerful fertility symbols.

The other possibility that the ceramic duct flutes of the Sinú were symbols of power for male sexual aggression versus female sexual invitation is based on the Tukano's sound symbolism metaphor for whistling.

Among them, whistling sounds (such as those performed on the Tukano ceramic flute described earlier [Reichel-Domatoff 1971, 115]) symbolize female sexual invitation, which, when joined with buzzing sounds (such as those of a bamboo trumpet), together represent "a synthesis of opposites, . . . an act of creation in which male and female energy have united" (Reichel-Dolmatoff 1971, 116). By way of ethnographic analogy with this Tukano interpretation of sound symbolism, I combine the whistling sound of the Sinú ceramic duct flute with the flute's phallic shape to represent that act of creation. The combination of the two ideas may also be symbolic of male sexual aggression (the phallic shape of the flute shape plus the male symbolism of the superimposed animals) versus female sexual invitation (the whistling sound of the instrument). The aural and physical fertility symbolism of the Sinú flutes, combined with the fertility symbolism of the animals superimposed on the flutes, perhaps assured the people of the Sinú River basin long life, large families, fertile crops, or a place in the hereafter, according to their belief system.

These interpretations are based on ethnographic analogy that does not have direct geographic proximity, although native South Americans certainly shared many symbols and ideologies. In the next chapter about the Tairona, ethnographic analogy with close geographic proximity is indeed a reality, because the present-day Kogi claim to be the descendants of the Tairona.

Musical Effigy Figurines of the Tairona of Colombia

The Tairona of northern Colombia were among a select number of ancient cultures in the Western Hemisphere that reached a high level of technology, evidenced by the development of temples, agricultural terraces, irrigation canals, paved roads, and the perfection of metallurgy and pottery. Metallurgy was especially developed in the production of artifacts of gold; the term *Tairona*, in fact, means goldworkers (Enslow 1990, 30). The Tairona achievements in pottery include the fabrication of various types of globular and tubular duct flute–type aerophones, the former commonly referred to as ocarinas.

The Tairona (ca. A.D. 500–1550) were one of the first native South American cultures encountered by the Spanish conquistadores, beginning in 1502. The Spaniards, driven by the legend of El Dorado, first set foot on the northeastern coast of present-day Colombia in search of gold. In response, many Tairona withdrew into the dense forests and rugged terrain of the Sierra Nevada de Santa Marta. Today the Kogi native Americans are thought to be their modern descendants (Reichel-Dolmatoff 1965, 148).

Archaeology and grave robbing have provided most of what is known today about the Tairona. Thousands of ceramic objects have been found that detail many aspects of Tairona life and beliefs; hundreds more are musical instruments (globular and tubular flutes) made in the shapes of humans, animals, and highly stylized versions of both. I call these small edge-blown instruments musical effigy figurines. They were, I believe, powerful magical tools for the individuals who used them.

During organological research of private and museum collections in Bogotá in 1974, at the Field Museum of Natural History in Chicago in 1982, and at the Metropolitan Museum of Art in New York in 1983, I photographed, measured, and recorded myself playing over 300 of these musical instruments. I originally hypothesized that each of the various aerophone categories would demonstrate a systematic tone system, and would have been constructed with as much concern for pitch organization as for their elaborate exterior detail. I also hypothesized that the musical tone systems of the musical instruments would be related to their types, shapes, and iconography. One of the goals of this chapter is to present my conclusions relative to these hypotheses. The primary purpose, however, is to suggest possible uses and significances of the Tairona ceramic flutes.

Tairona Background

The Tairona probably represented only one tribe among several in the vicinity of the northern and western slopes of the Sierra Nevada de Santa Marta, in the Colombian department of Magdalena. The term *Tairona* may be a misnomer, since the Spanish chronicler Juan de Castellanos (writing in 1545–46) used it to refer to the geographic location of a native American group known as Tairo (cited in Reichel-Dolmatoff 1951, 58). Nevertheless, the name is consistently used today for a dense population of native people who inhabited the area mentioned and shared a number of cultural traits.

Archaeological investigation has determined that the Tairona lived in numerous large village federations consisting of hundreds of circular dwellings placed on stone ring foundations. The villages had stone burial vaults, stone irrigation systems, stone walled terraces, and stone paved roads, stairways, and bridges leading from one village to the other. Warwick Bray writes, "Since 1973, more than two hundred archaeological sites have been discovered, ranging from small settlements of no more than thirty houses to large towns with a thousand or more dwellings spread over an area of several hectares" (1978, 45). In addition, the Tairona established numerous ceremonial centers in mountain retreats to which they made pilgrimages.

The Tairona were also adept at ceramics and metallurgy, as Reichel-Dolmatoff explains: "Life in a Tairona village must have been colorful and busy. Here were a people who loved to manufacture with care and taste the simplest utensils of everyday life, to decorate them and to individualize them. They took pleasure in the smooth and shining surfaces of their black pottery. . . . There must assuredly have been skilled artisans in many different crafts: potters, goldsmiths" (1965, 155). Much of their pottery and gold work suggests the Tairona were a culture strongly influenced by the supernatural. People and animals, for example, were depicted with combined traits in a highly stylized manner, suggesting shamanistic transformation from human to animal. People are sculpted with various types of elaborate clothing, headdresses, and ornaments, perhaps indicating a religious hierarchy. Chroniclers in the early decades of the sixteenth century also mention that the Tairona wore elaborate feather headdresses and shawls, with golden jeweled ornaments for their arms and chests, and earlobe and nose plugs for the men (cited in Reichel-Dolmatoff 1951, 83–84). Although the historical description of dress does not necessarily indicate religious expressions, the molding in clay and gold of highly stylized physical features combining humans and animals, often with elaborate headdresses, collars or necklaces, earlobe plugs, shawls, breastplates, and so forth, suggests ceremony, ritual, or some form of mortal-immortal nexus.

Spanish chroniclers discuss Tairona beliefs in ethnocentric terms, and most often Tairona religion is referred to as devil worship. Castellanos, for example, wrote the following in the Spanish poetic style of the sixteenth century: "They adore the planets and the signs received from the heights of hills; there are many female and male diviners, and a large quantity of charmers who say millions of nonsensical things about the future; they give to the demon things that it doesn't merit, painting him into their art" (cited in Reichel-Dolmatoff 1951, 94).[1] The last statement most certainly refers to Tairona pottery, because no paintings exist among them. The types of musical instruments presented in this chapter could have been among the "demon" forms that Castellanos saw during his 1545–46 explorations.

Music Archaeology and Iconology

The provenience of Tairona globular flutes (described as ocarinas or whistles in the literature) and tubular flutes cannot always be ascertained, because most of them are not documented. Even some of the ceramic ocarinas in the Field Museum of Natural History, which were carried from Colombia by John Alden Mason (1931, 1939) in the 1920s, were purchased from grave robbers, as were many of the musical artifacts I found in commercial stores and public museums throughout Bogotá.

Nevertheless, Mason also excavated numerous ceramic globular flutes, which he lists as coming from either of two areas within certain sites: graves or houses (but not temples). The following items from Mason's field notes (for May 1922 through April 1923) refer to grave sites:

(1) . . . an urn of C (possibly A) type, protected by a cover, and containing traces of bones, probably those of a child. . . . In the earth of the urn, in addition to the human bones, were found five black pottery whistles. . . . a small stone ax-head, a copper frog, the bones of a small animal. . . .

(2) Five black pottery whistles were found in one C urn, apparently with a burial of a child. . . .

(3) The principal object of interest found in this site is a small, stone-lined grave or boveda. . . . Little was found in this grave. . . . Above this grave was found a broken olla [jar] of polished black ware containing . . . two pottery figurine whistles.

(4) A small stone-lined grave found. A red stone ax found, another green ax-head, some beads and a small black olla of polished ware with long ornament of green stone and two figurine whistles of black pottery.

Evidence for the presence of clay globular flutes in house contexts comes from Reichel-Dolmatoff, who, like John Alden Mason, had first-hand experience as an archaeologist in Tairona territory. In the following account, he gives important clues about the use of certain musical instruments: "The center of the house is clean and free of furniture, but along the curve of the wall there lie the odds and ends which once belonged to each member of the family and which were left lying on the floor. . . . in a corner there will be a few polished stone celts, a fish-hook of stone, net sinkers, a couple of bird-shaped clay whistles, and perhaps some ceremonial object such as a finely polished monolithic ax. That the opposite side of the house was occupied by the women is suggested by the pottery, the children's necklaces, and the scraping and grinding tools of daily food preparation" (Reichel-Dolmatoff 1965, 148).

Mason also writes about objects found within the ring of stones forming the foundation of a house: "Many other buried objects were found on this site. . . . These were found in all parts of the circles, but mostly to the north and least to the south, and apparently without any plan of interment. A vase of dark pottery . . . contained a monolithic ax. . . . Nearby was a pottery whistle in the form of a bat" (1931, 66).

Bray, however, explains that ceramic whistles were found in ceremonial houses rather than in common houses: "The ceremonial houses were much larger than the ordinary dwellings, and were sometimes provided with causeways, multiple entrances, stairways, columns and stone tables or benches. One of the Pueblito ceremonial houses contained caches of ritual stone objects buried in pots or underneath stone slabs. Beneath the threshold slab was a terracotta whistle, beads of quartz, forked 'sceptres' or staffs, and winged *placas sonajeras* [stone chimes] of polished stone. Beside the entrance was a jaguar skull" (1978, 45–46). In a drawing of the inside of a Tairona house, the men's side includes "stools, axes, whistles, fishhooks, ceremonial gear" (46).

These findings suggest that only the Tairona men used certain types of clay globular flutes, as suggested by Mason's statement that "the opposite side of the house was occupied by the women" and by Bray's drawing. In many native South American cultures, ceremonial, hunting, and fishing paraphernalia and edge aerophones (flutes and ocarinas) are usually reserved for males. The several archaeologists' field notes and commentaries cited above strongly suggest a ritual significance for the Tairona aerophones, and for that reason I call them musical effigy figurines, a nomenclature also inspired by Reichel-Dolmatoff: "Elaborate clay ocarinas constitute a special category of objects, ranging from simple bird shapes to very complex figurines of warriors or priests, with high feathered head-dresses, nose ornaments, clubs, and other paraphernalia. Some of these effigies show people wearing animal masks or sometimes a human face peers through the open jaws of a jaguar or reptilian monster" (1965, 150–51).

Another archaeologist-explorer, Gregory Mason (1940, 308; unrelated to John Alden Mason), considers the Tairona effigy figurines of clay,

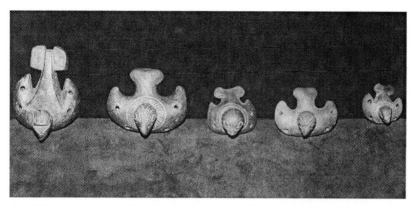

10.1. Tairona ceramic realistic bird globular duct flutes with four fingerholes each. Measurements of flute second from left: length 9.1 cm, height 5.1 cm, wing span 12.1 cm. Guillermo Cano Collection, Bogotá.

stone, metal, shell, and bone as evidence of totemism among the Tairona. Indeed, the number of animals represented in Tairona sculpture is large, and includes realistic birds (figs. 10.1, 10.6) such as kites, owls, parrots, eagles, hawks, and doves; stylized birds with jaguar or reptilian heads (fig. 10.2); mammals such as bats (figs. 10.3, 10.8), coati, dogs, foxes, or opossums (fig. 10.4), jaguars, pigs, and monkeys; and reptiles and amphibians such as crocodiles, frogs or toads (fig. 10.13), turtles (fig. 10.5), lizards, and stylized snakes with jaguar or cayman heads (see fig. 5.1). About these and their symbolism Gregory Mason writes, "I am con-

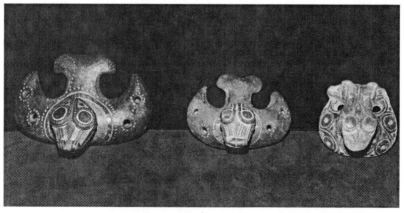

10.2. Tairona ceramic stylized bird globular duct flutes with four fingerholes each (listen to audio track 43). Guillermo Cano Collection, Bogotá.

10.3. Tairona ceramic flying-bat globular duct flute with four fingerholes. Length 11.5 cm, wing span 17.2 cm. Estampillas y Monedas Arqueología Collection, Bogotá.

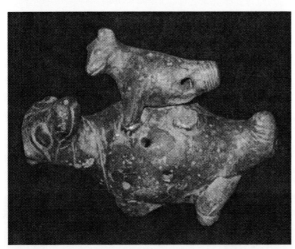

10.4. Tairona ceramic double globular duct flute of a mother opossum or coati with baby on her back (listen to audio track 46). Length 12 cm, width 5 cm, height 8.5 cm. Guillermo Cano Collection, Bogotá.

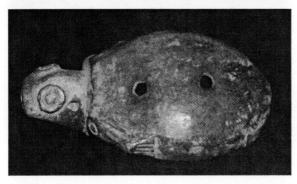

10.5. Tairona ceramic turtle globular duct flute with four fingerholes (listen to audio track 39). Length 10.8 cm, width 7.9 cm. Guillermo Cano Collection, Bogotá.

10.6. Tairona ceramic bird globular duct flute with six fingerholes (listen to audio track 42). Length 5.6 cm, width 4.1 cm. Guillermo Cano Collection, Bogotá.

vinced that these representations are not the haphazard result of the free play of Indian whim. Indians never give free play to their imaginations. Every stroke in an Indian drawing, every geometric line incised on Indian pottery, means something. The meaning, for the South American Indians, is more often concerned with magic than with anything else. Totemism is founded deeply in magic. . . . That is why I suggest that (1) the animal figures found in Tairona art are the eponymous symbols of matrilineal exogamic clans . . . and that (2) the curious pig-like creature, the . . . 'visor-god,' is nothing more than . . . a pig, a wild pig, a peccary, and a totem of a clan" (1940, 309).

I agree with Gregory Mason when he argues that totemism is the reason for the Tairona animal figures. The musical effigy figurines especially (because of the added dimension of sound) must have had some supernatural use, perhaps as a part of shamanism, totemism, or magical protection. As for Mason's statement that "Indians never give free play to their imaginations" and his inference that they did everything for a purpose, however, I disagree. Based on the musical instruments of the Tairona I studied, I found there was no standardization of pitch among them, suggesting that their pitches were haphazardly determined. Indeed, even graphic and geometric designs may not have meaning or supernatural use, in spite of what Mason writes, as suggested by Gebhart-Sayer for the Shipibo-Conibo of the Peruvian Amazon: "My prime informant insisted that once materialized on textiles, ceramics, or other media, a design loses its spirit . . . and thus its potency" (1985, 152). This type of emic information is very important simply because it suggests evidence to possibly counteract commonly held etic opinions that are not often based on fact, such as that of Gregory Mason cited above.

To substantiate my own etic analyses, I classified the 300 musical instruments I studied into twelve animal types: bird, bat, opossum (coati?), fish, frog or toad, jaguar, lizard (cayman?), mouse, monkey, sea creature, snake, turtle (snail?). In addition, I subclassified them according to body design and position.

Based on an analysis of my photographs of the Tairona tubular and globular flutes, I placed the instruments in typological categories according to my own taxonomy, beginning with the method of sound production (duct or ductless mouthpieces), followed by basic shape (tubular or globular). Next is specific information about the chamber(s): tubular flutes are either cylindrical, sausage, or double-cone, and globular flutes have either one, two, or three chambers or are crescent-shaped. Another criterion is design: plain, zoomorphic, anthropomorphic, or anthrozoomorphic, with the taxonomy organized from general to specific. I devised an animal and position code that includes sixteen animal types and specific characteristics such as realistic, stylized, sitting, standing, flying, and swimming. The identification code key offers a systematic method of classification for Tairona ceramic aerophones, relative to my working hypotheses (formulated before I began my laboratory analysis) that (1) each of the various aerophone categories would demonstrate a systematic tone system and would have been constructed with as much concern for pitch organization as for the instruments' elaborate exterior detail, and (2) the tone systems of the instruments would be related to their types, shapes, and iconography.

Using my identification code, I classified the 300 Tairona ceramic aerophones into fifty-two categories; however, only twenty-six categories were usable because they contained a sufficient number of instruments in each to provide a random sampling (the other twenty-six categories included either only a single instrument or instruments that were not playable). In all I analyzed 147 Tairona musical instruments in the twenty-six usable categories.

My systematic measurement of pitches is based on my performance of sustained tones using fingerings that include all possibilities for producing pitches without changing air pressure or using half-holes (i.e., only partially covering a fingerhole). In the laboratory at the Florida State University I transcribed all the musical tone systems into Western notation and then notated the cents deviation from A = 440 with a stroboscopic frequency meter (Stroboconn 6T5). As with my study of Sinú tubular flutes, my Tairona comparisons are based on two relationships: foundation interval and overall span interval.

The following observations, organized according to selected examples from the twenty-six categories, are based on the systematic analyses of the instruments.

Five tubular cylindrical flutes: Each has a duct mouthpiece, standing and stylized anthropomorphic design, and four fingerholes (fig. 10.7). Since these instruments are tubular flutes, their fingering possibilities

10.7. Three Tairona ceramic tubular duct flutes with four fingerholes each. Guillermo Cano Collection, Bogotá.

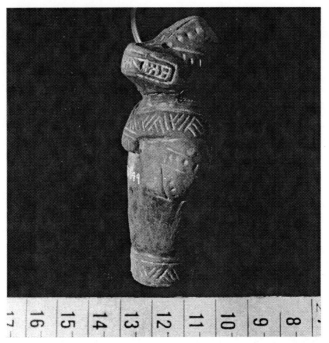

10.8. Tairona ceramic stylized standing-bat tubular duct flute with two finger-holes and a small distal hole. Scale in cm. Field Museum of Natural History Collection, Chicago.

yield interesting results and clearly indicate that they share similar characteristics. For the most part, the flutes in this group support my first working hypothesis that the instruments were not produced haphazardly. Analysis clearly indicates, for example, that the foundation intervals produced by the Western fingering method are similar in four of the five instruments, and the Q'ero fingering method produces foundation intervals of a perfect fourth in all five instruments (with a difference, however, of as much as 67 cents between two of the flutes). Other fingering styles (Warao method, reverse Warao method, and reverse Western method), however, show no consistency of foundation interval. Although these tubular flutes share physical similarities as well, it is my feeling that the sampling in this category is too small to determine whether or not the musical and structural similarities were intentional.

Fifteen tubular flutes: Each has a duct mouthpiece, a stylized bat design (fig. 10.8), two fingerholes, and a distal hole that can easily function as a bottom fingerhole. Using the distal hole to produce a foundation interval, however, reveals little consistency except for minor and neutral thirds taken together as one type of interval (8 flutes). The overall span, however, is approximately a perfect fifth in nine of the instruments. If we consider the neutral and major thirds as the same interval (and indeed, many cultures do), the tone systems without the distal hole are very similar: eleven flutes produce a type of major trichord (i.e., the first three notes of a major scale). A careful comparison of the similar flutes with the dissimilar ones, however, reveals no substantial differences in ornamentation and design.

Six sausage-shaped flutes: Each has a duct mouthpiece, four fingerholes, and an abstract design (fig. 10.9). Three of these instruments have very similar tone systems. Although each instrument's principal tone differs from the others by about a half step, their intervallic relationships and exterior details are nearly identical, tempting one to suggest that they were made by the same potter. Each of these flutes has a major second foundation interval, and four of them have an overall span of a perfect fifth.

Six double-cone flutes: Each has a duct mouthpiece, two fingerholes, a distal hole, and batlike heads. Four of them have a major second foundation interval; one has a minor third and another a major third foundation

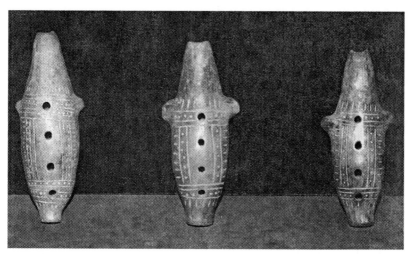

10.9. Three Tairona ceramic sausage-shaped tubular duct flutes with four fingerholes each (listen to audio track 1). Guillermo Cano Collection, Bogotá.

interval. Their overall spans vary from a minor third to an augmented fourth.

Forty-three globular flutes: Each has a duct mouthpiece, four finger-holes, and a bird shape featuring one of two basic types: realistic (see figs. 10.1 and 10.6) and stylized with jaguar characteristics (see fig. 10.2). Because of the importance of birds and jaguars in many South American native cultures (both animals are associated with shamanism), these musical instruments strongly suggest supernatural use. In spite of the obvious physical variations between the two bird types, there are no outstanding musical differences except pitch range. Slight physical variations observed among the stylized bird-jaguar ocarinas include figurines with two types of heads (one a horizontal head with eyes on the side and bulbous sacred mushrooms on top, and another a vertical head with eyes on the side) and one with double jaguar-headed tail. There are no musical differences between them. Foundation intervals vary, including a major second (13 ocarinas), a minor third (17), and a major third (8). The most common overall span is a minor sixth (16 ocarinas).

Nineteen globular flutes: Each has a duct mouthpiece, from one to four fingerholes, and an animal design, including dog or opossum (coati), jaguar, mouse, fish, sea creature, turtle, frog, snake, and others that are not identifiable. Regarding classification of zoomorphic iconography in pre-Columbian artifacts, Wilbert writes, "Because of the high degree of conventionalization in some of the designs, unequivocal zoological classification is not possible and must remain a matter of personal choice and probability rather than of proof" (1974, 57). Nevertheless, I have grouped the ocarinas together on the basis of animal motif rather than number of fingerholes; their tonometric data, therefore, are based only on an analysis of their foundation intervals. My analyses indicate that there is *no* connection between animal type and intervals employed, except in the case of the frog or toad motif. Three of the four frog or toad globular flutes are based on a minor third as their foundation interval which, I believe, is only a coincidence. One of the most interesting instruments in this group is a double globular flute in the shape of an opossum (or a coati or similar mammal) with its baby on her back (see fig. 10.4). The mother is a globular flute with two fingerholes, while the baby is a very-high-pitched globular flute without fingerholes.

Twenty-four globular flutes: Each has a duct mouthpiece, four finger-holes, a crescent shape, and stylized anthropomorphic designs that are

10.10. Three Tairona ceramic globular duct flutes with stylized priest/shaman sitting on crescent throne and four fingerholes each (listen to audio track 50). *Flute on left*, length 9.1 cm, width 8.4 cm; *center*, length 10.1 cm, width 7.6 cm; *right*, length 8.7 cm, width 8.7 cm. Guillermo Cano Collection, Bogotá.

usually seated human-animal combinations (fig. 10.10). I have subclassified these elaborate and beautiful ocarinas into three groups: without facial deformation, with extended tongue, and with jaguar mask. Each of the human figures is seated on a crescent base (which perhaps represents a boat or a throne) that terminates in jaguar heads. The ornate feather headdresses incised into the pottery seem to indicate a high-ranking social class for each figure represented, such as that of priest/shaman. The elaborate renderings of extended tongue and jaguar mask on many of the specimens, as well as the stylized elements of the others, suggest that these ocarinas functioned in ceremonial contexts. As with all the globular flutes studied so far, there is also no particular musical characteristic unique to the subgroups. There is, however, a preponderance of the minor third used for the foundation interval (15 ocarinas). In fact, when the minor third, the neutral third, and the major third (which may not have been heard as a different interval by the Tairona) are taken together, they constitute nearly four-fifths of the sampling (19 ocarinas).

Twenty-nine tubular flutes: Each has a ductless (cross-blown) mouthpiece on one end, two fingerholes, a crescent shape, and an anthropomorphic or zoomorphic design (figs. 10.11, 10.12). These tubular flutes are unique among pottery musical instruments. Although each flute has two fingerholes, it is capable of two basic tone systems; one tone system is

10.11. Four Tairona ceramic crescent-shaped ductless tubular flutes with various motifs (listen to audio track 52). Guillermo Cano Collection, Bogotá.

produced with the distal end open, and the other with it closed. My analyses of the foundation and overall intervals of both sets of tone systems indicate no standard arrangement and no relationship between choice of interval and exterior motif. The evidence simply shows that with the distal end open the primary foundation intervals are the major

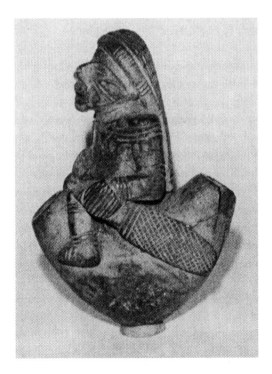

10.12. Tairona ceramic crescent-shaped ductless tubular flute shaped like a man astride a boat holding a paddle (listen to audio track 51). Museo Arqueológico Collection, Banco Popular, Bogotá.

second (18 flutes) and minor second (8), and with the distal end closed they are the minor third (11), major second (6), and major third (5). Furthermore, with the distal end open the most frequent overall intervals are the minor third (11), major second (6), and major third (6), while with the distal end closed they are the perfect fourth (7), augmented fourth (6), and perfect fifth (5) (figs. 10.11, 10.12).

The iconographic symbolism of these musical instruments is a mystery. On the one hand the crescent-shaped chamber upon which the person or animal is sitting or lying resembles a throne, but on the other hand it also resembles a boat. In most cases the creature sits with knees up high on one side of his seat; but in others he sits astride it and some figurines depict the creature on his back. Some of the human figures are playing tubular flutes; some are chewing coca. Others have their tongues extended, and some seem to be wearing masks that represent transformation into an animal. The most frequent animal shape seems to be that of a jaguar or some other fanged beast. The designs on the seats or vessels themselves often include geometric motifs such as steps and spirals, and some suggest faces (the fingerholes are the "eyes"). In several, the animal or man is itself a globular flute without fingerholes. In one example (fig. 10.12), the coca-chewing person who sits astride his seat is actually a two-holed duct globular flute with its window in the middle of the long hair that extends down the person's back to his waist. The seat or base itself seems to represent a boat (perhaps a craft similar to the totora-reed tule boats of the Moche, who lived on Peru's north coast), because the person appears to hold a paddle at his left side.[2]

My analyses, therefore, have revealed that pitch combinations (tone systems or scales) of Tairona ceramic tubular and globular flutes are haphazard, and that my first hypothesis is false. They have also revealed that the musical instruments were *not* made in a manner that systematically related exterior motif with tone system structure. Thus, while I originally hypothesized that all the bird ocarinas had similar pitch relationships or scales, all the bats had their own scales, all the humans had theirs, and so forth, this is not the case. Therefore, my second original hypothesis is also false. What the ceramic musical instruments of the ancient Tairona *can* tell us is that the Tairona had a great concern for exterior detail of their musical effigy figurines, and that while pitch variation was a concern because it existed, recurring pitch relationships (as conceived of in modern Western terms) between instruments of similar design were apparently not of concern to them.

The next modes of inquiry in the methodological model enable us to probe more deeply into the possible uses and significances of these ancient musical artifacts. For this analysis I will apply a Kogi classification of animal type to the Tairona musical effigy figurines.

History

Although the number of Spanish chroniclers who were present during the encounter with the Tairona was small compared to those during the conquests of the Aztec or Inca, several early writers have provided information relating to the uses of musical instruments, ceramics, ornaments of everyday dress, and other physical and cultural attributes of the Tairona that may elucidate the cultural context of the musical effigy figurines.

Spanish chronicler Gonzalo Fernández de Oviedo y Valdés (cited in Reichel-Dolmatoff 1951, 93) mentioned several musical instruments of the Tairona and other Santa Marta native people in 1514, describing large slit drums that were suspended from the rafters inside Tairona temples: "large drums from about six or seven palms in length, [are] made from the hollow trunk of large trees."[3] In other paragraphs he described "cornetas" and conch shell trumpets, instruments of "loud sounds" and possible ceremonial use by priest or congregation. However, since he never mentioned small ceramic globular and tubular flutes, Tairona individuals probably used them for private use rather than in a ceremonial setting. Their exclusion from the historical writings suggests that the Spanish were not aware of their existence or the cultural framework within which they were used.

In addition to Oviedo y Valdés, Pedro Simón and Antonio de Herrera y Tordesillas (cited in Reichel-Dolmatoff 1951, 86) also wrote about the ceramics of the Santa Marta people; however, they described only large painted urns that were used for holding water and wine, and made no mention of ceramic globular or tubular flutes, again suggesting that such instruments were either kept out of sight of the Spanish or simply not noticed.

Chroniclers also explained that the Tairona made extensive use of body ornaments, including necklaces of stone, shell, and gold (cited in

Reichel-Dolmatoff 1951, 83–85). Although some of the ceramic musical effigy figurines have suspension holes in them and could have been worn around the musician's neck, no mention is made by the chroniclers that they were. It is probable, therefore, that the musical effigy figurines were worn neither during everyday village activities nor at ceremonies where the Spanish were present.

Regarding the use of the animal-shaped musical effigy figurines, the following information also is relevant. The chroniclers Juan de Castellanos and Pedro Simón wrote that the native people of Santa Marta did not eat land animals (or birds), but only corn, roots, fruits, and fish (cited in Reichel-Dolmatoff 1951, 82). Therefore, the music performed on the animal-shaped ceramic flutes was probably not used to attract animals (and birds) nor to appease the spirits of the animals the instruments represented in order to kill the animals for food, as is the tradition among the Cuna (McCosker 1974, 15).

The significant uncertainties resulting from this historical analysis are perhaps obvious. Although it is important to consider chroniclers' accounts when creating a complete picture of the Tairona, the following must be understood: the historical accounts must be carefully weighed because of the ethnocentrism of the writers, and the accounts must be considered incomplete, because the native people at the time of their encounters with the Spanish probably had no desire to share their religious knowledge with the foreigners. Therefore, the possibility of error, omission, or distortion is too great for the historical descriptions to count as reliable empirical facts.

Ethnographic Analogy

By way of ethnographic analogy I suggest it is possible to make scientifically derived assumptions about the use and significance of Tairona musical artifacts. With regard to the Tairona, ethnographic analogy involves an important variable—*survivor validity*. One must ask whether Tairona survivors actually exist today, removed in time by hundreds of years.

Chroniclers have not precisely mentioned to which part of Colombia the Tairona escaped when they fled the Spaniards. Nevertheless, it is most commonly believed that the Kogi are the descendants of the Tairona (Reichel-Dolmatoff 1965, 148). However, other native American groups, such as the Chocó and the Cuna, may also be descendants since they "can be assumed to represent, in the surviving aspects of their aboriginal cultures, remnants of groups which once inhabited precisely that region where the archaeological remains of Tropical-Forest type are often characterized by the occurrence of small clay figurines" (Reichel-Dolmatoff 1961, 230). Using the occurrence of small clay figurines as a criterion, this statement would include the Tairona culture as among the most prolific makers of the small clay figurines. Reichel-Dolmatoff, however, continues: "This is not meant to say that these modern tribes are the direct descendants of the ancient Indians who made these figurines but in some aspects a continuity of a common cultural heritage might perhaps be observed" (ibid.). Although the Chocó and the Cuna are geographically close to the Santa Marta region of Colombia where the Tairona lived, the variable of *spatial proximity* is challenged by the following question: What physical distance (space) is required for such continuity of a common cultural heritage to exist? Because the Kogi are geographically the closest living culture to the Tairona, they will be given the greatest consideration in this chapter.

Reichel-Dolmatoff, the foremost authority of the Tairona and their descendants, the Kogi, presents a rationale for ethnographic analogy: "The investigation about the subject in question obviously should neither limit itself to the copying of information written by the chroniclers nor to speculations derived from archaeology, but should also make ample use of modern ethnological facts" (1975b, 201).[4] Therefore, I employ specific ethnographic analogies with the Kogi, while I make comparative ethnological analogies in a broader sense with other indigenous groups that seem to share certain cultural traditions with the Tairona.

Kogi Background

The Kogi (Cogui, Kogui), also known as the Cágaba (Kagaba), number less than 2,000 people who inhabit the northern foothills of the Santa Marta sierra. Their language is classified as Chibchan and their relatively unacculturated life style and belief system are guarded by their isolation and profoundly religious nature. The Kogi claim to be the descendants of the Tairona, and they make many references to the Tairona and even use certain ancient Tairona artifacts for religious purposes. Because of the thorough ethnographies of Reichel-Dolmatoff and others, Kogi ideas about their own religious beliefs, life-death cycle, magical protection, and other ideologies may help to explain the use and significance of the Tairona musical effigy figurines.

Reichel-Dolmatoff writes in particular about the Kogi's use of certain Tairona ceramic whistles and how they functioned as representations of totemic animals in times past: "A very typical element in Tairona archaeology, and still in use today among the Kogi, are ceramic whistles (*huíbiju*). They are suspended around the necks of the dancers who play them at particular times during the dances in imitation of birds. The different zoomorphic representations (e.g., jaguars, owls, foxes, bats, etc.) of the whistles seem to be originally related to totemic animals, and according to my informants, each Túxe [a Kogi clan] used to use whistles to represent its corresponding animal. Today, this distinction is not made, and the whistles only serve as musical instruments without pertaining to a particular social group" (1953, 43).[5] This quotation is the only Kogi reference I found about how the Tairona might have used their ceramic globular flutes. However, since only a small percentage of the Tairona flutes have suspension holes enabling them to have been carried around the necks of the individual players, we must seek other explanations for the numerous musical figurines that do not have suspension holes.

Central to the Tairona religion, according to the Kogi Indians of today, was a jaguar-god known as Cashindúcua. Stylized jaguar imagery is often displayed in Tairona gold iconography, and even more frequently in the ceramic globular and tubular flutes. To perhaps better understand the significance of Tairona jaguar imagery, let us review the concept of totemism.

Kogi Totemism

Totemism may have been important in Tairona culture, as it is today among the Kogi. According to Lévi-Strauss, however, there are several types of totemism, and he establishes a dichotomy in order to explain what they are: "The term totemism covers relations, posed ideologically, between two series, one natural, the other cultural. The natural series comprises on the one hand [animal] categories, and on the other [animal] particulars; the cultural series comprises [human] groups and persons." The two modes of human and animal existence, collective and individual, can be associated in four ways, "two by two, belonging to the different series," as presented in table 10.1. Using examples taken from literature

Table 10.1. Totemic series (after Lévi-Strauss 1963)

	1	2	3	4
Natural (animal) series	Category	Category	Particular	Particular
Cultural (human) series	Group	Person	Person	Group

and possibly his own research, Lévi-Strauss explains the following about his diagram: "only the first two have been included in the sphere of totemism . . . , while the other two have been only directly related to totemism, one [number 3] as a preliminary form . . . and the other [number 4] as a vestige" (1963, 15–17). Since these questions (i.e., whether or not the Tairona musical effigy figurines are examples of totemism, pre-totemism, or posttotemism) are not crucial to the current study, I will not elaborate on his complete system further. I am interested, however, in his third category, which pertains to a relationship between a particular animal and a particular human.

Lévi-Strauss continues to explain totemism in a way that strengthens this one-to-one relationship. The etymology of the word *totem*, he explains, is from the "Ojibwa, an Algonquin language of the region to the north of the Great Lakes of northern America. The expression ototeman . . . means roughly, 'he is a relative of mine.' . . . [It is a] collective naming system not to be confused with the belief, held by the same Ojibwa, that an individual may enter into a relationship with an animal which will be his guardian spirit." This guardian spirit is known by the Ojibwa "as nigouimes, [which] has nothing to do with the word 'totem' or any other term of the same type" (18–19). He also writes, "the acquisition of a guardian spirit came as the consummation of a strictly individual enterprise which girls and boys were encouraged to undertake when they approached puberty" (23).

This detailed discussion of totemism is necessary to establish a framework within which the phenomenon of magical protection among the Tairona can be discussed. With Lévi-Strauss's categories it is clear that one should not attach a totemic use to the Tairona musical effigy figurines as Gregory Mason (1940, 309) has done, unless one is thinking in terms of the particular animal–particular person category, as discussed above. In other words, the musical effigy figurines cannot be considered with totemism as an aspect of clan affinity whereby an animal type is associated with a group of people. Rather, the type of totemism that associates a particular "natural" element (e.g., an animal) with a "cultural" person element (e.g., a Tairona individual) is, I believe, that which best establishes the power relationship between what a musical effigy figurine represents and who uses it.

Kogi Magical Protection

Kogi males have a tremendous concern about their mortality. "The Kogi are deeply preoccupied with death . . . [and] the common people will constantly mention death and dying in daily talk," writes Reichel-Dolmatoff (1984, 83), who also gives the following detailed description of the Kogi preoccupation with death: "For young people . . . death is a horrifying specter. He who dies young will be old in the Beyond in proportion to the phase of life in which he died. The wish of every Kogi is to die old and be reborn young in order to live life over again and enjoy all those gratifications which the first life had withheld. For this reason one must 'die in time.' Among the Kogi the death of a young person is seen as a misdemeanor, a lack of responsibility toward society. Such a death is always thought to be a supernatural punishment and is directly the fault of the deceased. . . . The ideal life-span is ninety years and he who dies at twenty will arrive in the Beyond at the age of seventy. Young people 'have no right to die'" (65). Within Kogi culture it is necessary, therefore, to teach a male child to strictly follow the culturally determined behavioral path, lest he be exposed to all types of dangers (Reichel-Dolmatoff 1977a, 217). Through the world of mythology boys are taught about the potential supernatural dangers of natural and atmospheric phenomena, including lightning, thunder, rainbows, echoes, trees, and stones. They are taught that these are mythical creatures in whose presence one must tread carefully. This concern about life and its continuation is central to my hypothesis that musical effigy figurines were employed by Tairona men for magical protection.

"Nevertheless," continues Reichel-Dolmatoff, "no technique or practice of protection is taught to the boys; only the adult males can acquire power in the form of a *sewá* [power object] to counteract these dangers" (1977a, 217). With the acquisition of such power objects as "small archaeological necklace beads of stone, of different minerals, shapes, colors, and textures," the Kogi male is entering into the office of *mama*, or shaman-priest, one who is a specialist in cosmological knowledge (Reichel-

Dolmatoff 1976, 280–81). The Kogi children, nevertheless, have their own techniques of dealing with danger: "Upon finding themselves face to face with strangers, the reaction of the children is always that of fear, whereupon they try to immediately run away. If they are surprised in a place where they cannot flee, they smile in a forced manner and remain completely still and silent" (Reichel-Dolmatoff 1977a, 220). The similarity between Kogi adults and children is that techniques of protection exist for both. Even though the Kogi adult males employ their power objects for magical protection during an initiation period into shamanism, nearly all adult Kogi males follow their religious beliefs, making the difference between a Kogi shaman and nonshaman very slight.

In another source Reichel-Dolmatoff, writing about the *Túxe* and *Dáke* (Kogi clans), describes the importance the Kogi give to animals for protection against disease and misfortune: "All the *Túxe* or *Dáke* recognize a genealogical root and declare their relationship with a particular animal, plant, object, natural phenomenon. . . . They consider these animals directly as ancestors: 'We all came from animals. Long ago animals were people.' The relationship of the group and of the individual with a particular animal is multiple. . . . Having completed with his offerings, an individual has nothing to fear and the animal will defend him against illnesses or disgraces; but if the offerings are not made, the animal will punish him by sending calamities" (Reichel-Dolmatoff 1949–50, 261–63).[6] Therefore, the Kogi make use of a particular individual relationship in which a particular animal offers magical protection. One method for obtaining the magical power is through dance and song, as Reichel-Dolmatoff explains: "These animal imitation dances and songs, and those that are performed as a means of asking the animals for help, are the strict 'property' of those individuals who descended from a particular ancestral animal" (ibid.).[7] The importance of animal imitation among the Kogi was also explained by Father Alvarez Don José Nicolas de la Rosa in 1739: "The dances are named after different birds, animals, or people, which are supposed to be imitated in the performance" (in Nicholas 1901, 642).

Thus, the preoccupation with animal imitation and human death among Kogi males of all ages, shamans and nonshamans alike, has prompted them to acquire culturally learned methods for facing danger and ultimately preventing death. This concern for prolonged life is possibly derived from their pre-Columbian past, since intangible elements of belief systems, such as concern for the life-death cycle, are commonly

more resistant to change than tangibles, such as the use of physical paraphernalia. I believe that the Tairona employed their ceramic globular and
tubular flutes as musical guardian spirit effigies for individual magical
protection, in a manner philosophically similar to how the Kogi perpetu-
ate their own mortal existence by protecting themselves from danger.
These include remaining completely still and silent, employing power
objects for magical protection during an initiation period into shamanism, and asking animals for protection against disease and misfortune.
The magical protection hypothesis is further supported by the results of
my detailed iconographic analyses of the Tairona ceramic musical instruments themselves.

Kogi Animal Classification

The Kogi classify animals into four large groups: worms, birds, quadrupeds, and insects (Reichel-Dolmatoff 1949–50, 261–63). I will use a
slightly altered version of the Kogi classification to classify the Tairona
musical effigy figurines. For example, because none of the Tairona flutes
resemble insects, that Kogi group is not used; an additional group, bipeds, is added; and turtles are placed into the worm group.

Several of the Tairona animals represented by the musical effigy figurines fall within the Kogi worm group, including the snake, lizard or cayman, fish, snail, frog or toad, sea creature, and turtle. The animals within
this group are, according to the Kogi, generally aquatic and cold-
blooded. Similarly, they are considered to be ugly, but have special qualities because they symbolize the male sexual organ. They are animals with
"a magical, mysterious, and somewhat obscene character" (Reichel-Dolmatoff 1949–50, 261).

Many of the Tairona animals fall within the bird group of the Kogi,
including birds in their many positions of flying or sitting. Bats also be-
long to this group. Like worms, birds also symbolize the penis according
to the Kogi, especially those with long beaks or the color red (or both).
Bats, placed in a subcategory with night birds, are considered malicious
and have an association with death and misfortune.

The large group of quadrupeds is divided into wild and domestic animals. The Kogi consider the animals of the cat, deer, rodent, and fox
families to be especially important, as well as four-legged animals with
shells. From the Tairona musical effigy figurines, the coati, jaguar, monkey, mouse, opossum, and turtle can be included. While the deer is im-

portant to the Kogi, none of the Tairona ceramic objects includes that animal.

Finally, because of the large number of musical effigy figurines with two legs, I include an additional category: (natural and stylized) bipeds. Table 10.2 lists all subcategories of worm, bird, quadruped, and biped musical effigy figurines that I studied, arranged according to the Kogi animal taxonomy. For my iconographic analyses I have chosen representative examples from each of the main categories.

Worm Group. I have selected for analysis three musical effigy figurines that I place into the worm category: a double-headed snake, a frog or toad, and a turtle.

The double-headed snake instrument (see fig. 5.1) is circular with a head at each end of the body. Each highly stylized snake (crocodile?) head contains a fipple flute mouthpiece with one main air duct that branches off into each of the mouths of the snake's two heads. The window of each mouthpiece is at the throat of each head, and the snake's body is divided into left and right chambers with one fingerhole per chamber (these parts of the snake's body are separated by a partition within the tube). The instrument can, therefore, produce two tones simultaneously (listen again to audio track 11).

According to Wilbert, who is writing in general about South America, the snake is one of the most common symbols of fertility, life, death, and rebirth: "The symbolic meaning of snakes varies from place to place, but, if one may generalize, on the whole it is ambiguous, symbolizing good and evil, life and death, etc. The snake's identification with fecundity and perennial life is generally assumed to be due to its striking habit of periodically shedding its skin, and with it—so it is widely believed—old age and death. Seemingly in possession of the secret of eternal life, the snake became the hoped-for companion of the shaman as he entered upon the cure of the patient" (1974, 91). The Kogi also paradoxically believe the snake to be immortal, because through molting it rejuvenates itself, while at the same time it is a symbol of death (Reichel-Dolmatoff 1949–50, 269). Two-headed snakes are found in the mythologies of ancient Americans, from the Moche of Peru to the Aztec of Mexico. Among the ancient people of Mexico, Hommel writes, "the two-headed serpent is found as a fertility symbol worn by the maize goddess" (1969, 12).

The Tairona dragon-like snake heads seen in this circular flute may actually be those of crocodiles or caymans (see chapter 9), about which

Table 10.2. Kogi animal classification and Tairona musical effigy figurines

Kogi	Tairona	Number of items
A. Worms:	Worms:	16 total
snake	snake	2
lizard	lizard	2
fish	fish	2
frog	frog	6
toad	–	–
shrimp	sea creature (?)	2
lobster	–	–
worm (*lombrice*)	–	–
churrusco (?)	–	–
general aquatic animals	aquatic turtle	2
B. Birds (including bat):	Birds (including bat):	97 total
with prominent beak (toucan, heron, woodpecker, hummingbird)	with prominent beak	1–40 (?)
red	–	–
owl	owl	4
bat (leaf-nosed and vampire)	bat	32
hunting type with curved beak	curved beak	13
–	regular beak	1–40 (?)
–	stylized (jaguar head)	8
C. Quadrupeds (only jungle animals):	Quadrupeds:	29 total
tigres (tigers, meaning jaguar, puma, *tigrillo* or small wild cat)	jaguar	19
deer (includes the *guatinaja*, a large gnawing animal)	–	–
rat (includes the squirrel)	mouse	7
fox	opposum or coati	2
animals with a shell	–	–
oso (bear, generally grouped with the *tigres*)	monkey	1
D. Insects:	Insects (none)	–
house-type (flea, cockroach, scorpion)	–	–
butterfly	–	–
fly and mosquito	–	–
social-type (ant, bee, wasp)	–	–
E. –	Bipeds (normal or stylized)	78 total

Labbé writes: "Although the dragon may be modeled after a cayman, its meaning in the iconography of Colombia, Panama, and parts of Costa Rica appears to be related to the shamanic concept of *tinguna*, an emanation of power or energy from the 'soul body' of a shaman or supernatural shamanic being. *Tingunas* are often portrayed in the prehispanic art of Central Panama as serpentine projections with cayman-like heads" (1998, 43). The dual nature of the two-headed snake-cayman-dragon has been further interpreted by Donald Lathrap (1975), whose descriptions of cayman mythology I presented in chapter 9 with regard to the cayman iconography on Sinú tubular flutes. Labbé continues Lathrap's interpretations with a description of reptile dualism: "This dual-natured deity is at one and the same time the phenomenal universe we experience and the source of all things within it (Lathrap 1975, 56–57). . . . Since all phenomena result from the interaction and dynamic tension between these two complementary forces, it is in this sense that the two caymans are the source of all things and are conjoined. Their polar aspects, sky (male) and water-underworld (female), derive from an underlying oneness. The dynamic current engendered by their interaction is what is called fertility, and a prime role of the shaman is to act as the guardian of fertility" (1998, 44).

The next musical effigy figurine type represents a frog or toad with two fingerholes and one fipple mouthpiece, with a blowhole on top of the animal's head and a window underneath, by the animal's throat (audio track 38). All the Tairona frog or toad examples are very realistically designed; each is tailless and has bulging eyes, a big grinning mouth, and a ridge down its back outlining the spinal column (fig. 10.13). It is not clear if the animal represented in Tairona iconography, however, is a frog or a toad, and the distinction is perhaps an important one because "the frog lives only in the water, while the toad lives on both the land and in the water, making the toad a transitional animal" (Seibold 1992, 174). Such transition is important in the central Andes about which Seibold is writing because the toad is associated with the start of the rainy season. Like snakes, both frogs and toads are also important symbols of rebirth because of their metamorphosis from an aquatic fishlike creature to an air-breathing amphibian (Wilbert 1974, 95). In addition, certain frogs are extremely fecund and have a rapid gestation period when environmental conditions are wet enough. Wet conditions are found in the lowlands where the Tairona lived, but are not as frequent in the highlands of the

10.13. Tairona ceramic frog or toad globular duct flute with two fingerholes. Length 11 cm, width 4 cm, circumference 12.8 cm. Field Museum of Natural History Collection, Chicago.

Santa Marta sierra where the Kogi live. Nevertheless, among the Kogi the frog is metaphorically associated with fertility—it is symbolic of the female sexual organ in "its aggressive state"; as the frog devours worms so the vagina devours the penis, say Kogi men, who view the frog with disgust (Reichel-Dolmatoff 1949–50, 268). Could the frog or toad musical effigy figurines of the Tairona have been used as individual totemic guardian spirits providing protective powers for females? Or could they have been used as individual musical fertility amulets?

Perhaps supporting the magical protection hypothesis is the natural repellent of some frogs. Wilbert (1974, 95) explains that certain Central American and South American frogs belonging to the family Dendrobatidae secrete powerful poisons. Some native people apply such toxins to their weapons. A Tairona individual may have believed it possible to capture the frog's poisonous defensive character with the use of a frog musical effigy figurine. Another interpretation for the protection quality of a frog is based on its nearly invisible nature due to its excellent camouflage within jungle vegetation. One of the Tairona frog figurines, for example, has its head down and its body low, as if it were hiding. This ability to remain motionless and to blend into nature recalls how Kogi children, when confronted by strangers (potential dangers), grin and remain completely still and silent.

The realistic turtle-shaped musical effigy figurine seen in figure 10.5 has four fingerholes, and as a musical instrument, it sounds like all the other globular flutes with four fingerholes (audio track 39). Because of the turtle's aquatic nature, it is related to the frog and toad; like them, it may be important in a type of water ideology. Moreover, because of its carapace, the turtle is a natural symbol for magical protection.

Bird Group. Among the musical effigy figurines of the Tairona, there is an abundance of animals in the bird category, many of them within the subdivision of "flying birds" with extended wings forming a crescent (see figs. 10.1 and 10.2). Generally, each bird wing possesses two fingerholes while the tail contains a fipple mouthpiece (the blowhole is at the very tip of the tail and the window is at the bottom of the bird's body). The head and neck of the bird are solid. Most exemplars of realistic birds include incised neckbands to indicate extravagant plumage; their beaks are prominent, a characteristic that is symbolic of the phallus and fertility among the Kogi. Some of the regular bird figurines have small or hooked beaks, the latter being a characteristic of hunting birds, which tear apart the flesh of their prey with their sharp beaks. In many parts of the world "the bird has been a symbol of spiritual transcendence from time immemorial" (Wilbert 1974, 33). As an animal that traverses two planes, land and sky, it is a symbol of shamanistic power.

Musically, the Tairona bird ocarinas are capable of a wide range of pitches. The smaller flying birds naturally have higher pitch possibilities (audio track 40) than the larger and rounder flying birds (audio track 41). Some of the flying birds have sharp beaks and extravagant plumage, while others have short beaks and little indication of plumage. It is difficult to identify the types of birds modeled by the Tairona, which may range from doves with low pitches to songbirds with high pitches.

The figurine seen in figure 10.6 is a small standing bird with elaborate plumage. Musically it is unique because it has six fingerholes, making it capable of a wide range of pitches (audio track 42). The distal end of this globular flute is open, allowing it to function as a seventh fingerhole.

The many musical effigy figurines that are a combination of bird and jaguar (or cayman) have perhaps an even greater magical protection quality because of the cosmic power of the jaguar. These ocarinas (three examples are shown in fig. 10.2) feature almost reptilian heads, similar to other ceramic and gold Tairona figurines shaped as a stylized jaguar deity. Besides the bulging eyes and the many bared teeth, the tail of the bird-jaguar (cayman) ends in monstrous double heads. In addition, these (and other stylized Tairona figurines) include many geometric designs with unclear meaning: "Unfortunately, we lack the necessary insights to unlock the meaning of the non-representational designs . . . remembering only . . . that no primitive artist ever made a meaningless design" (Wilbert 1974, 102). Although the bird-jaguar (cayman) ocarinas contrast the plain bird ocarinas because of their elaborate designs and juxtaposition of dissimilar animals, their melodic capabilities and sound (audio track 43) are very similar to the sounds produced on the realistic bird instruments (compare with audio track 41).

A musical effigy figurine in the shape of a flying bird with a superimposed bat on its top shows that the Tairona, like the Kogi, categorized bats with birds (see fig. 10.3). This instrument, like the flying bird ocarinas, has four fingerholes situated on the wing portions of the artifact. The bat itself is superimposed on the ocarina with its head at the mouthpiece end and its body and rear feet on the large crescent. Most of the bat musical effigy figurines, however, are completely designed as that animal. With only two fingerholes, they are very small, some shaped as seated bats with wings folded (see fig. 10.8) and others as flying bats with their wings open. All the bats feature ferocious faces with bared teeth.

A unique Tairona globular flute features a leaf-nosed bat's head fused onto a human body (fig. 10.14). As if describing this very Tairona artifact, Wilbert writes, "By combining the vampire's blood-seeking teeth and the leaf-nosed bat's aggressive air with a human body, the Indian artist succeeded in creating a powerful symbol of numinous qualities" (1974, 102).

The leaf-nosed bat (*Lonchophylla handleyi*) is one of the most commonly portrayed bats in the native art of Latin America, along with the vampire bat. "Leaf-nosed bats grow an erect and fleshy 'leaf' from the tip of their nose, a membrane which has been linked to spearheads, swords,

10.14. Tairona ceramic globular duct flute in stylized human shape with leaf-nosed bat face (listen to audio track 44). Length 12.5 cm, width 10.5 cm, back of head to tip of nose 4.5 cm. Galería Alonso Collection, Bogotá.

and, in the case of Mexican picture writing, to flint knives. This leaf, together with the alert eyes and big upright ears, give leaf-nosed bats a certain fierce en garde appearance" (Wilbert 1974, 55). In spite of the elaborate designs of this artifact, its musical capabilities are similar to other Tairona globular flutes with four fingerholes (audio track 44).

Although some non-Western cultures, including the Kogi, associate the bat with negativism, darkness, and death, many ancient South American peoples exalt the animal as the epitome of duality and transformation (Wilbert 1974, 55). As such, the bat is associated with power, and its fierce appearance gives it protective powers for the individual.

Quadruped Group. Tairona musical effigy figurines in the Kogi quadruped category include fierce-looking animals with jaguar features and nonaggressive animals with natural composures. It is no accident that jaguar symbolism emphasizing ferocious fangs seems to dominate Tairona art. Among the Kogi the jaguar (*Felis onca*) is an important shamanistic animal (Reichel-Dolmatoff 1949–50, 265), and the Kogi consider themselves and their ancestors to be the jaguar people. Reichel-Dolmatoff (1975a, 45) explains that the Kogi reserve special feline names for people of importance, as he writes: "The Kogi name for jaguar is *nebbi* (*nabi*), and the root *neb-*, *nem-*, or *nam-* occurs frequently in the names of mythical priests or chiefs, divine personifications, important mythical ancestors, and constellations of stars. Among the many names of mythical ancestors, most of whom are reported to have been chieftains or priests, we find *Namaku* (jaguar-lord), *Namsiku* (jaguar-man), *Namsaui* (jaguar-devourer), all of them referring explicitly to jaguar-people (*nebbi-kive*)."

While such feline attributes must have also existed among the Tairona, realistic jaguar representation in their musical effigy figurines is rare. Among the hundreds of musical effigy figurines examined, only one is shaped like a four-legged animal that slightly resembles a jaguar. It features a wide mouth showing many bared teeth; is incised with many geometric lines that emphasize the animal's eyes, nose, ears, and body; and has a curious mane that protrudes from the top of its head to the middle of its back. The mouthpiece blowhole is also at the top of the head, while the window is under the head and between the front legs, in the general vicinity of the animal's throat. Four fingerholes are situated on the figure's body, with two per side, and its musical capabilities are similar to other Tairona ocarinas (audio track 45). A small suspension hole pierces the jaguar's neck just beneath its ears.

In other Tairona jaguar representations, vertical animals (possibly masked humans) are seen, either standing on their hind legs or sitting. Jaguar-man or jaguar-god figurines that feature stylized jaguar faces with human bodies are quite common among the Tairona (they are discussed in detail under the biped group). Figures such as these are similar to the were-jaguars depicted in the art of the Andes and Mesoamerica. With these musical instruments a Tairona individual could possibly have secured the aid of the fearless jaguar, a jaguar ancestor, or a jaguar deity for magical protection against dangerous supernatural forces. The instruments also could have served as a sonic metaphor for an individual's magical transformation into a jaguar, much as wearing a jaguar skin served as a visual metaphor for the same purpose. It was reported by

Simón (cited in Reichel-Dolmatoff 1975a, 45), for example, that the Tairona wore robes made from the skins of jaguars.

Similar metaphors are also found among the Kogi, who employ jaguar masks that, with their protruding fangs, long mouths, and often protruding tongues, are apparent continuations of Tairona motifs (Reichel-Dolmatoff 1949–50, 265). As a part of their religion, the Kogi wear such masks while dancing with jaguar movements and sounds. The jaguar is not considered dangerous to the Kogi but is highly respected for its hunting prowess, its domination over other animals, and its mysterious and nocturnal habits. In other regions of western Latin America, such as Mexico, Central America, and the Andes, the jaguar "was symbolically linked with earth, fertility, night and moon, the Otherworld, and more indirectly with the Sun" (Wilbert 1974, 69).

The Tairona double instrument seen in figure 10.4 represents a mother opossum (*Didelphidae*) or coati (*Nasua* spp. [Legast 1987, 33]) and her baby. It is characterized by the mother animal, a three-fingerhole globular flute, carrying her baby, a smaller ocarina with two fingerholes, on her back. The tail of each animal functions as the air duct of each mouthpiece, while a window is under the base of each tail (audio track 46). In this artifact, the mother looks back at her offspring. Exterior details are minimal but realistic, including incised lines for the closed mouths, lines on the mother's neck to indicate the turning of her head, and circular lines around the legs and tails of both animals. What are the significant characteristics of opossums and coatis, relative to native belief systems and ocarina usage?

The opossum has an effective built-in defense mechanism: it defends itself by playing dead (Wilbert 1974, 82).[8] By lying on its side with its eyes closed and its tongue hanging out, and by giving off an unpleasant odor, the opossum fools its enemy. If the trick does not work the animal can also be a hardy fighter. By analogy, the opossum could have functioned as a guardian spirit for a particular Tairona individual who, with an opossum-shaped musical effigy figurine, could have acquired magical protection power from having it near and making it speak its musical voice.

The coati, related to the raccoon, gathers its food either on the ground or in the canopy of the trees in the rainforest. Having the capability to traverse these two worlds enables the animal to protect itself by eluding its predators. "It makes a constant whining sound, a possible reason that ocarinas were sometimes made in its image," writes Benson (1997a, 44).

The coati's constant whining may also be one of its protective manner-isms.

Biped Group. Bipeds constitute a large group of "animals" not distin-guished by the Kogi in their animal taxonomy (except as jaguar-men or jaguar-gods, as discussed above). Among the Tairona musical effigy figu-rines in this group, stylization occurs in many forms: anthropomor-phized tubular flutes, standing human globular flutes, jaguar-man or jag-uar-god globular flutes, seated man globular flutes, and others.

Anthropomorphic characterization occurs in Tairona tubular flutes with four fingerholes (see fig. 10.7), although because of the tubular shape of such flutes, human body features are very abstract. The most common human characterization includes arms bent upward at the elbow, either in a gesture of prayer or offering. The humanoid figures wear necklaces and high hats, etched into the clay. Like the Sinú flutes, the Tairona tubular aerophones are also duct flutes with fipple mouthpieces (audio track 48), and they have suspension holes, which probably enabled them to be car-ried around an individual's neck.

The standing human globular flutes have four fingerholes. The blow-hole of each duct mouthpiece apparatus is in the top of the figure's head, while the window is at the back of its neck (audio track 47). In the figu-rine pictured in figure 10.15, a human with a disfigured face is holding something in each hand, probably a bag of coca leaves in one and a con-tainer for *cal* (crushed limestone used as a catalyst to extract cocaine as the coca leaves are masticated) in the other. A human heart dangles around his neck, and his clothing includes a protruding hat and an ornate cape or coat with a checkered design in back. He appears to have a short tail, although the protrusion may be an extension of his cape or coat.

Numerous biped musical effigy figurines are crafted as human bodies with jaguar facial characteristics (fig. 10.16). Most prominently featured are jutting jaws that reveal sharp fangs, protruding ears, and beady eyes. The globular flute in figure 10.16 has two fingerholes and a duct mouth-piece (the blowhole is in the top of its head and the fipple is at the back of the neck and shoulder blade area) (audio track 49). This jaguar-man is wearing a long cape that is fastened around his neck, biceps, and head; forming a crown, his cape extends from his head and shoulders to the middle of his back. He also wears two side breechcloths attached at the waist, leaving his genitals exposed. With his arms outstretched, he ap-pears to be ready to attack any danger.

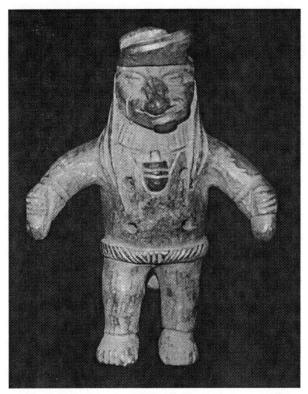

10.15. Tairona ceramic stylized man globular duct flute with a human-heart neck-lace (front view). Length 15 cm, width 10.4 cm, circumference 13.9 cm. Guillermo Cano Collection, Bogotá.

The most remarkable jaguar-man musical instrument of the Tairona, however, is a triple globular flute with three chambers and three mouth-pieces (see fig. 5.2). This artifact is shaped as a biped with enormous bi-ceps, each functioning as a chamber without fingerholes, while the torso is another chamber, with the navel functioning as a single fingerhole (the complex multiphonic sounds of this instrument are discussed in chapter 5 and heard in audio track 12). Armand Labbé also describes this figurine (pictured in Labbé 1998, 100, fig. 78), which he calls "figural whistle: priest in ritual attire": "The monumentality of this small figural sculpture is characteristic of Tairona art. The image of an anthropomorphic feline suggests a shamanic figure is intended. Powerful shamans were said to be able to transform their vital force spirit to take on the appearance of a jaguar."

The vast majority of Tairona musical effigy figurines with anthropomorphic characteristics possibly represent priestly personages; with zoomorphic faces (possibly masks) and large crescent headdresses (see fig. 10.10), they are perhaps sitting upon boats or crescent thrones. These globular flutes have four fingerholes (two on each half of the crescent), a blowhole at the top of the headdress, and a window at the back of the head. Musically, they sound similar to the flying bird figurines (audio track 50). Two types of crescents are observed: (1) plain, similar to the wings of the flying bird globular flutes, and (2) ornate, with the points of the crescent terminating in stylized reptile or jaguar heads. The elaborate incising on each biped suggests a feathered headdress, elaborate clothing, waistband, necklace, diadem, and large earlobe plugs. These are apparently representations of personages of great importance.

10.16. Tairona ceramic stylized man globular duct flute with jaguar face (listen to audio track 49). Length 12.2 cm, width 8.5 cm. Galería Alonso Collection, Bogotá.

Several scholars have offered interpretations of these elaborate pieces. Sam Enslow, for example, writes that such bipeds on crescents represent "*Caciques* [chiefs] riding in boats . . . , a common subject of Tairona art. The boats resemble in design the reed craft often associated with Lake Titicaca on the Peru-Bolivia border. Such craft would not be suitable for navigation in the many small streams and rivers of Santa Marta. The historical record fails to provide clues as to why boats of this design appear. There is no archaeological evidence to suggest a contact between the Tairona and the cultures of Peru and Bolivia. The people represented on the boats are generally referred to as *caciques*, but the description may be incorrect" (1990, 33). While the position of the human figures is not conducive for riding on boats (it would be a sidesaddle position rather than a straddling position), another piece (discussed below) does indeed seem to represent a human astride a watercraft. It is more likely that the majority of the ocarinas represents an important person seated on a throne or elaborate bench, as explained by Labbé:

> In the figural art of the Tairona the image of a dignitary seated on a double-headed dragon bench is a stock theme closely associated with ceramic *ocarinas*, multitonal musical instruments. Shown wearing an elaborate headdress, the central figure most likely represents the solar deity seated on his double-headed dragon bench, an image still used by the Kogi Indians in their mythology. At the base of the headdress is a band of complementary inverted triangles symbolizing fertility. Similar bands are seen on the figures in the Malagana style of the Calima region. The headdress itself appears to represent rays emanating from the head of the solar deity. In actual ritual these may have been symbolized by feathers. Framing the "rays" is a band containing two rows of dots. Dots were commonly used in pre-Columbian art to represent seeds, potential new life. Indians throughout the Americas viewed the sun as the source of life. The Aztecs of Mexico called the rays of the sun Xiucoatl or "fire-serpents," the life-giving "semen" of the sun. In Mesoamerican iconography the long split distended tongue is also associated with the sun. (1998, 35, cat. no. 13)

Another similar crescent-shaped ocarina depicts a personage seated upon a wing-shaped bench, about which Labbé explains: "Ceramic *ocarinas* in the form of a winged figure are peculiar to the Tairona culture. The incised decoration is highlighted by a white substance, the use of which may have had symbolic significance. The image of an anthropomorphic winged figure likely represents a shaman in 'soul flight.' Shamans were believed capable of leaving their bodies to fly about from place to place, including interdimensional travel to the 'Upper World' and 'Lower World.' Winged anthropomorphic personages are found over wide areas of South and Central America and are depicted in both the graphic and plastic arts" (1998, 32, cat. no. 9). These interpretations are valuable for the development of my hypothesis that these globular flutes had magical use. Labbé continues to explain the Kogi mythology of a similar personage: "In the belief system of the Kogi, the solar deity is described as sitting on a bench in the sky chewing coca, dispensing life in the form of sun rays. Elaborate dress and jewelry accentuate his high estate" (1998, 43). However, since ethnographic analogy with the Kogi offers no interpretative evidence of the significance of these globular flutes beyond that suggested by Labbé, I interpret them to be guardian spirit effigies because of their emphasis on zoomorphic facial characteristics that possibly indicate either a masked or transformed human (perhaps a priest, shaman, or both) or solar deity, which Labbé explains "was considered the First Shaman, the source of all subsidiary shamanic power" (1998, 44).

Another related category of crescent globular flutes is the cross-blown type (see figs. 10.11 and 10.12). Each of the ends of the crescent is open, and blowing across either end produces tones; pitch changes are created by closing and opening the distal end (the end of the crescent opposite the mouthpiece) as well as by using the two fingerholes. These are the only cross-blown flutes found among the Tairona, and my performance on them produced a variety of disjunctive pitches because of the complex fingering possibilities. A coca-chewing man on a boat (fig. 10.12), for example, is heard in audio track 51.

External designs on these unique musical effigy figurines feature stylized bipeds and quadrupeds, each abreast or seated on a crescent, reminiscent of the Moche totora-reed boats. To argue that these are representations of water craft, however, is conjectural, although the artifact in figure 10.12 appears to depict a coca-chewing male astride his "boat" with a "paddle" in hand.[9] Spirit boats are frequently found in shamanistic cultures, where supernatural boat trips are made for guardian spirit retrievals (Harner 1980, 91–94). These globular flutes could have functioned differently than those described above; that is, they could have been used for guardian spirit retrieval in addition to offering protection, as suggested by their unusual construction. In addition, several of these artifacts are two instruments in one; the figure seated on the crescent, for example, is a tiny fipple ocarina, although it was not playable because its mouthpiece duct was clogged (see fig. 10.11, second from right, and listen to audio track 52.)

Tairona Magical Protection

A careful examination of the mouthpieces of the Tairona musical effigy figurines and the positions of the creatures when they are played reveals that in most of the cases the mouthpiece air ducts are fabricated in such a way that the animals face the same direction as the performers. In this manner, each figurine and its voice (its music) are ahead of or in front of the performer and are, therefore, in a position to meet potential dangers before they reach the individual performer. In most of the musical instruments the musician must blow into the tail or back of the animal, causing the front of the animal to face away from the performer. In other instruments the air duct is in the top of the animal's head and once again the creature faces away from the musician because the instrument is held vertically, with the feet of the animal or human either down or facing out, away from the performer. In very few examples does the animal face the performer when the instrument is played. In the worm category, for example, frogs often have their backs toward the danger. These characterizations would seem to be realistic portrayals of the creatures in real life defense situations. While birds and mammals, for example, protect themselves with their beaks and teeth, frogs either flatten themselves down to blend in with their surroundings, or their backs emit poisons.

The iconology of the ancient musical instruments of the Tairona says a great deal about the fauna and its supernatural connections for that culture. When joined with ethnographic analogies, such as analyses derived from the Kogi and other native South American cultures that may have shared similar cultural characteristics, the musical instruments take on dimensions that are important in the native life-death cycle. It is very likely that these animal-shaped musical effigy figurines were individually used musical instruments having supernatural power, perhaps for personal protection.

Likewise, the globular flutes that depict a biped sitting upon or astride a bench, boat, or wings, and who "fits the ethnographic descriptions of the Kogi solar deity who sits in the heavens, radiating his life force in order to engender, nourish, and sustain life on earth" (Labbé 1998, 92), are perhaps also intended for personal use, such as magical protection and well being. Also included in this biped category are the numerous highly stylized standing figures. As a whole, all the Tairona globular and tubular flutes were perhaps types of guardian spirit musical effigy figurines, some for use by shamans or priests or both, and others for use by common people. They were all extraordinary musical instruments, on par for their musical craftsmanship with the highly cherished Tairona gold ware.

Part IV

≈

Conclusion

Sounding the Silent Flutes of El Dorado

I summarize the conclusions of my research by returning to the four categories that correspond to the four modes of inquiry presented in my methodological model, employed throughout this book. While these conclusions are derived from the data and interpretations presented throughout this study, only those based on the music archaeology mode of inquiry are made with confidence; many of the others must remain as speculations, suggestions, or at best plausible possibilities. Such is the nature of the discipline I have termed ethnoarchaeomusicology—only the music archaeology mode of inquiry can be quantified. As the study ventures into the other modes of inquiry, its qualitative analyses are basically interpretations. Nevertheless, it seems that the value of such interpretations lies in the fact that they provide a picture, whether blurred, hazy, reflective, or refractive. This is perhaps better than no picture at all.

Music Archaeology Mode of Inquiry

The following five conclusions are made with considerable certainty because of the scientific nature of the tonometric analysis methodology employed with the musical instruments themselves.

First, ancient South American musical instrument makers constructed their flutes with what they perceived as precise pitches or pitch relationships in mind. This standard of construction, of course, is based on the particular culture's own standard for precision, which can never be determined. Nevertheless, the music technology used to manufacture musical instruments with distinct melodic capabilities strongly suggests that particular pitches were chosen and preferred, for whatever purposes yet precisely unknown.

Second, while the pentatonic, or five-tone, scale may have existed in archaeological cultures, its predominance as the standard for South American archaeological cultures is not warranted. This is evidenced by the large variety of scales produced on archaeological flutes, making it impossible to establish any particular scale as being predominant. If any series of tones can be suggested as a standard, it would have to be a type of "thirdness" foundation interval. However, tonal measurements have shown that a wide variety of foundation intervals also exists.

Third, both single-unit panpipes and double-unit panpipes existed in ancient Peru, perhaps even within the same cultures. While it can be surmised that both types were played in ensembles, at least on occasion, the evidence is slim that the ensembles were as large as they have been known to be today. Nevertheless, ensemble panpipe playing as a performance technique definitely existed in the ancient Andes.

Fourth, some globular flutes, such as those with two or three chambers, are capable of producing multiple pitches simultaneously, indicating that their makers had advanced acoustical awareness and employed a high level of technology. When sounded together, the multiple pitches produce difference and summation tones that create beat frequencies of great acoustic intensity. This fact suggests that the globular flutes were not constructed haphazardly. Indeed, the proven practice of manufacturing ocarinas from molds by the Moche suggests that the musical potters had an awareness of predetermined acoustical properties.

Fifth, the ceramic globular and tubular flutes of ancient South America were *not* made in a manner that systematically related exterior motif with tone system structure, and there was no particular musical scale associated with a particular animal or other representation. This has especially been shown with the large sampling of Sinú flutes and Tairona musical effigy figurines.

Iconology Mode of Inquiry

Within this mode of inquiry, I make six conclusive statements with some confidence because of the scientific nature of the comparative and interpretative analysis methodology used, as applied to the musical instruments and the music iconographic representations themselves.

First, the musical instrument makers of ancient South America had a great concern for exterior detail (including shape and design) when they constructed their musical instruments and musical effigy figurines. The visual representation of human and animal figures (and combinations of these) was important to them, as was the aural representation. Although there was no apparent connection between the figure represented and musical variation, as concluded above, it was perhaps not the details of the musical sounds themselves (the product—i.e., the scales, intervals, etc.) that formed the bond between the visual and the aural, but rather the act of simply making the sounds (the process—i.e., the performance on the instruments).

Second, vertical flutes were possibly associated with shamanic transcendence, flights of ecstasy, and life-giving power. Analysis of the possible contexts within which musical events may have occurred suggests individual or group ritualistic use, or both, for notch flutes and panpipes in Peru.

Third, music iconology is a useful tool for determining forgery in musical effigy pottery. Specific knowledge of performance techniques with particular musical instruments (how they are held, body position relative to the instrument, etc.) can provide insight into whether or not a potter produced a true and realistic representative performance situation.

Fourth, panpipes were possibly symbols of transfiguration or death, or both. The panpipe musicians of the Moche can be seen on a physical-condition continuum from normal to death, suggesting a transfiguration theme.

Fifth, a possible context for panpipes and panpipe musicians from the southern coast of Peru may have been to musically provide magical protection for seafarers. This conclusion is reached because of the panpipe ensemble iconography on leeboards that were used on seaworthy balsa rafts among the southern coastal inhabitants.

Sixth, a possible context for transverse flutes on the north coast of Peru was an ancestor cult of the dead. This is suggested by an archaeological discovery by Santiago Uceda Castillo in the Moche Temple of the Moon of a wooden model representing a Chimú ceremonial plaza from Chan Chan in which transverse flute players are depicted. According to Uceda

Castillo, the modeled musicians are possibly performing their instruments during a death or ancestor ritual.

History Mode of Inquiry

This mode of inquiry is supported by ethnographic writings. Because of the possible biases of the chroniclers, only one tripartite conclusion is made: The ceramic vertical flutes of the Sinú were possibly employed for some type of ritual use involving water ideology, fertility, or male sexual aggression versus female sexual invitation (or any combination thereof). These three possible ritually inspired uses are respectively derived from the attitudes toward cayman and fish as reported in historical and ethnographic sources, the phallic shape of the instruments and the animals molded onto them, and their male physical symbolism versus their female whistle sound symbolism.

Ethnographic Analogy Mode of Inquiry

From this mode of inquiry, the most speculative of the four modes, I make the following four conclusions.

First, ancient Peruvian globular flutes or ocarinas were instruments that were possibly used for calling and communicating with the supernatural. The knowledge and opinions of Calderón and other curanderos from Peru's northern coast have led to this conclusion. Even though present-day Peruvian shamans use archaeological ocarinas for their curing rituals, a similar use for ocarinas in the archaeological cultures themselves is only a plausible possibility.

Second, a dichotomy between life giving and life taking presently found in northern Peruvian curing practices among shamans suggests the existence of a similar dichotomy among the ancient Moche (this is also supported by Moche iconography). This conclusion is also held by Christopher Donnan and Douglas Sharon, and its relevance for music is that ancient ocarinas, rattles, and sometimes conch shell trumpets are employed by present shamans, who place them on their curing altars (usually within the life-taking field). No Moche iconography, however, depicts such instruments being displayed on shaman's altars or being used during curing rituals, unless individual ceramic pots depicting ocarina players represent shamans in their life-giving or life-taking roles.

Third, some stirrup spout ceramic pots of the Moche were possibly used as repositories for the spirits (encantos and desencantos). This conclusion is also supported by Calderón, who points out the similarity to Catholic icons that are viewed as repositories for the Christian spirits, such as a statue of the Virgin Mary or a Roman Catholic patron saint.

Fourth, the importance given to magical protection against death among the Kogi suggests that the musical effigy figurines of the Tairona were used for magical protection. The elaborate totemic belief system of the Kogi and their attitudes toward life and death, plus the fact that the Kogi use Tairona ocarinas in their rituals, supports this conclusion.

While many of these latter conclusions are interpretative rather than scientific (i.e., they cannot be scientifically measured), they have been determined by the rigorous application of my methodological model for ethnoarchaeomusicological inquiry. Therefore, I consider them plausible possibilities that can provide other archaeomusicologists with comparative materials for future use.

Music of El Dorado and the Nature of Value

An important theme is woven throughout this book: the musically related artifacts from the realm of El Dorado must have been valued highly by the musicians or other people who used them. While in archaeology this statement may appear to be derived from a "psychological preference," that is, "using explanations based upon assumed states of mind of prehistoric people for which there is no direct evidence," Colin Renfrew continues to argue the following: "a concept like value [may be regarded] as belonging to . . . an 'emic' category: something existing primarily in the thoughts and minds of individual members of a given community. But value can also be an 'etic' category: something that acts upon the material world in a manner that can be observed and evaluated cross-culturally, for which the modern observer can therefore gather relevant material evidence" (1986, 143). So many topics and subtopics dealing with relevant material evidence have been studied in this book, however, that "the nature of value and the way in which it is appropriately conceptualized" must be clearly dealt with (Thomas 1991, 30). For example, we have seen that some instruments were played by mutilated or diseased men, others by death figures, and still others by elite priests or shamans; panpipes seemed to have been intentionally smashed into pieces, ocarinas were buried in graves next to the mouths of men or in burial urns, and flutes were suspended around musicians' necks; globular flutes were shaped like any number of animals or zoomorphized bipeds, tubular flutes were shaped like humans and fish, and fanged deities emerge from conch shell trumpets; tubular flutes emit extremely high-pitched sounds, some globular flutes produce piercing clusters of pitches, and other ocarinas produce wide ranges of sounds from high to midrange levels. These are all aspects of value; but how can value be measured? Thomas suggests the following three ways: (1) "artifacts can have peculiarly personal value arising from some association with an individual's biography"; (2) "a perception of value creation [is] a process . . . that effectively reveal[s] persons . . . and artifacts, animals, or other . . . items in particular ways"; and (3) as "a classical labor theory of value [in which certain things] can be understood as objectified labor" (1991, 30–33). While Thomas is primarily interested in objects as exchange items, his perceptions on value have a certain relevance to this study. Specific applications of his perspectives on value within the musical realm of El Dorado, however, are moot. Nevertheless, several possibilities come to mind.

While it is impossible to recreate complete biographies of individuals in archaeological cultures, and while it is equally impossible to know which individuals played musical instruments or used effigy pots in the past, archaeologists like Walter Alba and Christopher Donnan have suggested partial biographies of Moche kings and deities, such as the lord of Sipán and the fanged deity. By using Moche iconography, Donnan has carefully analyzed cultural contexts that include music and dance as performed by individuals in the service of such lords and gods. Likewise, Julio C. Tello, Helaine Silverman, and others have recreated partial biographies of Nasca priests and others who may have been involved with panpipe construction, performance, and destruction. However cursory these biographical attempts are, they do suggest a high value placed on rituals and their music.

Likewise, the level to which humans, animals, and sacred space are revealed as being musical or musically related says much about the value of music in the realm of El Dorado. Moreover, music and dance events can often be seen as processual, such as the Moche life-death continuum, the Moche dances of death, the Nasca panpipe procession, and the Tairona/Kogi animal taxonomy as a hierarchy (e.g., worm group to biped group) applied to musical instruments. If such temporal and spatial creations are viewed as process, then these and perhaps other examples reflect music value.

Karl Marx was the first to suggest a labor value of commodities in 1867: "As values, all commodities are only definite masses of congealed labor time" (in Renfrew 1986, 157). Certainly the construction of ceramic musical instruments and musically related artifacts is labor intensive. I cannot think of any ceramic musical instrument produced in ancient times that must not have required careful construction and intensive labor. A flute will not sound, for example, if its mouthpiece is not carefully constructed; beat frequencies will not have their effect if the two or more simultaneous tones are not precisely tuned; and panpipes played in ensemble must be precisely tuned. The labor involved is objectified and done with a purpose in mind—to make ritual music as the culture defined it. This is the highest value.

I now return to the value I consider to be the most important for understanding the music of El Dorado, stated earlier in a quote by Lawrence Sullivan: "Sound identifies and gives shape to societal values and structures" (1986, 15). In the above perspectives on value by Thomas and Marx, sound is merely suggested as a consideration; however, only until sound becomes a sonic phenomenon rather than a verbal one, can music as value truly be appreciated. I believe that the research presented in this book, coupled with the audio examples of the instruments themselves, have shown that music, musical instruments, and music making were highly valued in South American archaeological cultures. Within the realm of El Dorado, music was indeed the most exquisite of all things.

Glossary

aerophone. A musical instrument whose sound is usually produced by the vibration of a column of air within a tube that is activated by the musician's breath. *See* **flute; ocarina; whistle.**

antara (Quechua). A single-unit panpipe, found mostly in Peru.

aperture. *See* **window.**

arca. *See* **siku.**

beat frequency. An acoustical phenomenon that produces an interference wave when two tones (pitches) sound simultaneously and whose frequencies (measured in hertz, or vibrations per second) are very close together. Their particular sonic relationship produces a wavering tone that can be slow (like a vibrato) or fast (like a buzz), depending on the distance of the two tones. The term comes from the clash (beat) of the two sound waves, whose high and low points create interference.

blowhole. The open end of a duct mouthpiece apparatus into which the musician blows air directly.

bombo. A double-skin membranophone from the Andes, characterized by a deep cylindrical wooden body, rims, and lacing.

cents. A pitch-measuring system devised by Alexander Ellis in the late 1800s which divides an octave into 1,200 equal parts called cents. Each of an octave's twelve semitones (distance between two adjacent keys on a piano keyboard) is divided into 100 equal parts. Machines such as stroboscopes (Stroboconn and Korg tuners) register the cents of a pitch, and musicians often use such machines for learning how to play in tune. Stroboscopes that register in cents are used to measure precise pitches of musical instruments.

cents deviation. A scientific measuring of pitches that calculates how many cents flat or sharp a tone is from a standard (based on A = 440 Hz).

cipher notation. A musical notational system that uses Arabic numbers for the notes of a scale in Western countries and in China (do = 1, re = 2, mi = 3, fa = 4, sol = 5, la = 6, ti or si = 7). The middle range of the scale uses plain numbers; the second octave uses a dot above each number; and the octave below uses a dot beneath each number. A backward slash (\) through a number indicates a half step flat, and a forward slash (/) through a number indicates a half step sharp.

container idiophone. An idiophone whose sound is produced by materials (seeds, stones, or other small objects) that are placed within a container (gourd, calabash, ceramic vessel, cane tubes, etc.) and which strike the inside of the container when the container is shaken. *See* **container rattle.**

container rattle. Another term for *container idiophone.* The most common name for this instrument when it is made from or shaped like a gourd or calabash with a handle is maraca, a term borrowed from the Arawak or Tupi language.

cross-blown. Describing the type of ductless edge aerophone mouthpiece assembly that consists of an embouchure hole that is blown across directly by the musician, thus producing the sound. The Western orchestral flute is a cross-blown horizontal tubular flute.

difference tone. An acoustical principle whereby two tones (pitches) are played together, and their particular relationship produces a third tone that is the difference between the other two. The term comes from the mathematical process of subtracting the frequencies (hertz) of each of the two tones, and their difference equals the frequency of the third tone; for example, if a tone of 400 hertz is played on one instrument and a tone of 700 hertz is played simultaneously on another, a third tone of 300 hertz (the difference) will also be heard, even though only two instruments are being played.

distal end. The end of an aerophone that is most distant from the musician's mouth.

double-unit panpipe. A panpipe that consists of two halves, each half traditionally played by a separate individual (requiring two persons to play one instrument). *See* **panpipe; siku.**

drum. Usually a membranophone in Western cultures, although when preceded by an adjective it can also be an idiophone (steel drum), a container (oil drum), an auto part (brake drum), or a body part (ear drum). Thus, the term can be misleading unless the context is known.

duct fipple mechanism. Another term for duct fipple mouthpiece assembly, although the implication here is that the mouth is not employed as a source of air (as with whistling bottles). *See* **whistling bottle.**

duct fipple mouthpiece assembly. An assembly in which the musician blows into a mouthpiece duct or small tube, which channels the air and forces it against a small hole or window with a sharp edge. The forced air stream is split when it hits the sharp edge of the window, thus creating sound waves within the chamber or tube to which the duct is attached.

duct flute or ocarina. A tubular or globular flute with a fipple mouthpiece assembly.

ductless flute or ocarina. A tubular or globular flute without a fipple mouthpiece assembly; the former includes cross-blown, notch, and panpipe edge aerophones.

edge aerophone. Commonly called a flute in English; a wind instrument of any shape whose sound is produced by a thin stream of air that strikes an edge, whether duct or ductless.

embouchure. The formation of the musician's mouth (lips, teeth, and jaw) required to play a particular aerophone.

embouchure hole. A cross-blown hole or mouthpiece; the musician blows directly across the hole as if playing a Western transverse flute.

fingerhole. A small hole on most edge aerophones that, when covered and uncovered by a finger, respectively, lengthens or shortens the tube, causing a drop or rise in pitch.

fipple. A duct mouthpiece assembly, found on some tubular and globular flutes.

flute. An aerophone instrument of any shape whose sound is produced by a thin column of air that strikes an edge, whether duct or ductless. *See* **edge aerophone.**

foundation interval. The distance from the lowest pitch or principal tone to the next highest pitch on a musical instrument or in a musical performance, whether played, sung, or whistled. *See also* **interval; overall span interval.**

globular flute. An aerophone flute shaped as a globe or vessel whose sound is produced by a thin column of air that strikes an edge, whether duct or ductless. *See* **ocarina.**

hertz. A unit that expresses vibrations per second. Abbreviated Hz.

hocket. From the European (Latin) term *hoketus,* which referred to a technique of alternating vocal parts in the medieval era. Today *hocket* refers to the manner in which two (or more) instruments play a melody by interlocking or alternating their musical notes; siku pan-pipes play this way because they are double-unit instruments. *See* **siku.**

huancar (Quechua). A large membranophone used by the Inca people.

idiophone. An instrument whose sound is produced by the vibration of a hard surface that can be activated by a variety of means. *See* **container idiophone; container rattle.**

interval. In musical acoustics, the distance between any two notes. Intervals are generally named sequentially, as steps on a ladder: such as second, third, fourth, fifth, sixth, seventh, and the octave (these terms generally correspond to the white keys on a piano, from C to C, which is a major scale). An interval can be major or minor (the latter are one-half step lower [flat] than the former). An interval can also be microtonal if its distance is smaller than found on a piano. *See also* **cents.**

kena. *See* **quena.**

lip concussion aerophone. A trumpet-type of instrument where the sound is produced by the buzzing of the musician's lips into a cup-shaped mouthpiece or a hole.

membranophone. An instrument whose sound is produced by the vibration of a stretched skin that can be activated by a variety of means. *See* **bombo; drum; huancar; tinya.**

mode. A predetermined sequence of pitches that usually has cultural meaning and can create a mood for a particular culture.

mouthpiece. The end of the aerophone instrument into which the musician blows air. *See* **mouthpiece assembly.**

mouthpiece assembly. The precise configuration or assembly of parts that produces the sound on an edge aerophone. Each flute instrument type has a particular mouthpiece assembly that determines whether it is a duct flute, ductless flute, or notch flute (see Rawcliffe 1992, 60).

notch flute. A tubular flute with a mouthpiece assembly that consists of a U- or V-shaped notch cut into the top rim of the tube. *See* **quena.**

ocarina. An Italian and Spanish term for a globular or vessel flute. *See* **globular flute.**

octave. In musical acoustics, the distance between two notes one of whose frequencies is precisely double that of the other. For example, a tone with 200 hertz and another with 400 hertz are tuned to the octave. The term comes from the distance between eight successive pitches of a diatonic scale (from C to C on a piano, for example). An octave contains 1,200 cents. *See also* **cents; interval.**

overall span interval. The distance or span from the lowest pitch to the highest pitch on a musical instrument or in a musical performance, whether played, sung, or whistled. *See also* **foundation interval; interval.**

panpipe. A series of tubular ductless edge aerophones with closed ends (i.e., a series of closed tubes) and without fingerholes that are rafted together and blown across (*see* **antara; rondador; siku**). Some may have a second open or closed row that resonates but is not blown directly. A panpipe is either single-unit or double-unit. Bundle panpipes (where the pipes are bundled together rather than rafted) are rare in South America. *See* **double-unit panpipe; single-unit panpipe.**

pinkullo (southern Peruvian Quechua; also pinkillo, pinkollo, pingullo, and others). A tubular duct flute. Throughout the Quechua-speaking Andes this instrument has many orthographic and physical variations.

pipe and tabor. A one-person combination whereby a single musician plays a duct flute (usually with two or three fingerholes) with one hand and a drum with the other (the drum is suspended from the musician's shoulder, arm, or wrist).

pito (also **pitu;** Spanish, whistle). Generally a transverse cross-blown flute in the Andes; elsewhere also a vertical duct flute or a whistle.

principal tone. The lowest, or basic, pitch of any instrument, and the beginning of each ascending scale.

proximal end. The end of an aerophone that is the closest to the musician's mouth. *See* **mouthpiece.**

quena (also **kena;** from Aymara *kina-kina* or *quina-quina*). A tubular flute with a notch mouthpiece assembly and usually from three to seven fingerholes; common in the central Andes.

recorder. An English term for a tubular duct flute developed in the Renaissance. Recorders were introduced into South America by Jesuits. The term is occasionally used generically for *duct flute.*

roncador (Spanish, snorer). A tubular duct flute with three fingerholes played in pipe-and-tabor fashion by a single musician in the department of Ancash, Peru. It is called snorer because its sound is harsh, due to the manner in which the musician must overblow to obtain the required pitches.

rondador (Spanish, one who makes the rounds, i.e., a night watchman). A single-unit panpipe from Ecuador, characterized by a series of alternating unequal lengths of closed tubes rafted together, so named because it was played by the night watchmen who made their rounds in Quito during colonial times.

scale. An arbitrary sequence of pitches in ascending or descending order, as steps on a ladder, usually for analytical purposes. *See also* **tone system.**

siku (Aymara). A double-unit panpipe, found in southern Peru, Bolivia, northern Chile, and northern Argentina.

single-unit panpipe. A panpipe that consists of one part, played by one individual. *See* **antara; rondador.**

summation tone. An acoustical principle whereby two tones (pitches) are played together, and their particular relationship produces a third tone that is the sum of the other two. The term comes from the mathematical process of adding the frequencies of each of the two tones, and their sum equals the frequency of the third tone; for example, if a tone of 400 hertz is played on one instrument and a tone of 300 hertz is played simultaneously on another, a third tone of 700 hertz (the sum) will also be heard, even though only two instruments are being played.

tinya (Quechua). A small double-skin membranophone with a shallow wooden body and laces, found in Peru.

tone system. Another term for *scale,* an arbitrary succession of pitches on a musical instrument (or in a song) in ascending or descending order. *See also* **scale.**

tubular flute. An edge aerophone shaped as a tube whose sound is produced by a thin column of air that strikes an edge, whether duct or ductless. *See* **pinkollo; quena.**

whistle. A colloquial term in English for a small edge aerophone without great melodic possibilities because of a usual lack of fingerholes.

whistling bottle. A ceramic vessel (ancient or modern) which houses a duct fipple mechanism within its spout that produces whistle sounds when air passes through it; the air is activated either by human breath or by a sloshing of water that displaces the air and forces air through a fipple.

window. A square, rectangular, oval, triangular, or round hole (aperture) on the front or back of a duct flute mouthpiece assembly, a few centimeters from the proximal opening of the duct into which the musician blows. The distal end of the window contains the sharp edge against which the thin ribbon of air emanating from the musician's mouth and into the duct hits and is split, causing the edge aerophone to produce a sound.

Notes

Chapter 1

1. Throughout this book I attempt to refrain from using such Western terms as *flute* (unless qualified with an adjective such as *notch* and *duct*) and *whistle*, because of what they mean in English. I will use the word *whistle* only when it is found in secondary sources about many of the cultures studied in this book. The term *globular flute* (sometimes called ocarina, an Italian word, or vessel flute), which can be either a duct or ductless instrument, subsumes the so-called whistle type. *Whistle* usually refers to a globular (or vessel) flute without fingerholes. To be consistent and eliminate any ethnocentric bias concerning its simplicity of construction, I prefer to call such an instrument a globular flute without fingerholes. No fingerholes versus several, for example, is not a criterion for complexity.

Likewise, I have refrained from using current Andean indigenous terms for ancient instruments, unless reference is made specifically to those instruments as ethnographic specimens. My reason for rejecting the continuous use of Aymara and Quechua terms for ancient instruments is the same as for my rejection of the English terms: they refer to a particular type of instrument in each language, and we do not know (except for the Inca, who spoke Quechua) what the ancient Andean peoples called their instruments.

Chapter 2

1. The conference, held April 18–19, 1998, was organized by Jeffrey Quilter, director of Pre-Columbian Studies, and Dorie Reents-Budet. My paper for that conference was entitled "Borrowing from Ethnoarchaeology: The Usefulness and Validity of Ethnographic Analogy in 'Ethnoarchaeomusicology': An Application to the Tairona of Northern Colombia."

2. Although Peter Crossley-Holland (1980, 34–35) refers to these as "paired fingering" and "closed fingering," I prefer to use the terms "Q'ero method" and "Warao method," because the other terms are confusing. Although "paired finger-

ing" is clear, "closed fingering" is not, since all fingerings are based on the closing and opening of a musician's fingers.

3. *Etic* and *emic* can be explained in the simplest way as forms of analysis borrowed from linguistics (Kenneth Pike) and anthropology (Marvin Harris): *etic* means studied from outside the culture and *emic* means studied from within (Headland 1990, 22).

Chapter 3

1. In Venezuela, an archaeological bone flute with a notch mouthpiece was discovered near the lower Orinoco River, pertaining to the La Cabrera style in Venezuelan archaeology (pictured in Cruxent and Rouse 1958, pl. 38A). It has a U-shaped notched mouthpiece with rounded corners, and three fingerholes.

2. "Así mismo, las quenas que resonaban en torno a los muertos en el ceremonial indígena, probablemente no tenían intención luctuosa, sino, eran hechizos de vida y resurrección."

3. "connotación fálica del instrumento, cuya voz mágica derrota a la muerte y promueve la vida."

4. See Donnan 1975 for a discussion of the thematic approach to iconology.

5. Benson (1975, 117, fig. 10), for example, incorrectly calls trumpets quena flutes; Harcourt and Harcourt call strings of seeds rattles ("un personnage qui agite, en guise de grelots, des grains enfilés") (1925, 2, pl. 2), while Jiménez Borja wisely says of them, "It is not possible to say with certainty if they are traders poised in the act of trading, or musicians playing strung rattles" ("No es posible decir con certeza si ellos son traficantes en actitud de ofrecer mercancía o músicos sacudiendo sonajas enfiladas") (1951, pl. 1). Donnan calls the same artifacts "Individual[s] holding strands of espingo seeds," and writes the following about the seeds: "Although Eduardo uses espingo seeds to cure supernatural disorders, a sixteenth-century Spanish account tells of their use for stomachaches, hemorrhages, and other illnesses. The Indians also used them as offerings for their idols, shrines, and sacred objects" (1976, 101).

6. "Esta flauta se tañe a tiempo que comienzan las grandes lluvias. . . . Antes de tañer el instrumento se remoja en chicha, alcohol o agua. La coincidencia de estas fiestas con la llegada de las aguas y el ceremonial del remojo de la madera antes de labrarla y del instrumento antes de tañer es muy significativa."

Chapter 4

1. Paracas may be the earliest phase of Nasca, although archaeologists are not in agreement about the relation between the two. Its name is derived from the cemetery Paracas Necropolis, which is situated on the peninsula of Paracas in the department of Ica (Cáceres Macedo 1985:32).

2. "Lo importante del estudio de las antaras de esta tumba es que los sonidos de todas ellas estaban interrelacionados; como si todas las antaras hubieran per-

tenecido a un conjunto instrumental, muy parecido a como actualmente los *sicuris* aymaras acostumbran a organizar—para hacer música—sus antaras de caña, que llaman *sicus*. Se reunen grupos de dos o mas pares de ejecutantes, hasta a veces conformar grandes conjuntos en los que cada uno, en su *sicus,* tiene parte de la gama de sonidos de su escala musical."

3. "Es probable que para los mochicas el sexo significara creación, multiplicación de seres vivientes y fuente de vida, no únicamente sensualidad y mucho menos pornografía. Tal vez los mochicas intentan a su manera, con su abundante imaginería, expresar su preocupación por estos temas. También suponemos que el sexo, la vida y la muerte fueron una tríada inseparable para los mochicas y que, por ello, en sus imágenes los situaron en constante diálogo."

4. "del pellexo hizo tambor y de la cauesa mate de ucuer chicha y de los guesos antara."

5. "Estas flautas de huesos humanos, al igual que los tambores de piel humana, no debieron ser ordinarios instrumentos de música. Antes bien, considerando la impregnación de las partes: huesos, piel etc. por las esencias del todo, la voz en ellas debió ser tenida como algo vivo."

6. "La antara procedente de Sallaq Urcos, . . . se compone de 4 tubos de: 28, 27, 25 y 24 c. de longitud respectivamente. Los tubos están reunidos por una pita y brea fromando una sola hilera, muy firme. Uno de los tubos, el más largo, lleva en su extremo inferior varias vueltas de un hilo de lana blanca y un grabado en la caña, que representa una cruz. Este tubo no se toca pues trae la mala suerte a la comunidad; de modo tal que la antara solo tiene 3 tubos útiles. El 'cañari' funcionario encargado de tocar esta antara recorre desde muy temprano los caminos y las calles de la población. La voz de la flauta convoca a los campesinos a la ciega de trigo. Esta es la misión de la antara."

7. Alain Gheerbrant, editor of *The Royal Commentaries of the Inca*, writes the following about who the Collas were: "The Collas, often confused with the Aimaras, were in early Inca times a much more important tribe than the Incas, to the south of whose territory they lived, near Lake Titicaca. They are regarded by some authors as the heirs of the last Tiahuanaco culture. The absence of supporting documents makes any hypothesis as to their origin subject to the greatest caution" (Garcilaso de la Vega [1609] 1966, 84).

Chapter 5

1. A beat frequency can be defined as the phenomenon that occurs when two pitches "of equal amplitude and nearly equal frequency are sounded together, [creating in the listener an awareness] . . . of a single sound having definite pitch whose frequency is the average of the frequencies of the two original sounds, and whose loudness grows and shrinks with a frequency equal to their difference" (Benade 1960, 77). The growing and shrinking loudness, or "beats," occur when "two simple harmonic forces of slightly different frequencies get in and out of

step" (i.e., when their sound wave patterns are out of phase) (78). A difference frequency occurs when a pitch of frequency x is sounded together with a nearby pitch of frequency y (e.g., a third above or below). A third pitch is heard, the difference tone, which vibrates (vibrations or cycles per second, indicated as cps or Hz [hertz]) to the number of vibrations per second that is the difference between x and y. For example, if a pitch at 2000 Hz sounds with one of 1700 Hz, the difference tone vibrates at 300 Hz. Thus, "with loud sounds coming in, we can distinguish not only the two separate incoming sounds, but also a new note at the difference frequency. The two incoming sounds can be quite far apart in pitch and still produce a 'difference note'" (Benade 1960, 82–83). The cents measurements of the pitches used in this study have been made with a stroboscopic frequency meter (Stroboconn 6T5); these in turn have been converted into frequencies (Hz) using a logarithmic table.

    2. "Vasijas-silbato, ovoides zoomorfas, Chancay (Hacienda Lauri). Estos instrumentos fueron destinados a la interpretación musical colectiva. Cada músico ajecutaba en una vasija dos o tres notas de la melodía, apelando a un juego mecánico muy similar al que hoy usan los 'sikuris' del altiplano. La sonoridad de cada vasija está sujeta a sus dimensiones."

    3. "un pito de huaca, una ocarina para llamar a las huacas. La huaca chililí, ha huaca del sol, la huaca de la luna, la huaca boquerona, la huaca prieta, la huaca del gallinazo, la huaca rajada y todas las huacas que hay en el norte. O sea que a todos los gentiles se les llama con ese pito, con esa ocarina. En sus dos tonos, en la noche, se ajusta, se cuenta y vienen los gentiles."

Chapter 6

    1. "Figuras tan disímiles como, por ejemplo, las de seres humanos, felinos, monos, patos or loros emiten sonidos muy parecidos."

    2. "Emulando a los sacerdotes-astrónomos y constructores, los sacerdotes-músicos tenían un profundo conocimiento de su arte y de los fenómenos de la acústica. Se pueden citar como ejemplos los ingeniosos Vasos Silbadores, que más que instrumentos musicales se antojan ser objetos rituales o mágicos o exvotos a deidades relacionadas con la música. Este artefacto consiste de dos vasos de barro unidos por un tubo, uno de ellos está cerrado con un adorno zoomorfo o antropomorfo al cual se le adapta un silbato. El otro vaso tiene su abertura libre por el cual se medio llena con agua y al moverse o inclinarse el agua es impulsada dentro del vaso cerrado y al aumentar el volumen del agua ésta comprime el aire y lo envía a través de la embocadura del silbato produciendo un sonidito prolongado y sugerente que sorprende por su belleza y procedencia. Es fácil imaginarse la impresión que causaría al pueblo el 'canto mágico' del vaso silbador en la penumbra del . . . templo al moverlo o inclinarlo el sacerdote."

Chapter 7

1. "La flûte traversière n'y a été signalée nulle part."

2. "El uso de flautas traverseras entre los antiguos peruanos ha sido puesto en duda."

3. "De este modo, la muerte y los muertos tuvieron vida propia: ellos bailan, festinan, se 'reproducen,' de la misma manera que en el mundo de los vivos."

Chapter 8

1. I gratefully thank Dr. Christopher B. Donnan, professor of anthropology at UCLA, former director of the Museum of Cultural History, and head of the Moche Archive, for his collaboration, inspiration, and provision of many of the photographs used in this chapter. I also thank Dr. Douglas Sharon, a Canadian anthropologist, UCLA colleague, curator of the Museum of Man in San Diego, and the foremost scholar of Moche curing, for his letter of introduction to Eduardo Calderón in 1974 and his willingness to provide me with a color photograph of Calderón's mesa.

2. "los instrumentos que frecuentemente se observan en estos contextos son, los idiófonos de sacudimiento, los de vaso con o sin agarradera. . . . No se encuentran instrumentos aerófonos ni membranófonos. . . . En las prácticas actuales, las sonajas con mango y silbatos son usadas. . . . Si se considera que las prácticas de medicina tradicional sustentan orígenes desde épocas prehispanas, entonces el sentido con que se usaron dichos instrumentos debió ser, sino igual, al menos parecido."

3. "Cada chamán tiene su silbo; cada Escuela, mejor dicho. La Escuela Norteña de Ferreñafe, de Punto Cuatro, de Salas y Penachí, de Chontalí. Ellos allí tienen sus silbos especiales que se llaman tarjos—cantos, inclusive. Canciones para cada actividad; tienen que llevar una canción específica, o sea su tarjo. Para amor, por ejemplo, un tarjo, un silbido. Para lucha, otro silbido; para curar, para rastrear; así, en fin, toda una serie."

"En realidad el silbido o canto se usa para el acto de meditación y concentración, para proyectarse después en el problema que se trata de encontrar o cuya solución se busca. Ahí es cuando uno puede crear con la mente una serie de cosas y llegar al punto que busca; con el silbido y la fuerza mental que en ese momento ocurre en el acto de la meditación. Eso es tradicional; todos los curanderos tienen que hacer su silbo, ponerse en contacto, en trance."

4. "La música juega un papel importante en la chamanería. Las octavas del sonido son importantes; también las del color. La octava de color es la secuencia dentro de su intensidad percibida tanto por el oído como por la vista para armonizar los chacras del hombre. En lo del color, entra en juego y depende del temperamento de cado uno. Hay los que son amarillos, otros verdes, otros azules. Depende del astral de cada uno. Eso es lo importante."

5. Calderón's understanding of the chakra concept differs slightly from the new age understanding. The following summaries are from the Internet website for Holistic Healing,
http://healing.about.com/health/healing/library/blterms chakras.htm
and are for the purpose of making a comparison between Calderón and current ideas about the concept. Holistic Healing provides the following information about chakras.

Definition: energy centers that are the openings for life energy to flow into and out of our aura. Their function is to vitalize the physical body and to bring about the development of our self-consciousness, and they are associated with our physical, mental, and emotional interactions.

Chakra 1, Sacral = Red. This chakra is the grounding force that allows us to connect to the earth energies.

Chakra 2, Sacral = Orange. A well-functioning second chakra helps one to maintain a healthy yin-yang existence.

Chakra 3, Solar Plexus = Yellow. This intuitive chakra is where we get our "gut instincts" that signal us to do or not to do something.

Chakra 4, Heart = Green. Physical illnesses brought about by heartbreak require that an emotional healing occur along with the physical healing.

Chakra 5, Throat = Sky Blue. The healthfulness of the fifth chakra is in relation to how honestly one expresses himself or herself.

Chakra 6, Third Eye = Indigo. Achieving the art of detachment beyond "small-mindedness" is accomplished through developing impersonal intuitive reasoning.

Chakra 7, Crown = Violet/White. This chakra is often pictured as a lotus flower opening to allow spiritual awakening in an individual.

6. "La Mesa tiene que ser de noche, porque la noche es más importante, por la razón de que los espíritus encarnados están en descanso. En el momento del descanso uno hace la apertura del subconsciente, por el principio de transitoriedad, o sea abre su frecuencia para captar y emitir sus ondos, sus vibraciones. Y justamente en la noche, cuando uno está en descanso, se opera eso."

7. "es una *tutuma* horadada por el medio con una manija de palo de chonta y alrededor de toda la chungana hay incisiones que son dibujos esotéricos y místicos, y huecos para tener sonoridad. La chungana lleva al centro semillas de chira, cuentas de lapislázuli, pedernal y turquesa, para que tenga sonido en la noche y salga como chispa de fuego. Ese sonido se usa para llevar el ritmo del canto del silvo que tiene su influencia, su poder de abstracción a la persona."

8. "tradicionalmente las hay con figuras de lechuzas, serpientes, genios y dioses; de auquis también. La figura de animal que más se ve es la de la lechuza; a veces son dos, lechuzas dobles, gemelas. La lechuza es el símbolo de la sabiduría, de la Ciencia Hermética. Las figuras de las chunganas ya no se usan tradicionalmente. Al menos yo no las he visto. . . . Yo a la mía le he puesto figuras, grabados, símbolos. La cruz, el símbolo del espiral, la firma de los tres ángeles de luz, el sol

y la luna, el Espíritu Santo, el tríptico del triángulo; y así. Y yo procedo así porque he estudiado y lo creo conveniente. A ningún otro chamán le he visto usar esas cosas; quiero decir, las que yo he ideado y dispuesto. En fin, es mi modalidad, mi manera de proceder."

9. "Los que son muy tradicionales usan un tamborcito; eso es por lo general en la sierra; en la costa no. Aquí, maraca no más, chungana; chungana de bronce, de huaca; chungana de tutuma o chungana de barro cocido."

10. According to Cáceres Macedo (1985, 30), the term *Vicus* is used for this culture from the department of Píura, north of the Moche valley, because that is the name of the cemetery site where most of the pottery was found.

11. "Después tenemos esta concha que está ajustada con la cuenta de San Juan Bautista, o sea que es una concha para el bautisterio, con agua bendita. Y aqué [*sic*] hay una conchita que está ajustada con la Virgen del Rosario, para dar las tomas, una especie de platito."

12. "En medio tenemos una pequeña concha de abanico que se llama *Mano para Servir*, juntamente con otra concha, una moradilla, que la uso solamente yo, el maestro. Al lado derecho está una chungana."

13. "Ahora el lado negativo, el ganadero, el de la Magia Negra. Comencemos, como siempre, por la izquierda. Un caracol grande o un tritón, lo cual significa un rollo especial para el trabajo de recepción, de abstracción y desenvolvimiento de algún problema, de algún asunto de una secuencia."

14. "de abstracción y desenvolvimiento de algún problema, de algún asunto de una secuencia."

Chapter 9

This chapter is a revised and expanded version of a paper titled "The Ethnomusicology of Archaeology: A Model for Research in Ethnoarchaeomusicology," which I read at the 32nd Annual Meeting of the Society for Ethnomusicology, Ann Arbor, Michigan, November 7, 1987, and published in *Selected Reports in Ethnomusicology* 8 (subtitled "Issues in Organology"): 175–97. In addition, some of the material on the Sinú has been published in an enlarged form as "The Magic Flutes of El Dorado: A Model for Research in Music Archaeology as Applied to the Sinú of Ancient Colombia," in *The Archaeology of Early Music Cultures,* selected papers from the Third International Meeting of the ICTM Study Group on Music Archaeology (1988), 305–28; reprinted by permission.

1. I made a startling and disturbing discovery several years before the completion of the first draft of this book and approximately thirteen years after conducting my research in Bogotá: a book entitled *La música precolombina* was published in 1985 by Luís Antonio Escobar, in which serious ethical problems are involved. A portion of his publication is translated and discussed here at some length because of the scholarly and ethical questions it raises. In his book, Escobar includes the following chapter about a number of ceramic flutes found in the Gold Museum of the Banco de la República in Bogotá (my translation of pp. 117–18):

Malibu Flutes

In the basement of the Bank of the Republic's Gold Museum in the city of Bogotá is a collection of pre-Columbian ceramics which holds a very important treasure. I refer to the Malibu Flutes, which represent a musical advancement comparable to that of the Mayas of the eighth century, who made quadruple flutes. This is a great surprise, because they were found in a region of Colombia that has not had a trace of important musical culture. Besides, the locale, in the territory of lower Magdalena, near the Sierra Nevada of Santa Marta, where the "male and female *gaitas*" and the precious Tairona ocarinas come from, signifies that a new pre-Columbian cultural and musical zone of sufficient quality continues to be evaluated. But let's look at some of the facts related to the Malibu Flutes.

From the colonial period the Sinú region was marked as one of the places from where gold and such clay objects [the Malibu Flutes] came, and because of their beauty a great culture was clearly denoted. In addition, various archaeologists have said that the objects came from the lower San Jorge River. Nevertheless, as recently as the summer of 1976 a large and very well conducted investigation began. Two archaeologists from the Bank of the Republic's Gold Museum, Clemencia Plazas and Ana María Falchetti de Sáenz, directed the project. During their investigations they not only definitively studied the now famous artificial irrigation canal system, a pre-Columbian work of gigantic proportions that is indicative of the power and creativity of the Indians of that region, but also located towns and cultures, one of them the Malibu site in the Momposina Depression and on the banks of the Magdalena River. According to these archaeologists, the site where they found the ceramic flutes corresponds to the Malibu culture, with the approximate date of the thirteenth century. Professor Gerardo Reichel-Dolmatoff has already investigated this region and writes that "the Malibus of the lower Magdalena River were cultivators of corn, sweet yucca and wild yucca; this was an agricultural production carried out from primordial times in fields near their clay barns and houses." Further significant studies of this region, conducted by Dr. Orlando Fals Borda, complement the importance of this zone. Nevertheless, we should still not be satisfied with small conclusions, and yes, the long-gone inhabitants of the culture tell us nothing. The most intriguing aspect is the appearance of some beautifully finished flutes, which present themselves to our view without any antecedent.

Characteristics of the Malibu Flutes. In the first place, something that is not common in the pre-Columbian world is the manufacture of instruments all having the same form, as if we were dealing with a flute designed to be reproduced, as in our present consumer society. It is well known that the pre-Columbian artisan "created" a new work with each of his instruments insofar as he put together different figures, or at least different lines, designs, incisions, or new colors. The Malibu Flutes, however, have a sense of uniformity because all known exemplars are adorned with the same small cayman, or *babilla,* placed in the upper part of the flute and always in the same position. They all have the same proportions, including their share of little details that suggest that they were for children. They are all made from the same quality of clay, in conical form, and with a duct mouthpiece.

As ceramic artifacts, these flutes present a style that is very well defined, with the fineness of their surfaces, their proportions, and the delicacy of their ornaments.

Regarding the form, it is without a doubt the culmination of a process in the search for beautiful sounds that probably began several centuries before. These instruments cannot be the products of only a few years of experience.

The quality of the sound these flutes emit is something truly exceptional. They produce beautiful, sweet tones, better than those of the wooden or plastic flutes presently manufactured. Perhaps the conical form or the quantity of air in the mouthpiece could be the reason they are so harmonious.

Regarding the pitches of the sounds, those of some flutes are identical. Some produce a series of five notes with the following tones: C, D, E, F-sharp, and G-sharp. Others produce C, E-flat, F-sharp, G-sharp, and A-sharp. Several flutes clearly produce a diatonic scale. The close simultaneity of sounds for some groups of flutes suggests a religious use for the flutes. Furthermore, the groups of small flutes, as if intended for children, could indicate their significance as instruments for mere musical enjoyment, for musical games, or perhaps for the preparation of the child for the liturgy. The flutes average 25 cm in length by 5 cm in diameter.

These Malibu Flutes present, then, a synthesis of musical advancement unsuspected in our history of the music. Together with the male and female *gaitas* they comprise the most important melodic instruments from the pre-Columbian cultures of Colombia.

Escobar's (1985, 117) claim that the so-called Malibu Flutes were excavated in 1976 by two archaeologists in the employ of the Gold Museum is unjustified, based on my research. When I compared his very detailed, high-quality photograph of several flutes in the Gold Museum (1985, 118) with my equally good photographs taken at the museum in 1974, none were similar. Then, realizing that his instruments nevertheless looked very familiar to me, I compared them with the Sinú flutes I photographed in 1974 from the Guillermo Cano private collection. A total of six of the nine flutes in Escobar's photograph (1986, 118) turned out to be the identical instruments from the Cano collection I studied, and one of them is not Sinú (or Malibu, as he calls them) at all, but is Tairona. Two of these appear as illustrations in two of my earlier publications: the flute in the lower left-hand

corner of Escobar's photograph can be seen in Olsen 1988 (318), and the Tairona
flute in the upper middle of his photograph (the only anthropomorphic example)
appears in Olsen 1986a (126, far right). I have compared these photographs with
such great detail (counting scales on the reptiles' backs, comparing repair marks,
depressions, discolorations, numbers of incisions in motifs, etc.) that there is ab-
solutely no question in my mind that Escobar's flutes are from the Cano collection
I photographed in 1974. Therefore, they were not discovered in 1976 by the cited
Gold Museum archaeologists, and are falsely passed off as recent discoveries,
rather than being correctly attributed to the Cano collection.

The late Guillermo Cano, a very well known and controversial editor of a
Bogotá newspaper, was brutally assassinated years ago. It is apparent that his collection was given or sold to the Gold Museum of the Bank of the Republic. It is an
atrocity that portions of his wonderful collection are being falsely attributed to a
recent discovery, and that no credit is given to Guillermo Cano, who was so de-
voted to archaeology. Furthermore, Escobar's analysis of the instruments is a total
contradiction of my analyses of many of the same instruments, as a comparison of
his discourse with the present chapter will reveal. Escobar's simplifications, generalizations, and conclusions are highly suspect.

Original text of "Flautas malibues"

En los sótanos del Museo del Oro del Banco de la República en la ciudad de
Bogotá, existe una colección de cerámica precolombina que guarda un
tesoro muy importante. Se trata de las "FLAUTAS MALIBUES" que
representan un avance musical comparable al de los Mayas del siglo VIII
que lograron las flautas cuádruples. Gran sorpresa, pues en territorio colombiano no havía rastros de culturas musicales importantes. Además la
localización, región del Bajo Magdalena, cercanía de la Sierra Nevada de
Santa Marta, de donde proceden las "gaitas macho y hembra," y del territorio de las preciosas ocarinas taironas, todo ello significa que se está en
mora de valorar una nueva zona cutural precolombina de suficiente calidad,
al menos en lo musical. Pero veamos algunos datos relacionados con las
flautas malibúes.

Desde los tiempos de la Colonia la región del Sinú quedó marcada como
uno de los lugares de donde procedían objetos de oro y arcilla que por su
belleza denotaban claramente una gran cultura. Varios arqueólogos también
habían advertido que los objetos procedían del bajo río San Jorge. Sin embargo, solamente en el verano de 1976 se comenzó un trabajo amplio y muy
bien encausado. Lo dirigían dos arqueólogas del Museo del Oro del Banco
de la República, Clemencia Plazas y Ana María Falchetti de Sáenz. Debido
a estas investigaciones no solamente estudiaron de manera muy definida los
ahora ya famosos canales artificiales de irrigación, obra precolombina de
gigantescas poporciones e indicadora de la pujanza y creatividad de los

indígenas de aquella región, sino que localizaron pueblos y culturas, una de éstas del Grupo Malibú en la Depresión Momposina y las riberas del río Magdalena. Según las arqueólogas mencionadas, el sitio donde se encontraron las flautas de cerámica corresponde a la cultura de estos Grupos Malibúes con fecha aproximada al siglo XIII. El profesor Gerardo Reichel-Dolmatoff ya había investigado aquella región y dice que, "los Malibúes del bajo Magdalena eran cultivadores de maíz, yuca dulce y yuca brava, producción agrícola que realizaban primordialmente en huertas cercanas a los caseríos o viviendas de barro." Estudios de mucha significación, realizados por el Dr. Orlando Fals Borda sobre esta región, complementan la importancia de esta zona. Sin embargo, apenas debemos contentarnos con poquísimas conclusiones y sí aparecen muchos inquietantes interrogantes. Lo que más intriga es la aparición de unas flautas hermosamente acabadas que se presentan a nuestra vista sin ningún antecedente.

CARACTERISTICAS DE LAS FLAUTAS MALIBUES. En primer lugar, algo que no es común en lo precolombino, la hechura de instrumentos con el mismo patrón de forma, como si se tratara de una flauta modelo para reproducir, como en nuestra sociedad de consumo. Bien sabemos que el hombre precolombino en cada uno de sus instrumentos "creaba" una nueva obra a la cual le agregaba figuras, o en último caso, rayas, diseños, incisiones or colores nuevos, diferentes. Las flautas malibúes tienen el sentido de la uniformidad y todas las que se conocen están adornadas con el mismo pequeño caimán o babilla colocado en la parte inferior de la flauta y siempre en la misma posición. Todas tienen las mismas proporciones, inclusive un lote de pequeñas que dan la idea de que fueran para niños. Todas tienen la misma calidad de barro, forma cónica y embocadura de pico.

Como obra de cerámica, estas flautas presentan un estilo muy definido en la finura de las paredes, las proporciones y la delicadeza de adornos.

En cuanto a la forma, es sin duda la culminación de un proceso en la búsqueda de sonidos bellos que debió comenza varios siglos atrás. No pueden ser instrumentos producto de pocos años de experiencia.

Algo verdaderamente excepcional es la calidad de los sonidos que emiten estas flautas. Producen bellísimos y dulces sonidos, mejores que los de las flautas de madera o plástico que se elaboran actualmente. Tal vez la forma cónica o cantidad de aire en el recipiente pueda ser la causa para que sean tan armoniosos.

En cuanto a la altura de los sonidos, los de algunas flautas son idénticos. Unas producen una serie de cinco notas por tonos seguidos: do, re, mi, fa sostenido y sol sostenido. Otras producen: do, mi bemol, fa sostenido, sol sostenido y la sostenido. Varias flautas emiten claramente la escala diatónica. La casi simultaneidad de sonidos por grupos de flautas sugieren el uso para fines religiosos. También los grupos de flautas pequeñas como para niños podrían indicar el sentido de gozo musical, de juguete musical o de preparación infantil para la liturgia.

El promedio del largo de las flautas es de 25 centímetros por cinco de diámetro.

Estas flautas malibúes presentan pues una síntesis de adelanto musical insospechado en nuestra historia de la música. Junto con las Gaitas macho y hembra se convierten en los instrumentos melódicos más importantes de la cultura precolombina en Colombia.

2. "las figurinas: casi siempre son zoomorfias y ornitomorfas . . . cuyas formas son lagartos, aves y otra clase de animales indefinidos. Las aves se caracterizan por su pico largo y ancho y los largartos o caimanes por su realismo."

3. "Además de tener la forma de un pez, por la región bucal plana y el ángulo formado al nivel de la representación de la aleta dorsal, se puede deducir que se trata de un bagre de la familia Pimelodedae. Las branquias son visibles y las escamas o coloraciones de la piel están representadas. El género y la especie de esta figura no son identificables, pero se puede notar que la especie *Sorubin lima*, grande y de forma general muy parecida a esta representación, se encuentra frecuentemente en el río Sinú."

Chapter 10

This chapter is a slightly expanded version of a paper presented at the Thirteenth Annual Meeting of the American Musical Instrument Society at Arizona State University, March 1984, and published in *Journal of the American Musical Instrument Society* 12:107–36, copyright 1986 by the American Musical Instrument Society, Inc.; reprinted by permission.

1. "Adoran los planetas y los sinos regocijándose por los oteros; hay muchas adevinas y adevinos y grande cuantidad de hechiceros, que dicen un millón de desatinos acerca de los tiempos venideros: dan al demonio lo que no merece pintándolo del arte que parece."

2. Compare this representation of the ancient Tairona boat and boatman with those of the Moche as pictured in Donnan (1976, 92–93).

3. "atambores grandes de seys o siete palmos de luengo, hechos de un tronco vacuo de árboles gruessos y encorados."

4. "La investigación sobre el tema mencionado óbviamente no debe limitarse a la recopilación de noticias contenidas en los cronistas, o a especulaciones de carácter arqueológico, sino es necesario hacer amplio uso de datos etnológicos modernos."

5. "[Un] elemento muy típico para la arqueología *tairona* y aún en uso entre los *Kogi*, son silbatos de barro (*huíbiju*). Suspendidos del cuello de los bailarines, éstos los tocan en determinadas fases de sus danzas, imitando aves. Las diferentes representaciones zoomorfas (jaguares, buhos, zorros, murciélagos, etc.) de los silbatos parecen haberse relacionado originalmente con los animales totémicos y

según mis informadores, cada *Túxe* usaba silbatos representando su correspondiente animal. Hoy en día esta diferenciación ya no se observa y los silbatos sólo sirven de instrumentos musicales sin pertenecer a determinado grupo social."

6. "Todos los *Túxe* o *Dáke* reconocen una 'raíz' y se declaran relacionados con cierto animal, planta, objeto o fenómeno natural. . . . Estos animales se consideran directamente como antepasados: 'Todos venimos de animales. Ellos eran antes gente.' La relación del grupo y del individuo con este animal es múltiple. . . . Habiendo complido con las ofrendas un individuo no tiene nada que temer y el animal lo defenderá contra enfermedades o desgracias, pero si no cumple con las ofrendas, el animal lo castigará enviándole calamidades."

7. "Los bailes y cantos que imitan a estos animales y los cuales se ejecutan para pedir ayuda de ellos, son 'propiedad' estricta de los individuos quienes descienden de un animal ancestral."

8. Wilbert (1974, 82) explains that this is actually a physiological phenomenon whereby the breathing center in the opossum's brain becomes temporarily paralyzed.

9. Coca chewing, whereby the mastication of coca (genus Erythroxylum) leaves mixed with lime (calcium carbonate) produces small amounts of cocaine that is ingested into the body, is common among the natives of the Santa Marta region, as well as among Andean peoples. The juice is a mild narcotic that also functions as a hunger suppressant.

Bibliography

Abadía Morales, Guillermo. 1973. *La música folklórica colombiana* (Colombian folk music). Bogotá: Universidad Nacional de Colombia.

Alexander, George. 1976. "Shrills Are Music to Ears of Researchers." *St. Petersburg Times,* December 25, 5E (from *Los Angeles Times*).

Alba, Walter. 1990. "New Tomb of Royal Splendor." *National Geographic* 177/6 (June): 2–15.

Amaro, Iván. 1996. "Símbolo y sonido. Los instrumentos musicales figurativos del Perú antiguo" (Symbol and sound. Sculpted musical instruments from ancient Peru). In *Imágenes y mitos: Ensayos sobre las artes figurativas en los andes prehispánicos* (Images and myths: Studies about figurative arts in the pre-Hispanic Andes), ed. Krzysztof Makowski, Iván Amaro, and Max Hernández, 115–41. Lima: Australis, Fondo Editorial SIDEA.

Appadurai, Arjun. 1986. "Introduction: Commodities and the Politics of Value." In *The Social Life of Things: Commodities in Cultural Perspective,* ed. Arjun Appadurai, 3–63. Cambridge: Cambridge University Press.

Arango Bueno, Teresa. 1963. *Precolombia* (Pre-Columbia). 3d ed. Bogotá: Editorial Minerva.

Artesanía folclórica en el Ecuador. 1970–71. Guayaquil: Cromos.

Bankes, George. 1980. *Moche Pottery from Peru.* London: British Museum Publications.

Baumann, Max Peter. 1981. "Music, Dance, and Song of the Chipayas (Bolivia)." *Latin American Music Review* 2 (2): 171–222.

———. 1982. *Musik im Andenhochland* (Music in the Andean highlands). Museum Collection Berlin, MC 14.

———. 1985. "The Kantu Ensemble of the Kallawaya at Charazani (Bolivia)." *Yearbook for Traditional Music* 17: 146–65.

Becker, Judith. 1988. "Earth, Fire, *Sakti,* and the Javanese Gamelan." *Ethnomusicology* 32 (3): 385–91.

Bellenger, Xavier. 1983. *Peru: Ayarachi and Chiriguano.* UNESCO, MTC 1. Phonodisc and notes.

Benade, Arthur H. 1960. *Horns, Strings, and Harmony.* Garden City, N.Y.: Anchor Books.

Bennett, Wendell C. 1944. *Archeological Regions of Colombia: A Ceramic Survey.* Yale University Publications in Anthropology, no. 30. New Haven: Yale University Press.

Bennett, Wendell C., and Junius B. Bird. 1964. *Andean Culture History.* American Museum Science Books edition. Original ed., New York: The American Museum of Natural History, 1949.

Benson, Elizabeth P. 1972. *The Mochica. A Culture of Peru.* New York: Praeger.

———. 1975. "Death-Associated Figures on Mochica Pottery." In *Death and the Afterlife in Pre-Columbian America,* ed. Elizabeth P. Benson, 105–44. Washington, D.C.: Dumbarton Oaks Research Library and Collections.

———. 1997a. *Birds and Beasts of Ancient Latin America.* Gainesville: University Press of Florida.

———. 1997b. "Moche Art: Myth, History and Rite." In *The Spirit of Ancient Peru. Treasures from the Museo Arqueológico Rafael Larco Herrera,* ed. Kathleen Berrin, 40–49. New York: Thames and Hudson.

Berrin, Kathleen, ed. 1997. *The Spirit of Ancient Peru. Treasures from the Museo Arqueológico Rafael Larco Herrera.* New York: Thames and Hudson.

Bierhorst, John. 1988. *The Mythology of South America.* New York: William Morrow.

Bischof, Henning. 1964. "Canapote—An Early Ceramic Site in Northern Colombia. Preliminary Report." *Congreso internacional de americanistas* 36: 483–91.

Bohlman, Philip V. 1997. "Fieldwork in the Ethnomusicological Past." In *Shadows in the Field: New Perspectives for Fieldwork in Ethnomusicology,* ed. Gregory F. Barz and Timothy J. Cooley, 139–62. New York: Oxford University Press.

Boilès, Charles L. 1966. "The Pipe and Tabor in Mesoamerica." *Yearbook/Anuario* 2: 43–74.

Bolaños, César. 1981. *Música y danza en el antiguo Perú* (Music and dance in ancient Peru). Lima: Museo Nacional de Antropología y Arqueología, Instituto Nacional de Cultura.

———. 1988a. *Las antaras Nasca: Historia y análisis* (Nasca antaras [panpipes]: History and analysis). Lima: Instituto Andino de Estudios Arqueológicos.

———. 1988b. "La música en el antiguo Perú" (The music of ancient Peru). In *La música en el Perú* (The music of Peru), 1–64. Lima: Patronato Popular y Porvenir pro Música Clásica.

Boone, Elizabeth H., ed. 1982. *Falsifications and Misreconstructions of Pre-Columbian Art.* Washington, D.C.: Dumbarton Oaks, Trustees for Harvard University.

Bray, Warwick. 1974. "The Organization of the Metal Trade." In *El Dorado: The Gold of Ancient Colombia.* Catalogue from El Museo del Oro, Banco de la

República, Bogotá. Distributed by New York Graphic Society for Center for Inter-American Relations and American Federation of Arts.

———. 1978. *The Gold of El Dorado.* London: Times Newspapers.

Buchner, Alexander. 1972. *Folk Music Instruments.* New York: Crown.

Burger, Richard L. 1997. "Life and Afterlife in Pre-Hispanic Peru. Contextualizing the Masterworks of the Museo Arqueológico Rafael Larco Herrera." In *The Spirit of Ancient Peru. Treasures from the Museo Arqueológico Rafael Larco Herrera,* ed. Kathleen Berrin, 21–32. New York: Thames and Hudson.

Bushnell, G.H.S. 1957. *Peru.* New York: Praeger.

Bustillos, Freddy, Luís Oporto, and Roberto Fernández. 1981. *Música tradicional boliviana* (Traditional Bolivian music). La Paz: Instituto Boliviano de Cultura.

Cáceres Macedo, Justo. 1985. *The Prehispanic Cultures of Peru.* Translated by Daniel Sandweiss. Guide for the exhibitions in Peruvian archaeology museums. Lima: Perugraph Editores.

Calderón, Eduardo, Richard Cowan, Douglas Sharon, and F. Kaye Sharon. 1982. *Eduardo el Curandero: The Words of a Peruvian Healer.* Richmond, Calif.: North Atlantic Books.

Carvalho-Neto, Paulo de. 1964. *Diccionario del Folklore Ecuatoriano* (Dictionary of Ecuadorian folklore). Quito: Editorial casa de la Cultura Ecuatoriana.

Castro, José. 1938. "Sistema pentafónico en la música indígena precolonial del Perú" (Pentatonicism in the precolonial indigenous music of Peru). *Boletín latino-americano de música* 4 (4) (October): 835–48.

Castro Franco, Julio. 1961. *Música y arqueología* (Music and archaeology). Lima: Editorial Eterna.

Chamorro, Arturo. 1998. "Mexica (Aztec or Nahua People)." In *Garland Encyclopedia of World Music,* ed. Dale A. Olsen and Daniel E. Sheehy. Vol. 2, *South America, Mexico, Central America, and the Caribbean,* 555–62. New York: Garland Publishing.

Champion, Sara. 1980. *Dictionary of Terms and Techniques in Archaeology.* New York: Everest House.

Chang, Kwang-chih. 1967. "Major Aspects of the Interrelationship of Archaeology and Ethnology." *Current Anthropology* 8: 227–43.

Coba Andrade, Carlos Alberto G. 1981. *Instrumentos musicales populares registrados en el Ecuador* (Popular musical instruments documented in Ecuador). Vol. 1. Otavalo, Ecuador: Instituto Otavaleño de Antropología.

———. 1992. *Instrumentos musicales populares registrados en Ecuador* (Popular musical instruments documented in Ecuador). Vol. 2. Quito: Banco Central del Ecuador.

Coe, Michael D. 1975. "Death and the Afterlife in Pre-Columbian America: Closing Remarks." In *Death and the Afterlife in Pre-Columbian America,* ed. Elizabeth P. Benson, 191–96. Washington, D.C.: Dumbarton Oaks Research Library and Collections.

Cohen, John. 1966. *Mountain Music of Peru.* Ethnic Folkways Library, FE 4539.

New York: Folkways Records and Service Corp. Reissue, Smithsonian/Folkways, CD SF 40020 (2 compact discs), 1991.

———. 1998. "Q'ero." In *Garland Encyclopedia of World Music*, ed. Dale A. Olsen and Daniel E. Sheehy. Vol. 2, *South America, Mexico, Central America, and the Caribbean*, 225–31. New York: Garland Publishing.

Cordy-Collins, Alana. 1977a. "Chavín Art: Its Shamanic/Hallucinogenic Origins." In *Pre-Columbian Art History*, ed. Alana Cordy-Collins and Jean Stern, 353–62. Palo Alto, Calif.: Peek Publications.

———. 1977b. "The Moon Is a Boat! A Study in Iconographic Methodology." In *Pre-Columbian Art History*, ed. Alana Cordy-Collins and Jean Stern, 421–32. Palo Alto, Calif.: Peek Publications.

Crossley-Holland, Peter. 1980. *Musical Artifacts of Pre-Hispanic West Mexico: Towards an Interdisciplinary Approach.* Los Angeles: Program in Ethnomusicology, Department of Music, University of California, Los Angeles.

Cruxent, José María, and Irving Rouse. 1958. *An Archeological Chronology of Venezuela.* Washington: Pan-American Union, Organization of American States.

Cubillos Ch., Julio César. 1958. "Apuntes sobre instrumentos musicales aborígenes hallados en Colombia" (Points about aboriginal musical instruments from Colombia). In *Homenaje al profesor Paul Rivet*, 169–89. Bogotá: Academía Colombiana de Historia, Biblioteca de Antropología, Editorial ABC.

Cunninghame Graham, R. B. 1922. *Cartagena and the Banks of the Sinú.* London: Heinemann.

Dannemann R., Manuel. 1977. "The Musical Traditions of the Indigenous Peoples of Chile." *World of Music/Le monde de la musique* 19 (3–4): 104–13.

Davis, Martha Ellen. 1998. "The Dominican Republic." In *Garland Encyclopedia of World Music*, ed. Dale A. Olsen and Daniel E. Sheehy. Vol. 2, *South America, Mexico, Central America, and the Caribbean*, 845–63. New York: Garland Publishing.

Díaz Gainza, José. 1962. *Historia musical de Bolivia* (Musical history of Bolivia). Potosí: Universidad Tomás Frias.

Dickey, Thomas, John Man, and Henry Wiencek. 1982. *The Kings of El Dorado.* Chicago: Stonehenge Press.

Donnan, Christopher B. 1973. *Moche Occupation of the Santa Valley, Peru.* University of California Publications in Anthropology, vol. 8. Berkeley: University of California Press.

———. 1975. "The Thematic Approach to Moche Iconography." *Journal of Latin American Lore* 1 (2): 147–62.

———. 1976. *Moche Art and Iconography.* Los Angeles: UCLA Latin American Center Publications.

———. 1978. *Moche Art of Peru. Pre-Columbian Symbolic Communication.* Los Angeles: Museum of Cultural History, University of California, Los Angeles.

———. 1982a. "Dance in Moche Art." *Ñawpa pacha* 20: 97–120.

———. 1982b. "The Identification of a Moche Fake through Iconographic Analysis." In *Falsifications and Misreconstructions of Pre-Columbian Art*, ed. Elizabeth H. Boone, 37–50. Washington, D.C.: Dumbarton Oaks, Trustees for Harvard University.

———. 1990. "Masterworks of Art Reveal a Remarkable Pre-Inca World." *National Geographic* 177/6 (June): 16–33.

———. 1992. *Ceramics of Ancient Peru.* Los Angeles: Fowler Museum of Cultural History, University of California, Los Angeles.

Donnan, Christopher B., and Carol J. Mackey. 1978. *Ancient Burial Patterns of the Moche Valley, Peru.* Austin: University of Texas Press.

Donnan, Christopher B., and Donna McClelland. 1979. *The Burial Theme in Moche Iconography.* Studies in Pre-Columbian Art and Archaeology, no. 21. Washington, D.C.: Dumbarton Oaks, Trustees for Harvard University.

Dover, Robert V. H., Katharine E. Seibold, and John H. McDowell. 1992. *Andean Cosmologies through Time.* Bloomington: Indiana University Press.

El Dorado: The Gold of Ancient Colombia. 1974. Catalogue from El Museo del Oro, Banco de la República, Bogotá. Distributed by New York Graphic Society for Center for Inter-American Relations and American Federation of Arts.

Eliade, Mircea. 1972. *Shamanism: Archaic Techniques of Ecstasy.* Princeton: Princeton University Press.

Elsasser, A. B., and F. H. Stross. 1970. *Science and Archaeology.* Exhibition at R. H. Lowie Museum of Anthropology. Berkeley: University of California.

Emmerich, André. 1977. *Sweat of the Sun and Tears of the Moon.* New York: Hacker Art Books.

Enslow, Sam. 1990. *The Art of Prehispanic Colombia: An Illustrated Cultural and Historical Survey.* Jefferson, N.C.: McFarland.

Escobar, Luís Antonio. 1985. *La música precolombina* (Pre-Columbian music). Bogotá: Universidad Central.

Falchetti, Ana María. 1998. "Zenú Ceramics from the Caribbean Lowlands of Colombia." In *Shamans, Gods, and Mythic Beasts: Colombian Gold and Ceramics in Antiquity*, ed. Armand J. Labbé, 163–203. New York: American Federation of Arts; Seattle: University of Washington Press.

Fernández, Carlos A. 1998. "Costa Rica." In *Garland Encyclopedia of World Music*, ed. Dale A. Olsen and Daniel E. Sheehy. Vol. 2, *South America, Mexico, Central America, and the Caribbean*, 680–705. New York: Garland Publishing.

Furst, Peter T. 1965. "West Mexico, the Caribbean, and Northern South America: Some Problems in New World Inter-Relationships." *Antropológica* 14: 1–37.

———. 1972. *Flesh of the Gods: Ritual Use of Hallucinogens.* New York: Praeger.

García, Fernando. 1979. "Algunas notas sobre la zampoña de uso colectivo en Puno" (Some notes about the collectively used panpipe in Puno). *Folklore* 2 (January): 12–13.

Garcilaso de la Vega, El Inca. 1966. *The Incas: The Royal Commentaries of the Inca.* Second Avon Library. Edited by Alain Gheerbrant. Translated by Maria Jolas. New York: Avon Books, Orion Press.

Garrett, Steven, and Daniel K. Stat. 1977. "Peruvian Whistling Bottles." *Journal of the Acoustical Society of America* 62 (2) (August): 449–53.

Gebhart-Sayer, Angelika. 1985. "The Geometric Designs of the Shipibo-Conibo in Ritual Context." *Journal of Latin American Lore* 11 (2): 143–75.

Giacobbe, Juan. 1936. "Introducción al estudio de una etnofonía argentina" (Introduction to the study of Argentine ethnosound). *Boletín latino-americano de música* 2 (2) (April): 215–35.

Gillin, John. 1947. *Moche: A Peruvian Coastal Community.* Smithsonian Institution, Institute of Social Anthropology, publication no. 3. Washington, D.C.: Government Printing Office.

"Golden Ratio: Formula for Transcendence." 1981. *Coming Revolution,* Fall, 42–46.

González Bravo, Antonio. 1937. "Kenas, pincollos y tarkas." *Boletín latino-americano de música* 3 (3): 25–32.

Gordon, B. Le Roy. 1957. *Human Geography and Ecology in the Sinú Country of Colombia.* Ibero-Americana, no. 39. Berkeley: University of California Press.

Gostautas, Estanislao. 1960. *Arte colombiano* (Colombian art). Bogotá: Editorial Iqueima.

Grebe, María Ester. 1974. "Instrumentos musicales precolombinos de Chile" (Pre-Columbian musical instruments of Chile). *Revista musical chilena* 128: 5–55.

Greene, Oliver. 1998. "Belize," In *Garland Encyclopedia of World Music,* ed. Dale A. Olsen and Daniel E. Sheehy. Vol. 2, *South America, Mexico, Central America, and the Caribbean,* 666–79. New York: Garland Publishing.

Gushiken, José. 1977. *Tuno: El curandero* (Tuno: The shaman). Lima: Universidad Nacional Mayor de San Marcos.

Gutiérrez Condori, Ramiro. 1991. "Instrumentos musicales tradicionales en la comunidad artesanal Walata Grande, Bolivia" (Traditional musical instruments in the Walata Grande artisan community, Bolivia). *Latin American Music Review* 12 (2): 124–59.

Haeberli, Joerg. 1979. "Twelve Nasca Panpipes: A Study." *Ethnomusicology* 23 (1): 57–74.

Harcourt, Raoúl d', and Marguerite d'Harcourt. 1925. *La musique des Incas et ses survivances* (The music of the Incas and their survivors). Paris: Librairie Orientaliste Paul Geuthner. Reprint, 1990. *La música de los Incas y sus supervivencias.* Translated by Roberto Miro Quesada. Lima: Occidental Petroleum Corporation of Peru.

Harner, Michael J., ed. 1973. *Hallucinogens and Shamanism.* London: Oxford University Press.

———. 1980. *The Way of the Shaman.* Toronto: Bantam Books.

Headland, Thomas N. 1990. "Introduction: A Dialogue between Kenneth Pike and Marvin Harris on Emics and Etics." In *Emics and Etics: The Insider/Outsider Debate*, ed. Thomas N. Headland, Kenneth L. Pike, and Marvin Harris. Newbury Park, Calif.: Sage Publications.

Hernández de Alba, Gregorio. 1948. "Tribes of the North Colombia Lowlands." In *Handbook of South American Indians,* ed. Julian H. Steward, 4: 329–38. Washington, D.C.: Government Printing Office.

Herrera y Tordesillas, Antonio de. 1936. *Historia general de los hechos de los Castellanos en las islas y tierrafirme del mar océano* (General history of the accomplishments of the Spanish in the islands and continents in the Atlantic Ocean). Madrid: Academia de la Historia.

Hickmann, Ellen. 1983–84. "Terminology, Problems, Goals of Archaeomusicology." *Progress Reports in Ethnomusicology* (Department of Music, University of Maryland, Baltimore) 1 (3).

———. 1986. "Instrumentos musicales del Museo Antropológico del Banco Central del Ecuador, Guayaquil" (Musical instruments from the Anthropology Museum of the Central Bank of Ecuador in Guayaquil). Part 1, "Ocarinas." *Miscelánea antropológica ecuatoriana* 6: 117–40.

———. 1987. "Continuity and Change of South American Musical Instruments in the Environs of Precolumbian Cultures (Andean Countries)." *Archaeologia musicalis* 1: 19–20.

———. 1990. *Musik aus dem Altertum der Neuen Welt: Archäologische Dokumente des Musizierens in präkolumbischen Kulturen Perus, Ekuadors und Kolumbiens* (Music from the ancient New World: Archaeological documentation of musical life in pre-Columbian Peru, Ecuador, and Colombia). Frankfurt am Main: Peter Lang.

Hodder, Ian. 1982. *The Present Past.* London: B.T. Batsford.

———. 1986. *Reading the Past: Current Approaches to Interpretation in Archaeology.* Cambridge: Cambridge University Press.

Hole, Frank. 1979. "Rediscovering the Past in the Present: Ethnoarchaeology in Luristan, Iran." In *Ethnoarchaeology,* ed. Carol Kramer, 192–218. New York: Columbia University Press.

Holzmann, Rodolfo. 1986. *Q'ero, pueblo y música* (Q'ero, the people and their music). Lima: Patronato Popular y Porvenir Pro Música Clásica.

Hommel, William L. 1969. "Mythology in Ancient Peruvian Art." In *Myths of Ancient Peru.* Baltimore: Baltimore Museum of Art.

Hoyle M., Ana María. 1985. "Patrimonio musical de la cultura Moche" (Musical patrimony of the Moche culture). Master's thesis, Universidad Nacional de Trujillo (Peru).

Huamán Poma de Ayala, Felipe. 1978. *Letter to a King.* Translated by Christopher Dilke from *Nueva corónica y buen gobierno.* 1615. Reprint, New York: Dutton.

Huntley, H. E. 1970. *The Divine Proportion.* New York: Dover.

Instituto Nacional de Cultura. 1978. *Mapa de los instrumentos musicales de uso popular en el Perú: Clasificación y ubicación geográfica* (Map of the musical instruments in popular use in Peru: Classification and geographical location). Lima: Oficina de Música y Danza.

Izikowitz, Karl Gustav. 1970. Reprint. *Musical and Other Sound Instruments of the South American Indians.* East Ardsley, Wakefield, Yorkshire: S.R. Publishers. Original ed., Göteborg: Elanders Boktryckeri Aktiebolag, 1934.

Janusek, John W. 1999. "Craft and Local Power: Embedded Specialization in Tiwanaku Cities." *Latin American Antiquity* 10 (2): 107–31.

Jiménez Borja, Arturo. 1951. *Instrumentos musicales del Peru* (Musical instruments of Peru). Lima: Museo de la Cultura.

Joralemon, Donald. 1984. *Symbolic Space and Ritual Time in a Peruvian Healing Ceremony.* San Diego Museum of Man, Ethnic Technology Notes, no. 19.

Joralemon, Donald, and Douglas Sharon. 1993. *Sorcery and Shamanism: Curanderos and Clients in Northern Peru.* Salt Lake City: University of Utah Press.

Katz, Fred, and Marlene Dobkin de Rios. 1971. "Hallucinogenic Music. An Analysis of the Role of Whistling in Peruvian Ayahuasca Healing Sessions." *Journal of American Folklore* 84: 320–27.

Keen, Benjamin, ed. 1974. *Latin American Civilization. The Colonial Origins.* Vol. 1. 3d ed. Boston: Houghton Mifflin.

Kirkpatrick, Sidney D. 1992. *Lords of Sipan.* New York: Morrow.

Klein, Otto. 1967. *La cerámica mochica. Carácteres estilísticos y conceptos* (Mochica ceramics: Stylistic characteristics and concepts). Valparaiso: Universidad Técnica "Federico Santa María."

Knoll, Mark William. n.d. "The Minor Third and the Fibonacci Series." Unpublished paper, Florida State University.

Kramer, Carol, ed. 1979. *Ethnoarchaeology.* New York: Columbia University Press.

Kutscher, Gerdt. 1967. "Iconographic Studies as an Aid in the Reconstruction of Early Chimu Civilization." In *Peruvian Archaeology: Selected Readings,* ed. John Rowe and Dorothy Menzel, 115–24. Palo Alto, Calif.: Peek Publications.

Kvietok, D. Peter. 1989. "The Andean Trumpet: An Evocative Expression of Cultural Identity." Master's thesis, Columbia University.

Labbé, Armand J. 1998. "Symbol, Theme, Context, and Meaning in the Art of Prehispanic Colombia." In *Shamans, Gods, and Mythic Beasts: Colombian Gold and Ceramics in Antiquity,* ed. Armand J. Labbé, 21–119. New York: American Federation of Arts; Seattle: University of Washington Press.

Lanning, Edward P. 1967. *Peru before the Incas.* Englewood Cliffs, N.J.: Prentice-Hall.

———. 1974. "Western South America." In *Prehispanic America,* ed. Shirley Gorenstein, 65–86. New York: St. Martin's.

Lapiner, Alan. 1976. *Pre-Colombian Art of South America.* New York: Abrams.

Larco Hoyle, Rafael. 1966. *Peru.* Translated from the French by James Hogarth. Archaeologia Mundi Series. Cleveland: World Publishing Company; Geneva: Nagel Publishers.

Lathrap, Donald W. 1975. *Ancient Ecuador: Culture, Clay, and Creativity, 3000–300 B.C.* Chicago: Field Museum of Natural History.

———. 1977. "Our Father the Cayman, Our Mother the Gourd: Spinden Revisited, or a Unitary Model for the Emergence of Agriculture in the World." In *Origins of Agriculture,* ed. C. A. Reed, 713–51. The Hague: Mouton.

Legast, Anne. 1980. *La fauna en la orfebrería sinú* (Animals in Sinú goldwork). Bogotá: Fundación de Investigaciones Arqueológicas Nacionales, Banco de la República.

———. 1987. *El animal en el mundo mítico tairona* (Animals in the Tairona mythical world). Bogotá: Fundación de Investigaciones Arqueológicas Nacionales, Banco de la República.

Lévi-Strauss, Claude. 1963. *Totemism.* Translated from the French by Rodney Needham. Boston: Beacon Press.

———. 1973. *From Honey to Ashes.* London: Jonathan Cape.

List, George. 1983. *Music and Poetry in a Colombian Village: A Tri-Cultural Heritage.* Bloomington: Indiana University Press.

———. n.d. "The Conjunto de Gaitas of Colombia. The Heritage of Three Cultures." Unpublished paper.

Lombardi, Cathryn L., and John V. Lombardi, with K. Lynn Stoner. 1983. *Latin American History. A Teaching Atlas.* Madison: University of Wisconsin Press.

Lumbreras, Luis G. 1974. *The Peoples and Cultures of Ancient Peru.* Translated by Betty J. Meggers. Washington, D.C.: Smithsonian Institution Press.

Makeig, Scott. 1981. "Means, Meaning, and Music: Pythagoras, Archytas, and Plato." *Ex Tempore* 1 (1): 36–62.

Marroquín, Salvador. 1998. "El Salvador." In *Garland Encyclopedia of World Music,* ed. Dale A. Olsen and Daniel E. Sheehy. Vol. 2, *South America, Mexico, Central America, and the Caribbean,* 706–20. New York: Garland Publishing.

Martí, Samuel. 1968. *Instrumentos musicales precortesianos* (Pre-Cortezian musical instruments). Mexico City: Instituto Nacional de Antropología.

Marx, Karl. 1970. *Capital.* Vol. 1. London: Lawrence and Wishart.

Mason, Gregory. 1940. *South of Yesterday.* New York: Henry Holt.

Mason, John Alden. 1931. *Archaeology of Santa Marta Colombia, The Tairona Culture.* Part 1, *Report on Field Work.* Marshall Field Archaeological Expedition to Colombia 1922–23. Chicago: Field Museum of Natural History.

———. 1939. *Archaeology of Santa Marta Colombia, The Tairona Culture.* Part 2, section 2, *Objects of Pottery.* Marshall Field Archaeological Expedition to Colombia 1922–23. Chicago: Field Museum of Natural History.

———. n.d. Unpublished field notes. May–December 1922, January–April 1923. Archive of the Field Museum of Natural History, Chicago.

McClelland, Donna D. 1977. "The Ulluchu: A Moche Symbolic Fruit." In *Pre-*

Columbian Art History, ed. Alana Cordy-Collins and Jean Stern, 435–52. Palo Alto, Calif.: Peek Publications.

McCosker, Sandra Smith. 1974. *The Lullabies of the San Blas Cuna Indians of Panama.* Etnologiska studier, no. 33. Göteborg: Etnografiska Museum, 1974.

Mead, Charles W. 1903. *The Musical Instruments of the Incas.* Supplement to *American Museum Journal,* 3 (4) (July). Guide leaflet no. 2.

Meggers, Betty J. 1973. *Prehistoric America.* Chicago: Aldine Publishing.

Menzel, Dorothy. 1977. *The Archaeology of Ancient Peru and the Work of Max Uhle.* Berkeley: R. H. Lowie Museum of Anthropology, University of California.

Merriam, Alan P. 1964. *The Anthropology of Music.* Evanston: Northwestern University Press.

Merriam-Webster's Collegiate Dictionary. 1994. 10th ed. Springfield, Mass.: Merriam-Webster.

Moreno Andrade, Segundo Luis. 1949. *Música y danzas autóctonas del Ecuador* (Autochthonous music and dances of Ecuador). Quito: Editorial Fray Jodoco Ricke.

Moseley, Michael E. 1983. "Desert Empire and Art: Chimor, Chimú and Chancay." In *Art of the Andes: Pre-Columbian Sculpture and Painted Ceramics from the Arthur M. Sackler Collections,* ed. Lois Katz, 79–85. Washington D.C.: Arthur M. Sackler Foundation and AMS Foundation for the Arts, Sciences, and Humanities.

Nava L., E. Fernando. 1998. "Mixtec." In *Garland Encyclopedia of World Music,* ed. Dale A. Olsen and Daniel E. Sheehy. Vol. 2, *South America, Mexico, Central America, and the Caribbean,* 563–69. New York: Garland Publishing.

Netherly, Patricia J. 1988. "From Event to Process: The Recovery of Late Andean Organizational Structure by Means of Spanish Colonial Written Records." In *Peruvian Prehistory,* ed. Richard W. Keatinge, 257–75. Cambridge: Cambridge University Press.

Nicholas, Francis C. 1901. "The Aborigines of the Province of Santa Marta, Colombia." *American Anthropologist* 3: 606–47.

O'Brien-Rothe, Linda. 1998. "Maya." In *Garland Encyclopedia of World Music,* ed. Dale A. Olsen and Daniel E. Sheehy. Vol. 2, *South America, Mexico, Central America, and the Caribbean,* 650–58. New York: Garland Publishing.

Olsen, Dale A. 1978–79. "Musical Instruments of the Native Peoples of the Orinoco Delta, the Caribbean, and Beyond." *Revista/review interamericana* 7 (Winter): 588–94.

———. 1980a. "Magical Protection Songs of the Warao." Part 1, "Animals." *Latin American Music Review* 1 (2): 131–61.

———. 1980b. "Symbol and Function in South American Indian Music." In *Musics of Many Cultures: An Introduction,* ed. Elizabeth May, 363–85. Berkeley: University of California Press.

————. 1981. "Magical Protection Songs of the Warao." Part 2, "Spirits." *Latin American Music Review* 2 (1): 1–10.

————. 1986a. "The Flutes of El Dorado: An Archaeomusicological Investigation of the Tairona Civilization of Colombia." *Journal of the American Musical Instrument Society* 12: 107–36.

————. 1986b. "Towards a Musical Atlas of Peru." *Ethnomusicology* 30 (3): 394–412.

————. 1987. "The Flutes of El Dorado: Musical Guardian Spirit Effigies of the Tairona." In *Imago Musicae: The International Yearbook of Musical Iconography* 3 (1986): 79–102. Basel: Barenreiter Verlag; Durham, N.C.: Duke University Press.

————. 1988. "The Magic Flutes of El Dorado: A Model for Research in Music Archaeology as Applied to the Sinú of Ancient Colombia." In *Early Music Cultures,* selected papers from the Third International Meeting of the ICTM Study Group on Music Archaeology, Bonn, ed. Ellen Hickman and David Hughes, 305–28.

————. 1990. "The Ethnomusicology of Archaeology: A Model for Research in Ethnoarchaeomusicology." *Selected Reports in Ethnomusicology* 8 (Issues in Organology): 175–97.

————. 1992. "Music of the Ancient Americas: Music Technologies and Intellectual Implications in the Andes." In *Musical Repercussions of 1492: Exploration, Encounter, and Identities,* ed. Carol Robertson, 65–88. Washington, D.C.: Smithsonian Institution Press.

————. 1996. *Music of the Warao of Venezuela: Song People of the Rain Forest.* Gainesville: University Press of Florida.

————. 1998a. "Approaches to Musical Scholarship." In *Garland Encyclopedia of World Music,* ed. Dale A. Olsen and Daniel E. Sheehy. Vol. 2, *South America, Mexico, Central America, and the Caribbean,* 6–25. New York: Garland Publishing.

————. 1998b. "The Distribution, Symbolism, and Use of Musical Instruments." In *Garland Encyclopedia of World Music,* ed. Dale A. Olsen and Daniel E. Sheehy. Vol. 2, *South America, Mexico, Central America, and the Caribbean,* 28–42. New York: Garland Publishing.

Olsen, Dale A., and Daniel E. Sheehy, eds. 1998. *South America, Mexico, Central America, and the Caribbean* Vol. 2 of the *Garland Encyclopedia of World Music.* New York: Garland Publishing.

Olsen, M. Diane. 1978. *Precolumbian Exhibition: The John and Mary Carter Collection of Peruvian Precolumbian Artifacts and Textiles.* Tallahassee: Florida State University.

Otter, Elisabeth den. 1985. *Music and Dance of Indians and Mestizos in an Andean Valley of Peru.* Delft: Eburon.

Panofsky, Erwin. 1962. *Studies in Iconology: Humanistic Themes in the Art of the Renaissance.* New York: Harper and Row.

Paredes, Rigoberto. 1936. "Instrumentos musicales de los Kollas" (Musical instruments of the Kollas). *Boletín latino-americano de música* 2 (2): 77–88.

Parsons, James J. 1951. "Some Notes on the Geography of the Sinú Valley of Colombia." Manuscript, Berkeley.

———. 1952. "The Settlement of the Sinú Valley of Colombia." *Geographical Review* (January): 67–86.

Pferd, William, III. 1987. *Dogs of the American Indians.* Fairfax, Va.: Denlinger's.

Plotnitsky, Arkady. 1993. *In the Shadow of Hegel: Complementarity, History, and the Unconscious.* Gainesville: University Press of Florida.

Proulx, Donald A. 1983. "The Nasca Style." In *Art of the Andes: Pre-Columbian Sculpture and Painted Ceramics from the Arthur M. Sackler Collections,* ed. Lois Katz, 87–105. Washington D.C.: Arthur M. Sackler Foundation and AMS Foundation for the Arts, Sciences and Humanities.

Purce, Jill. 1974. *The Mystic Spiral.* London: Thames and Hudson.

Ramírez, Susan Elizabeth. 1996. *The World Upside Down. Cross-Cultural Contact and Conflict in Sixteenth-Century Peru.* Stanford, Calif.: Stanford University Press.

Ransom, Brian. 1998. "The Enigma of Whistling Water Jars in Pre-Columbian Ceramics." *Experimental Musical Instruments* (September): 12–15.

Rawcliffe, Susan. 1992. "Complex Acoustics in Pre-Columbian Flute Systems." In *Musical Repercussions of 1492: Exploration, Encounter, and Identities,* ed. Carol Robertson, 35–63. Washington, D.C.: Smithsonian Institution Press.

Reichel-Dolmatoff, Gerardo. 1949–50. "Los Kogi: Una tribu de la Sierra Nevada de Santa Marta, Colombia" (The Kogi: A tribe of the Sierra Nevada of Santa Marta, Colombia). *Revista del Instituto Etnológico Nacional* (Bogotá) 4 (1–2).

———. 1951. *Datos históricos-culturales sobre las tribus de la antigua Gobernación de Santa Marta* (Historical-cultural facts about the tribes of the ancient settlements of Santa Marta). Bogotá: Instituto Etnológico de Magdalena, Santa Marta. Imprenta de Banco de la República.

———. 1953. "Contactos y cambios culturales en la Sierra Nevada de Santa Marta" (Cultural contacts and changes in the Sierra Nevada of Santa Marta). *Revista colombiana de antropología* 1 (1) (June): 15–122.

———. 1954. "Investigaciones Arqueológicas en la Sierra Nevada de Santa Marta" (Archaeological investigations in the Sierra Nevada of Santa Marta), parts 1 and 2. *Revista colombiana de antropología* 2: 147–307.

———. 1957. "Momil: A Formative Sequence from the Sinú Valley, Colombia." *American Antiquity* 22 (3) (January): 226–34.

———. 1961. "Anthropomorphic Figurines from Colombia, Their Magic and Art." In *Essays in Pre-Columbian Art and Archaeology,* ed. Samuel K. Lothrop, 229–41. Cambridge, Mass.: Harvard University Press.

———. 1965. *Colombia.* Ancient Peoples and Places, vol. 44. New York: Praeger.

———. 1971. *Amazonian Cosmos: The Sexual and Religious Symbolism of the Tukano Indians.* Chicago: University of Chicago Press.

———. 1974. "Funerary Customs and Religious Symbolism among the Kogi." In *Native South Americans: Ethnology of the Least Known Continent*, ed. Patricia J. Lyon, 289–301. Boston: Little, Brown.

———. 1975a. *The Shaman and the Jaguar.* Philadelphia: Temple University Press.

———. 1975b. "Templos Kogi: Introducción al simbolismo y a la astronomía del espacio sagrado" (Kogi temples: Introduction to the symbolism and astronomy of the sacred space). *Revista colombiana de antropología* 19: 199–240.

———. 1976. "Training for the Priesthood among the Kogi of Colombia." In *Enculturation in Latin America: An Anthology*, ed. Johannes Wilbert, 265–88. UCLA Latin American Center Publications, vol. 37. Los Angeles: University of California, UCLA Latin American Studies.

———. 1977a. "La educación del niño entre los Kogi" (The education of the child among the Kogi). In *Estudios antropológicos*. Bogotá: Instituto Colombiano de Cultura.

———. 1977b. "Notas sobre el simbolismo religioso de los indios de la Sierra Nevada de Santa Marta" (Notes about the religious symbolism of the Indians of the Sierra Nevada de Santa Marta). In *Estudios antropológicos*. Bogotá: Instituto Colombiano de Cultura.

———. 1978. "The Loom of Life: A Kogi Principle of Integration." *Journal of Latin American Lore* 4 (1) (Summer): 5–27.

———. 1984. "Some Kogi Models of the Beyond." *Journal of Latin American Lore* 10 (1) (Summer): 63–85.

Reichel-Dolmatoff, Gerardo, and Alicia Reichel-Dolmatoff. 1957. "Reconocimento arqueológico de la hoya del río Sinú" (Archaeological recognition of the Sinú river basin). *Revista colombiana de antropología* 6: 31–157.

———. 1964–65. "Momil: Excavaciones en el Sinú" (Momil: Excavations in the Sinú area). *Revista colombiana de antropología*, 13: 111–333.

Reichert, Raphael X. 1977. "Pre-Columbian Ceramics: The Problem of Partial Counterfeits." In *Pre-Columbian Art History*, ed. Alana Cordy-Collins and Jean Stern, 393–406. Palo Alto, Calif.: Peek Publications.

Renfrew, Colin. 1986. "Varna and the Emergence of Wealth in Prehistoric Europe." In *The Social Life of Things: Commodities in Cultural Perspective*, ed. Arjun Appadurai, 141–68. Cambridge: Cambridge University Press.

———. 1987. "What's New in Archaeology?" In *Anthropology. Contemporary Perspectives*, ed. Phillip Whitten and David E. K. Hunter, 78–81. 5th ed. Boston: Little, Brown.

Roe, Peter G. 1982. *The Cosmic Zygote: Cosmology in the Amazon Basin.* New Brunswick, N.J.: Rutgers University Press.

Romero, Raúl R., ed. 1987. *Música andina del Perú* (Andean music of Peru). Lima: Archivo de Música Tradicional, Pontificia Universidad Católica del Perú, Instituto Riva Agüero. 2 LP discs with commentaries by Thomas Turino et al.

———. 1998. "Peru." In *Garland Encyclopedia of World Music*, ed. Dale A. Olsen and Daniel E. Sheehy. Vol. 2, *South America, Mexico, Central America, and the Caribbean,* 466–90. New York: Garland Publishing.

Rosenau, Pauline Marie. 1992. *Post-Modernism and the Social Sciences: Insights, Inroads, and Intrusions.* Princeton: Princeton University Press.

Rowe, John Howland, and Dorothy Menzel, eds. 1967. *Peruvian Archaeology: Selected Readings.* Palo Alto, Calif.: Peek Publications.

Sas, André. 1935. "Ensayo sobre la música inca" (Study about Incan music). *Boletín latino-americano de música* 1 (1) (April): 71–77.

———. 1938. "Ensayo sobre la música nazca" (Study about Nazca music). *Boletín latino-americano de música* 4 (4) (October): 221–33.

Sawyer, Alan R. 1961. "Paracas and Nazca Iconography." In *Essays in Pre-Columbian Art and Archaeology,* ed. Samuel K. Lothrop, 269–98. Cambridge, Mass.: Harvard University Press.

———. 1977. "Paracas and Nazca Iconography." In *Pre-Columbian Art History,* ed. Alana Cordy-Collins and Jean Stern, 363–92. Palo Alto, Calif.: Peek Publications.

Schaedel, Richard P. 1967. "Mochica Murals at Pañamarca." In *Peruvian Archaeology: Selected Readings,* ed. John Rowe and Dorothy Menzel, 105–14. Palo Alto, Calif.: Peek Publications.

Schechter, John M. 1998. "Ecuador." In *Garland Encyclopedia of World Music,* ed. Dale A. Olsen and Daniel E. Sheehy. Vol. 2, *South America, Mexico, Central America, and the Caribbean,* 413–33. New York: Garland Publishing.

Scruggs, T. M. 1998. "Nicaragua." In *Garland Encyclopedia of World Music,* ed. Dale A. Olsen and Daniel E. Sheehy. Vol. 2, *South America, Mexico, Central America, and the Caribbean,* 747–69. New York: Garland Publishing.

Seibold, Katharine E. 1992. "Textiles and Cosmology in Choquecanchca, Cuzco, Peru." In *Andean Cosmologies through Time,* ed. Robert V. H. Dover, Katharine E. Seibold, and John H. McDowell, 166–201. Bloomington: Indiana University Press.

Sharon, Douglas. 1972. "The San Pedro Cactus in Peruvian Folk Healing." In *Flesh of the Gods: The Ritual Use of Hallucinogens,* ed. Peter Furst, 114–35. New York: Praeger.

———. 1976a. "Becoming a *Curandero* in Peru." In *Enculturation in Latin America: An Anthology,* ed. Johannes Wilbert, 359–75. UCLA Latin American Studies, vol. 37. Los Angeles: UCLA Latin American Center Publications, University of California, Los Angeles.

———. 1976b. "A Peruvian *Curandero's* Séance: Power and Balance." In *The Realm of the Extra-Human: Agents and Audiences,* ed. Agehananda Bharati, 371–81. The Hague: Mouton.

———. 1978. *Wizard of the Four Winds: A Shaman's Story.* New York: Free Press.

Sharon, Douglas, and Christopher B. Donnan. 1974. "Shamanism in Moche Iconography." In *Ethnoarchaeology,* ed. Christopher Donnan and C. William

Clewlow Jr., 51–77. Institute of Archaeology Monograph 4. Los Angeles: University of California Press.

Sheehy, Daniel E. 1998. "Mexico." In *Garland Encyclopedia of World Music*, ed. Dale A. Olsen and Daniel E. Sheehy. Vol. 2, *South America, Mexico, Central America, and the Caribbean*, 600–625. New York: Garland Publishing.

Sherbondy, Jeanette E. 1992. "Water Ideology in Inca Ethnogenesis." In *Andean Cosmologies through Time*, ed. Robert V. H. Dover, Katharine E. Seibold, and John H. McDowell, 46–66. Bloomington: Indiana University Press.

Shimada, Izumi. 1994. *Pampa Grande and the Mochica Culture*. Austin: University of Texas Press.

Silva Sifuentes, Jorge E. 1978. *Instrumentos musicales pre-colombinos* (Pre-Columbian musical instruments). Serie Investigaciones, no. 2. Lima: Universidad Nacional Mayor de San Marcos, Gabinete de Arqueología, Colegio Real.

Silverman, Helaine. 1993. *Cahuachi in the Ancient Nasca World*. Iowa City: University of Iowa Press.

Siskind, Janet. 1973. "Visions and Cures among the Sharanahua." In *Hallucinogens and Shamanism*, ed. Michael J. Harner, 28–39. New York: Oxford University Press.

Skillman, R. Donald. 1990. *Huachumero*. San Diego Museum of Man, Ethnic Technology Notes, no. 22.

Slonimsky, Nicolas. 1946. *Music of Latin America*. New York: Thomas Y. Crowell.

Stern, Steve J. 1993. *Peru's Indian Peoples and the Challenge of Spanish Conquest: Huamanga to 1640*. 2d ed. Madison: University of Wisconsin Press.

Stevenson, Robert M. 1960. *Music of Peru*. Washington, D.C.: Organization of American States.

———. 1968. *Music in Aztec and Inca Territory*. Berkeley: University of California Press.

Stobart, Henry. 1998. "Bolivia." In *Garland Encyclopedia of World Music*, ed. Dale A. Olsen and Daniel E. Sheehy. Vol. 2, *South America, Mexico, Central America, and the Caribbean*, 282–99. New York: Garland Publishing.

Stone, Doris. 1966. *Introduction to the Archaeology of Costa Rica*. San José: Museo Nacional.

Sullivan, Lawrence E. 1986. "Sound and Senses: Toward a Hermeneutics of Performance." *History of Religions* 26 (1): 1–33.

———. 1988. *Icanchu's Drum: An Orientation to Meaning in South American Religions*. New York: Macmillan.

Thomas, Nicholas. 1991. *Entangled Objects: Exchange, Material Culture, and Colonialism in the Pacific*. Cambridge, Mass.: Harvard University Press.

Turino, Thomas. 1988. "The Music of Andean Migrants in Lima, Peru: Demographics, Social Power, and Style." *Latin American Music Review* 9 (2): 127–49.

———. 1989. "The Coherence of Social Style and Musical Creation among the Aymara in Southern Peru." *Ethnomusicology* 33 (1): 1–30.

———. 1993. *Moving Away from Silence: Music of the Peruvian Altiplano and the Experience of Urban Migration.* Chicago: University of Chicago Press.

Uceda Castillo, Santiago. n.d. "El culto a los muertos y a los ancestros: Representaciones en escultura dentro de modelos arquitectónicos en madera" (The cult of the dead and the ancestors: Sculptured representations among wooden architectonic models). Unpublished paper, Departmento de Arqueología y Antropología, Universidad Nacional de Trujillo (Peru).

Urton, Gary. 1985. "Animal Metaphors and the Life Cycle in an Andean Community." In *Animal Myths and Metaphors in South America,* ed. Gary Urton, 251–84. Salt Lake City: University of Utah Press.

Valcarcel, Luis E. 1938. *Músicos* (Musicians). Cuadernos de Arte, Antiguo Peru, no. 6. Lima: Museo Nacional.

Valencia Chacón, Américo Roberto. 1980. "Los Sikuris de la isla de Taquile" (The Sikuris from Taquile island). *Separata del Boletín de Lima* 8 (9): 1–23.

———. 1981. "Los chiriguanos de Huancané" (The Chiriguanos of Huancané). *Separata del Boletín de Lima* 12–14: 1–28.

———. 1983. *El Siku Bipolar Altiplanico* (The bipolar siku in the altiplano). Vol. 1, Los Sikuris y Pusamorenos. Lima: Artex.

———. 1989a. "El Siku Altiplánico" (The siku in the altiplano). *Conservatorio: Revista musical peruana* 2 (September): 13–22.

———. 1989b. *El Siku o Zampoña / The Altiplano Bipolar Siku: Study and Projection of Peruvian Panpipe Orchestras.* Lima: Artex.

Vargas, Teófilo. 1928. *Aires nacionales de Bolivia* (National Airs of Bolivia). Santiago: Casa Amarilla.

Velo, Yolanda M. 1985. "Los vasos silbadores del museo 'Dr. Emilio Azzarini'" (The whistling bottles from the Dr. Emilio Azzarini Museum). In *Segundas jornadas argentinas de musicología.* Buenos Aires: Instituto Nacional de Musicología.

Von Hagen, Victor W. 1964. *The Desert Kingdoms of Peru.* New York: New American Library.

———. 1978. *The Gold of El Dorado: The Quest for the Golden Man.* London: Paladin, Granada.

Watson, Patty Jo. 1979. "The Idea of Ethnoarchaeology: Notes and Comments." In *Ethnoarchaeology,* ed. Carol Kramer, 276–87. New York: Columbia University Press.

Weiss, Gerald. 1973. "Shamanism and Priesthood in Light of the Campa Ayahuasca Ceremony." In *Hallucinogens and Shamanism,* ed. Michael J. Harner, 40–48. London: Oxford University Press.

Whitten, Phillip, and David E. K. Hunter. 1987. *Anthropology. Contemporary Perspectives.* 5th ed. Boston: Little, Brown.

Wilbert, Johannes. 1974. *The Thread of Life. Symbolism of Miniature Art from*

Ecuador. Studies in Pre-Columbian Art and Archaeology, no. 12. Washington, D.C.: Dumbarton Oaks.

———. 1975. "Eschatology in a Participatory Universe: Destinies of the Soul among the Warao Indians of Venezuela." In *Death and the Afterlife in Pre-Columbian America,* ed. Elizabeth P. Benson, 163–358. Washington, D.C.: Dumbarton Oaks Research Library and Collections.

Yévenez S., Enrique. 1980. *Chile: Proyección folklórica* (Chile: Folkloric projection). Santiago: Edward W. Leonard.

Zemtsovsky, Izaly. 1997. "An Attempt at a Synthetic Paradigm." *Ethnomusicology* 41 (2): 185–205.

Index

aerophone, 17, 21, 113, 115, 126–27, 145, 170, 182–83, 194–95, 198, 202, 227. *See also* flute; ocarina; panpipe; trumpet

altar, 108, 147, 168–69, 176, 240. *See also* mesa

animals, 102, 106, 122, 178–79, 185, 189, 197, 206–11, 232, 240, 242; as ancestors, 216; blood of, 45; bones of, for flutes, 37, 47; calling of, 54; combined with humans, 196, 207, 227–28; dances in imitation of, 216; fertility of, 59, 89, 192; imitation of, 216; Koji classification of, 202, 209, 217–20; marking of, 89; masks of, 198, 207, 209; for protection, 84, 168, 216–17; relationship with music, 115, 130, 186, 206, 238; relationship with water, 187; shamanism and, 168–69, 206; shapes of, for flutes, 110, 126, 183, 194; sounds of, 130, 132; symbolism of, 168, 193, 199–200; as totems, 201, 213–15; types of, 202. *See also* biped; bird; fish; mammal; quadruped; reptile; worm

antara, 21, 62, 67, 87–89, 92

Appadurai, Arjun, 8, 9, 17, 55

archaeology, 9, 12, 28, 194, 212, 241; Colombian, 25, 213; dates in, 8; ethnomusicology of, 22; experimental, 22; museums of, 11, 13, 71, 165, 166; music, 17, 23–24, 30–31, 36, 62, 71, 101, 110, 119, 134, 145, 182, 190, 197, 237; New, 22, 23; scholars of Peruvian, 11

archaeomusicology, 11, 17, 22, 24; definition of, 8

Arundo donax, 93

Atacameño, 62

ayahuasca, 54

ayarachi, 92, 94, 96–97; definition of, 97

Aymara, 5, 36, 57, 74, 87, 90, 97; instruments of, 47, 58–59, 62, 68–69, 91–94, 96

axis mundi, 100

Aztec, 18, 72, 101, 116, 184, 210, 218, 230

Bahía, 101–2

Baumann, Max Peter, 59, 92–94, 99, 111

Benson, Elizabeth P., 35, 43, 74, 77–79, 83–86, 97, 144, 159, 226

biped, 101, 104–5, 218, 225, 227–31, 233, 242

bird, 88, 126, 128, 211; bones of, for flutes, 37; calling of, 54–55, 211; ceremonies about, 97; combined with animal or human, 159, 162, 199, 206, 223; dances in imitation of, 118, 213, 216; drummers as, 169; feathers of, 71, 191, 198; headdresses of, 84, 198, 229; imitation of, 118; Koji classification of, 217–18, 222–23; masks, 169, 178; for protection, 232; relationship with music, 209, 222–23, 229; shamanism and, 132, 162, 165; shapes of, for flutes, 102, 106, 110, 117–18, 122, 132, 188–89, 197–99, 202, 206, 223; sounds of, 40, 132; as spirit helper, 118; symbolism of, 132, 217, 222; as totems, 97

Dale A. Olsen is distinguished research professor of ethnomusicology and director of the Center for Music of the Americas at The Florida State University. He has more than eighty publications about music in South America, including an awarding-winning book, *Music of the Warao of Venezuela: Song People of the Rain Forest* (UPF, 1996). He is an editor of the *Garland Encyclopedia of World Music* and formerly the recording review editor for *Ethnomusicology.* He has served on the council, board of directors, and as first vice president of the Society for Ethnomusicology, as the board member for ethnomusicology of The College Music Society, and as president of The College Music Society and the Florida Folklore Society.

Printed in the United States
216970BV00001B/53/A